Commercialized Prostitution in
New York City

PATTERSON SMITH REPRINT SERIES IN
CRIMINOLOGY, LAW ENFORCEMENT, AND SOCIAL PROBLEMS

A listing of publications in the SERIES *will be found at rear of volume*

PUBLICATION NO. 52: PATTERSON SMITH REPRINT SERIES IN
CRIMINOLOGY, LAW ENFORCEMENT, AND SOCIAL PROBLEMS

Commercialized Prostitution in New York City

BY

GEORGE J. KNEELAND

With a supplementary chapter by
KATHARINE BEMENT DAVIS
Superintendent of the New York State Reformatory for Women

INTRODUCTION BY
JOHN D. ROCKEFELLER, JR.
Chairman of the Bureau of Social Hygiene

New Edition Revised to Date

Montclair, New Jersey
PATTERSON SMITH
1969

Copyright 1913, 1917, by The Century Co.
Reprinted 1969 with permission of Appleton-Century,
affiliate of Meredith Press, by
Patterson Smith Publishing Corporation
Montclair, New Jersey

SBN 87585-052-9

Library of Congress Catalog Card Number: 69-14937

CONTENTS

CHAPTER		PAGE
	Introduction	vii
	Preface to the Fourth Edition	xi
I.	Vice Resorts in New York City: (a) Parlor Houses	3
II.	Vice Resorts: (b) Tenement Houses, Hotels, Furnished Rooms, Massage Parlors	24
III.	Places which Cater to Vice	52
IV.	The Exploiters	77
V.	Prostitute and Customer	100
VI.	The Business of Prostitution; Its Cost	112
VII.	Prostitution, the Police, and the Law	137
VIII.	Comparison of Conditions in 1912 with Conditions in 1915 and 1916	163
IX.	A Study of Prostitutes Committed from New York City to the State Reformatory for Women at Bedford Hills	173
	Statistical Tables Accompanying Chapter IX	207
X.	Preventive, Reformative and Correctional Agencies in New York City	263
	Appendices	283
	Index	343

INTRODUCTION TO FIRST EDITION

In presenting to the public this volume, the first of four studies dealing with various aspects of the problem of prostitution, it seems fitting to make a statement with reference to the origin, work and plans of the Bureau of Social Hygiene.

The Bureau came into existence about two years ago, as a result of the work of the Special Grand Jury which investigated the white slave traffic in New York City during the first half of the year 1910. One of the recommendations made by the jury in the presentment handed up at the termination of its labors was that a public commission be appointed to study the social evil. The foreman of the jury subsequently gave careful consideration to the character of the work which might properly be done by such a commission and the limitations under which it would operate. In this connection, separate personal conferences were held with over a hundred leading men and women in the city, among whom were lawyers, physicians, business men, bank presidents, presidents of commercial organizations, clergymen, settlement workers, social workers, labor leaders and reformers. These conferences led to the conclusion that a public commission would labor under a number of disadvantages, such as the fact that it would be short-lived; that its work would be done publicly; that at best it could hardly do more than present recommendations. It was also believed that the main reason why more results of a permanent character had not been obtained by the various

Introduction

organizations which had dealt with the subject of the social evil during the past ten or fifteen years was that most of these organizations were temporary. While active, they materially improved the situation, but as their efforts relaxed, there came the inevitable return to much the same conditions as before. The forces of evil are never greatly alarmed at the organization of investigating or reform bodies, for they know that these are generally composed of busy people, who cannot turn aside from their own affairs for any great length of time to carry on reforms, and that sooner or later their efforts will cease and the patient denizens of the underworld and their exploiters can then reappear and continue as before.

So the conviction grew that in order to make a real and lasting improvement in conditions, a permanent organization should be created, the existence of which would not be dependent upon a temporary wave of reform nor upon the life of any man or group of men, but which would go on, generation after generation, continuously making warfare against the forces of evil. It also appeared that a private organization would have, among other advantages, a certain freedom from publicity and from political bias, which a publicly appointed commission could not easily avoid.

Therefore, as the initial step, the Bureau of Social Hygiene was formed in the winter of 1911. Its present members are Miss Katharine Bement Davis, Superintendent of the New York State Reformatory for Women at Bedford Hills, New York; Paul M. Warburg, of the firm of Kuhn, Loeb & Company; Starr J. Murphy, of the New York Bar; and John D. Rockefeller, Jr. As the work develops, new members may be added.

Introduction

One of the first things undertaken by the Bureau was the establishment at Bedford Hills, adjacent to the Reformatory, of a Laboratory of Social Hygiene, under Miss Davis's direction. In this laboratory, it is proposed to study from the physical, mental, social and moral sides each person committed to the Reformatory. This study will be carried on by experts and every case will be kept under observation for from three weeks to three months, as may be required. When the diagnosis is completed, it is hoped that the laboratory will be in position to suggest the treatment most likely to reform the individual, or, if reformation is impossible, to recommend permanent custodial care. Furthermore, reaching out beyond the individuals involved, it is believed that important contributions may be made to our knowledge of the conditions ultimately responsible for vice, and that the methods worked out may prove applicable to all classes of criminals, thus leading to lines of action not only more scientific and humane but also less wasteful than those at present followed.

In entering upon its labors, the Bureau regarded it of fundamental importance to make a careful study of the social evil in this country and in Europe. This problem, like any other great and difficult one, can be approached only through an understanding of the various factors involved — physical, moral, social and economic — and of the experience of other cities and countries in dealing with it. Arrangements were therefore made in January, 1912, to secure the services of Mr. George J. Kneeland, who had directed the Chicago Vice Commission investigation. Since that time Mr. Kneeland, with a corps of assistants, has been making a thorough and comprehensive

Introduction

survey of the conditions of vice in New York City, the findings of which are here presented.

The purpose of this volume is to set forth as accurately and fully as possible the conditions of vice as they existed in New York City during the year 1912. It should be clearly understood that the data upon which it is based are not presented as legal evidence, but as reliable information secured by careful and experienced investigators, whose work was systematically corroborated.

In presenting the facts contained in this report, the Bureau has no thought of criticizing any department or official of the city administration. The task which the Bureau set itself was that of preparing a dispassionate, objective account of things as they were during the period above mentioned, the forms which commercialized vice had assumed, the methods by which it was carried on, the whole network of relations which had been elaborated below the surface of society. The studies involved were made in a spirit of scientific inquiry, and it is the hope of the Bureau that all departments or officials whose work this book in any way touches may find the information therein contained helpful to them in the further direction and organization of their work.

In conclusion, it should be stated that the spirit which dominates the work of the Bureau is not sensational or hysterical; that it is not a spirit critical of public officials; but that it is essentially a spirit of constructive suggestion and of deep scientific as well as humane interest in a great world problem.

JOHN D. ROCKEFELLER, JR.
Chairman.

New York, May 1, 1913

PREFACE TO FOURTH EDITION

This volume, first issued by the Bureau of Social Hygiene in 1913, aims to describe in detail the situation as respects the practice of prostitution in New York City at that time. In 1915 the Bureau issued a pamphlet which endeavored to contrast conditions in that year with the conditions previously reported. In 1916 the Bureau again presented in pamphlet form a concrete statement of existing conditions as compared with those described in its two previous accounts. In the present edition a chapter has been added for the purpose of contrasting conditions found in 1915 and 1916 with the conditions as reported in 1912.

The contrast is in the highest degree striking and encouraging. Vice still exists; but its amount has been greatly reduced, and the damage caused has been immensely lessened. In 1912, prostitution was open, organized, aggressive, and prosperous; in 1916 it was furtive, disorganized, precarious, unsuccessful. This improvement is shown in the statistics in Chapter VIII; but, as a matter of fact, the real improvement is far greater than the statistics show. A single example will make this point clear. There were 142 parlor houses in 1912; in 1916 there were 22. On the face of the figures, the parlor houses have been cut down to one-seventh of what they were in 1912. But this understates the achievement. For the 142 houses in 1912 harbored over 1600 inmates;

Preface to Fourth Edition

they were notorious resorts, engaged in the active and open prosecution of their shameless business. The 22 houses reported in 1916 contained less than 50 inmates. They were hard to find, still harder to enter; they led a brief, uncertain, day-to-day existence. The same held true of vicious saloons, of vicious tenements, of street-walking, and of pimps. Thus, though commercialized vice continued in New York in 1916, it had been dealt a body-blow.

The credit for this achievement must be more or less widely apportioned. Civic organizations, such as The Committee of Fourteen, deserve to be prominently mentioned; the District Attorney's office and the Criminal Courts by successive convictions performed an admirable service. But the chief credit belongs to Mayor Mitchel and Police Commissioner Woods. An able, upright, clear-headed, and high-minded Police Commissioner pursued a sound and consistent policy, with all the backing, moral and official, that the Mayor could bring to his support. The results were obvious: The police force steadily improved in morale and efficiency; a new standard of public decency was set and maintained.

Prostitution was thus proved to be a "modifiable phenomenon." Whether the city has more of it or less of it depends very largely upon the policy which the municipal government pursues in dealing with it.

61 Broadway,
February 1, 1917.

COMMERCIALIZED PROSTITUTION IN
NEW YORK CITY

COMMERCIALIZED PROSTITUTION IN NEW YORK CITY

CHAPTER I

VICE RESORTS:[1] (a) PARLOR HOUSES

THE actual business of prostitution in New York City is conducted in buildings which are designated in this report as vice resorts. These resorts are of several kinds. Most prominent are the so-called parlor house or brothel, the tenement house apartment, the furnished room house, the disorderly hotel, and the massage parlor. The present chapter deals only with the first named.

A parlor house or brothel is a building used exclusively for the business of prostitution. It derives its name from the fact that its inmates gather in the parlor to receive their guests. There is, however, an exception to the definition, inasmuch as some parlor houses in New York City are situated on the upper floors of buildings, the ground floors of which are used for legitimate business enterprises.

During the period of this investigation, extending from

---

[1] Attention is called to the fact that the vice resorts described in the following pages are all situated in Manhattan, this being the only section of Greater New York considered in the present investigation.

Commercialized Prostitution in New York

January 24, 1912, to November 15, 1912,[2] 142 parlor houses were visited in Manhattan. Though this number does not include all the places of this character in Manhattan, it may be said to approximate the total. It is improbable that many were overlooked. Every one of the establishments investigated was visited two or more times on different dates by different individuals who have made affidavits as to their findings; and the findings of different investigators working in ignorance of one another have been carefully compared. The date and hour of the observation are given in connection with each report.

Of the 142 parlor houses thus investigated, 20 are known to the trade as fifty-cent houses; 80 as one-dollar houses; 6 as two-dollar houses; and 34 as five- and ten-dollar houses. The prices charged in the remaining two houses are unknown.

The majority of these houses are situated in the business section of Manhattan, namely, on Sixth and Seventh Avenues from West 23rd to West 42nd Streets, and in residential sections on side streets from West 15th to West 54th Streets between Fifth and Eighth Avenues. A few of them are located on the East Side on residential streets east of Third Avenue, and on Second Avenue. A still smaller number were discovered on the extreme East Side near the river and below East 14th Street. Not a few of these houses are found in the vicinity of public

[2] All statements made on the basis of our investigation are to be understood as of this period. There is no implication as to conditions before or after those dates. Where a statement under any other date is intended, that fact is noted. This caution applies to the entire book and will not be repeated.

Vice Resorts

schools, churches, and hotels; others occupy the upper floors over lunch rooms, jewelry shops, clothing stores, fur shops, and other business enterprises.

Private houses used exclusively for prostitution are usually three or four stories high; those of the cheaper type are in a dilapidated and unsanitary condition. For instance, the fifty-cent houses on the lower East Side are described as being practically unfit for human habitation. The rooms are dirty, the loose and creaking floors are covered with matting which is gradually rotting away, the ceilings are low, the windows small, the air heavy and filled with foul odors. The sanitary conditions in the majority of the one-dollar houses on the West Side streets between Sixth and Seventh Avenues are hardly less objectionable. No attempt is made to keep the houses clean. The floors are rotten and filthy; they sag as one walks across them. The small bedrooms are damp and unventilated; the atmosphere is heavy with odors of tobacco and perfumes, mingled with the fumes of medicine and cheap disinfectants.

Every step in the process of arranging for and conducting an establishment of this character is taken in the most businesslike fashion. Every detail is arranged in a cold, calculating spirit. It is first necessary to secure the consent of the owner or agent to use the property for the desired purpose. Negotiations may be conducted by the prospective keeper himself or through a go-between who is paid a bonus for securing a suitable building. In the majority of cases regular leases are drawn up and signed for stated periods. Usually two or more individuals enter into a regular partnership

Commercialized Prostitution in New York

agreement to conduct parlor houses. In the course of this investigation interesting data were obtained respecting the purchase, sale, and value of these shares,[3] which constantly fluctuate in value. Important factors in determining their value at a particular time are public opinion and the attitude of the city authorities toward vice. If the law is rigidly enforced and frequent arrests are made, the shares depreciate and there is a scramble among the partners to dispose of their holdings. If the business is fairly undisturbed, the shares increase in value and can hardly be purchased.

The house once secured and the owners being ready to begin business, a madame or housekeeper is hired by the month or on a percentage basis to take personal charge of the enterprise. She is usually a former prostitute who has outlived her usefulness in that capacity. To her the owners look for results. Every day she reports to them when they call to "make up" the books after business is over — generally during the early morning hours.[4]

Servants are employed to aid the madame: one or more cooks, according to the number of inmates boarding in the house; and maids, usually colored girls, who look after the rooms, tend the door, and aid in the sale of liquor to the customers during business hours. A porter is employed to care for the house and run errands, a "lighthouse," to stand on the street for the purpose of procuring "trade" and to give warning.

The prosperity of the business depends in the main upon the quality of the inmates. If they are young

[3] See Chapter II.   [4] See Chapter IV.

Vice Resorts

and attractive, and, as one madame was heard to say in another city, "especially womanly," success is assured. Thus the value of the manager depends in the first place on her ability to secure and hold the "right sort" of inmate. The girls must be contented; they must be stimulated to please; quarrels must be avoided, jealousies nipped in the bud. In the art of management, the madame must exercise all her ingenuity. If a girl is a good "money maker" the madame attaches her to herself in every possible way. Some of these unfortunate inmates become "house girls," remaining year after year, the unsuspecting victims of the madame's blandishments and exploitation.

Certain of the women are well known as "stars." Their reputation follows them wherever they go and madames vie with each other in securing them for their particular houses, in much the same way as a business firm is constantly looking for clever salesmen who have a reputation and a record for increasing business. The author has in mind a particular woman[5] whose customers follow her wherever she goes. There are in this business many such "stars" or "big money makers," looked upon with envy by their less attractive and less prominent rivals. The secret of their popularity lies

[5] X 2. The foregoing sign is the key by which the woman referred to can be identified in our records. At this point, I shall explain once for all a system which will be continued throughout this book. The persons, places, and exhibits mentioned or referred to in the text are invariably definite and concrete. A complete register of them has been made, each item being lettered and numbered. The sign X 2 in the present instance enables the writer promptly to put his finger on the name, address, etc., of the person designated. This is equally true of all future references similarly indicated.

frequently in the perverse practices to which they resort.

The manner of carrying on the business has been somewhat modified in recent years. Formerly, the madame gave the girl a brass check for each customer. After business hours she cashed in her checks, receiving her share of the proceeds, usually fifty cents on the dollar. Nowadays, madames or housekeepers have a punch similar to those used by railroad conductors. When a customer is secured, the inmate hands the madame a square piece of cardboard, in which she punches a hole. Among the exhibits obtained during this investigation is a series of sixteen such cards with the names of sixteen inmates written upon them. They are literally filled with holes, all representing the business done on July 9, 1912, in a notorious one-dollar house on West 28th Street. The largest number of holes punched on a single card that day was thirty.[6]

The madames are alive to the importance of assuring their customers that every precaution is taken to guard the health of their inmates. Hence, in practically all the houses here referred to the investigators were assured that the girls have in their possession medical certificates signed by physicians, certifying that the bearer has been examined and is free from venereal disease.[7]

In many houses the "doctor" is said to come every week; he makes a hasty and superficial examination, for which he is paid one dollar, one-half of which sum he turns

---

[6] For additional samples, see Chapter VI.
[7] Among our exhibits are several business cards belonging to the physicians here alluded to.

Vice Resorts

over to the owner of the establishment. Of these physicians, one, a member of the now notorious Independent Benevolent Association — a group of men individually interested either directly or indirectly in the business of prostitution in New York City — has a large practice among the inmates of the cheaper type of house. At times, physicians who make a specialty of this branch are also active in the local politics of their respective districts: these men are in demand, for the keepers hope thus to " stand in " with those " higher up." On April 27, 1912, for example, the proprietor [8] of a house in West 36th Street [9] related the fact that he had recently employed a physician [10] who was being " mentioned " as the next leader in his assembly district. He tried to induce another keeper [11] to take the same doctor [12] because of political advantages to be gained thereby.

The medical certificates obtained under the circumstances described are, of course, worthless. According to the best medical opinion the inmates are all dangerous,— in many of them disease is in an acute stage. When external indications develop, the women are sent to a hospital. One girl, in such a condition as to be utterly useless in the house, was removed by her cadet, who, covering up the signs of her disease, put her on the street. An equally unconscionable and characteristic incident is the following: A young traveling salesman was assured that an inmate was free from disease and a medical certificate stating this fact was shown to him. As a matter of fact, she was at that

[8] X 461.   [9] X 1.   [10] X 473.   [11] X 415-a.
[12] Discharging his present doctor, X 474.

Commercialized Prostitution in New York

time under treatment by the very physician who had given her the certificate. The visitor contracted venereal disease. When he complained to the madame, she gave him a card of introduction to the same doctor, in order that he too might receive treatment.

Since the general closing of parlor houses in 1907 [13] it is a matter of common complaint among owners that business is not what it was before. The falling off is explained by an alleged increase of disorderly flats in tenements and of massage parlors. An owner who conducted a house on West 24th Street before and after the cleaning up in 1907 declared that his receipts, before that date $3,500 per week from 25 women, have gradually declined until now they are about $2,000 per week. Another owner, in West 36th Street, gave the reason for this falling off: He had visited disorderly flats and had there seen the men who had formerly been his customers. "Why do the authorities bother us?" he remonstrated. "We are locked within four walls. Nobody sees anything; nobody hears anything. They pass tenement house laws. Why don't they raid the flats and let us alone?"

There is therefore a constant effort on the part of the keepers of parlor houses to undermine the business done by women on the street, in flats, and in massage parlors. They write anonymous letters to the Police Commissioner and the Tenement House Department; they send men to the flats to persuade their inmates to leave and enter the parlor houses on the pretense that much more money can be earned thus; street walkers

[13] For details and results, see Chapter VII.

Vice Resorts

are frightened away from the vicinity of these houses by threats of the police. The madame of an establishment in West 28th Street drove away a street walker who was soliciting men for a nearby tenement house by telling her that she would make a complaint against her for using a tenement for immoral purposes. There are cases on record where keepers have had officers on the beat and plainclothes men arrest street walkers; they have also been known to "beat up" girls loitering near their places.

If the getting and holding of attractive inmates is one important qualification in a madame, getting and holding trade is its necessary counterpart. Madames are selected who are known to be expert in soliciting trade and "keeping it in the house." They gradually accumulate lists of names and addresses of men and boys, keeping them up to date, and at stated intervals they send announcements of change of address or a veiled suggestion as to the "quality" of "goods" on display. One ingenious owner has a very neat printed folder reading, "Kindly call at our old place of business, as we have a Beautiful Spring Stock on view." Occasionally — as in the accompanying circular — no object at all is alleged:

"*Dear Sir:* — Kindly call at your earliest convenience at the below address.
"Respectfully yours,
"X 1. W. 36th Street."

This notice was sent to a long list of patrons — to sailors on board certain war vessels, to business men, and to clerks.

Runners, lookouts, lighthouses, and watchboys —

Commercialized Prostitution in New York

the names involve overlapping duties — also figure largely in procuring trade. The chief business of the lookout is to stand on the curb in front of the house or near the door and warn the inmates who solicit at the windows, or the madame in the house, when officers or suspicious-looking strangers approach. He opens the doors of cabs and taxis and conducts prospective customers to the entrance of the house. If a stranger appears to be " green," the lookout urges him to visit the resort, at the same time describing the inmates and the prices charged. One of his important duties is to see that street walkers do not solicit in front of his employer's house and " take the trade away." Together with the runner or lighthouse, the lookout is supplied with cards advertising the house, which he gives to men and boys in the street. He also goes wherever men and boys congregate — to saloons, restaurants, entertainments, prize fights, wrestling bouts, lobbies of theaters, hotels, and other public places, to distribute cards and to drum up trade. For example, on March 7, 1912, a runner, who was paid twelve dollars a week and tips for his services in behalf of a " fashionable house " on West 46th Street, went to the Sportsman's Show at Madison Square Garden to advertise his establishment. On June 24, 1912, a runner for a house on West 25th Street stood on the northwest corner of West 24th Street and Sixth Avenue, describing its attractions to passersby. At the noon hour or at closing time he stands in front of entrances to factories, department stores, and other places of business to accost the workmen and distribute cards.

Vice Resorts

These young men are usually pimps or ex-pimps, former waiters in saloons and restaurants, ex-prize fighters and wrestlers, gamblers, crooks, and pickpockets who have lost their nerve.[14] They form a class by themselves. They are the "down-and-outers" in the underworld, eager for any job no matter how poor the wage. Some of them are well known and take pride in their ability to "run in" a lot of customers. Saturday, July 15, 1912, one of them, Max by name, claimed that he had "hustled in" sixty-five customers that day. When an argument arose between him and a competitor as to who had been more successful, the latter produced a slip on which his business was recorded: for June 15, 16, 17 and 18 it showed $142, $117, $68, and $97, respectively.

Chauffeurs and cabmen also do a thriving business in soliciting customers for vice resorts,— a service for which they receive an ample commission. Standing at street corners or in front of hotels and restaurants, they urge men in low tones to go to houses or to "ladies' clubs," as they are sometimes called. "I know some good houses," "I'll take you to see the girls," "I know where there are a lot of chickens," are among the familiar expressions employed. In occasional instances, customers can gain access only if escorted to the door by the cabman, who tells the maid that the man he has brought is "all right."[15] "Louie," one of the most aggressive

[14] Among them X 189, X 470, X 472.
[15] Among the cabmen who are active in promoting this business are X 85, Joe X 22, Louis X 24, X 483, X 484, X 485, X 486, X 487, X 488, and X 489. As a rule the men do not own their cabs,

Commercialized Prostitution in New York

of these solicitors, is married to a woman [16] who herself conducts an assignation house: she has recently served thirty days in jail for participation in the robbery of a guest.

Finally, bartenders and waiters in disorderly saloons often act as agents for the procuring of customers: indeed, they are not seldom the pimps of the women for whom they act. Customers entering the saloon to drink are directed to the tables where their women sit or receive the business cards of the houses where their women are to be found.[17] Out-of-town visitors are not infrequently "steered" by hotel porters and clerks.

With the exception of the relatively small number of "exclusive establishments" already alluded to, the resorts here dealt with — something approaching one hundred and forty of them — were at the period of this investigation notorious and accessible. The advertising devices above described were openly employed; and visitors procured easy entrance at most places. External order is, however, usually preserved. Madames and inmate rarely and then very cautiously solicit trade from

but hire them by the day or night from proprietors of livery stables. In any case, they are supposed to have a license, which costs fifty cents per year.

[16] X 490.

[17] At 10.40 P. M., on March 25, 1912, the bartender in a saloon on Manhattan Avenue suggested to a man that he visit an apartment in a tenement house at (X 475) West 111th Street. A waiter in a disorderly saloon at (X 476) Seventh Avenue endeavored to persuade a man in the rear room to go to a house on the second floor of a building at (X 147) Broadway. The waiter said there were three women in this resort and the price was only $5. Liquor was sold there at $2 per round.

Vice Resorts

windows, doors, or stoops of their houses, as they did in former years. They do, however, practise this method to some extent at the present time, especially in connection with some of the one-dollar houses on the side streets between Sixth and Seventh Avenues.

The sale of wine and beer plays an important part in the prosperity of the parlor house. Deprived of this adjunct, business falls off to an alarming extent. There is no difference of opinion among owners and madames as to the importance of the sale of intoxicating liquors. Especially is this true in the five-, ten-, and twenty-dollar houses, frequented by a more pretentious type of customer. In such places a small bottle of wine is sold for five dollars. A "round of drinks," namely, a pint of beer served in very small glasses, brings two dollars. Very little wine or beer is sold in the one- or two-dollar parlor houses in New York City at the present time.

In the more exclusive parlor houses "circuses" or "shows" are also given by way of stimulating business. These exhibitions are too vulgar and degrading to be described. Suffice it to say that men have been known to spend fifty and seventy-five dollars for such exhibitions. So also, obscene books, photographs, etc., are sold or exhibited.

One more fact must be emphasized in connection with business management: alcohol is needed to keep the inmates to their task; but even more essential from the business standpoint are drugs. The girl must be kept gay and attractive; her eyes must look out upon the world of business bright and unfaltering. She must smile and laugh and sing and dance, or she becomes a

Commercialized Prostitution in New York

" has been," a " poor money maker," and so in danger of losing her " job." Is it any wonder that she becomes a drug fiend as well as a drunkard?

In the preceding account I have aimed to give certain general characteristics of the parlor house. By way of making the picture somewhat more vivid I shall briefly describe a few houses of each of the three types with which the account deals, namely, the fifty-cent house, the dollar house, the five- and ten-dollar house.

A well known place in Worth Street [18] is a fair sample of the cheapest establishment,— a frame building, four stories in height. The investigator who entered at 4.30 P. M., April 12, 1912, picked his way through a basement where a cobbler sat at his work. After climbing two flights of stairs he found himself in a large, loft-like room formerly used for manufacturing purposes. The rooms where prostitution is carried on are partitioned off by means of curtains. The only furniture in the receiving " parlor " are old leather couches and chairs. The curtains over the windows are of dark, heavy material, almost shutting out the light and air. The entire interior is in a condition of decay, a fit setting for the use to which it is put. Three of the five inmates were present, scantily dressed and all claiming to possess health certificates, issued by the house doctor.

In the parlor of a three-story house in Hester Street,[19] investigated at 1 P. M. on April 15, 1912, there were three inmates awaiting customers. A lighthouse, named Angelo, stood on the stoop, beckoning to passers-by to enter. Angelo is about thirty-five years of age, a short,

[18] X 3.   [19] X 4.

Vice Resorts

heavy man, with a black mustache; a cap sits upon his mass of black hair. The man is well versed in the art of "pulling" customers into the house for which he works. As men approach, he motions with his head and right thumb toward the door, and, at the same time an expressive look comes into his watery eyes. In the rear of the house is a large tenement building and little children were playing and running through the hall at the time.

In one of the houses of this type a large wooden bench was placed against the wall of the receiving parlor. Business was very brisk at the time the investigator entered. The bench was full of customers crowded close together, while others, who could not be accommodated with seats, stood about the room. At the foot of the stairs which led to the bedrooms above, a man was stationed. Every time a visitor came groping his way down the stairs, the businesslike and aggressive announcer would cry out, "Next!" At the word, the man sitting on the end of the bench nearest the stairs arose and passed up. As he did so, the men on the bench moved along and one of the men who were standing took the vacant seat.

Of the three grades of parlor house, the one-dollar establishment predominates in Manhattan. Eighty of them were discovered during this investigation. They differ from the fifty-cent houses just described only in the somewhat better character of their surroundings. One of them on Sixth Avenue [20] was visited at 12.45 A. M., March 1, 1912. A little woman admitted the investi-

[20] X 9.

gator to the receiving room, where sat nine inmates, all scantily dressed. At 9.30 P. M. on March 6, 1912, another investigator counted eighteen inmates at this same address; during the evening of October 8, 1912, still another investigator visited this house and counted ten inmates. The house is one of the most prosperous in the business; it is well advertised and has a large list of customers.

The receiving parlor of another house on Sixth Avenue [21] is reached by climbing a flight of winding stairs and passing through a red door with a little window in it. The bedrooms are small and dirty, with practically no furniture. But the madame is very energetic. As customers enter the house she does not allow them to sit about and talk with the inmates, but urges them to spend money or leave. At 12.45 A. M., March 14, 1912, twelve inmates in flimsy costumes were seated about the parlor with five men — one a forlorn peddler who had come in to sell fruit. The place was in an uproar. One of the inmates was quarreling with the madame; several were complaining of poor business. One of them showed the investigator a plain white card with seven punched holes, proving that up to that hour she had earned only seven dollars, half of which was hers. She stated that she has to pay two dollars per day for board whether she lives at the house or not. As a matter of fact, she as well as other girls in some of these houses lives at home, going home early in the morning and not coming to "work" until 6 P. M.

In an establishment in West 28th Street [22] — torn down

[21] X 11. [22] X 12.

Vice Resorts

during the summer to make way for a loft building — the business was so profitable in June that the keepers are said to have paid the wrecker a large sum to delay from week to week. July 9 was one of the hottest days of the year. The odors in the old house, dirty and falling into decay, were indescribable. Through the long hours the sixteen inmates sat, hot and sullen. The day before the madame had left for a resort in Sullivan County where many of her kind go during the summer months. She had placed in charge the housekeeper,[23] who did the best she could to keep the girls in good humor and to get through the day's business. On this hot July day there were 264 customers. So the records on the cards showed the next morning as the housekeeper sat with the "boss" making up the "books." Buster served 30 of these; Babie, 27; Charlotte, 23; Dolly, 20, and so on. But the "boss" was not satisfied. "Why were not more women on the job last night?" he demanded. The housekeeper replied that they had stayed away because of the heat,— they had been completely "done up" the day before. Then the fat and well-groomed owner of the business picked up a china cup and hurled it at his luckless representative, while he cursed loud and deep. "The trade must be taken care of" and if she could n't "do it" he would get "some one who could."

To the third group belong all houses where higher prices rule: sometimes twenty-five dollars, or even more, are demanded, according to the nature of the service performed. Men of standing have been heard to ad-

[23] X 13.

Commercialized Prostitution in New York

vise young men to patronize this class of house on the ground that there is less danger; everything is said to be sanitary, the inmates less vulgar, younger, and more intelligent. The external appointments are indeed good, and there is at times even an outward air of refinement. Costly dresses and valuable jewelry are worn; the women are young, sometimes attractive in appearance.

For several years a house in West 15th Street [24] has been a notorious resort of this description. The property is owned by the madame who conducts the business for a very exclusive trade. For some time it was impossible for the investigators to gain admittance. Finally, at 11.45 P. M., May 5, 1912, one of them was "introduced" by a man well known as a promoter of the business in former years. Six inmates were on hand at this hour, "house girls," as they are called,— that is, they are "steady" and leave all their earnings to the house, purchasing from the madame everything they require, dresses, hats, gloves, hose, cosmetics, etc., all at exorbitant prices. On one occasion a rich man remained here four days and spent $600. To use the madame's words, "He opened ninety pints of wine at five dollars a pint; that is, I charged him for ninety pints."

On this same street is another establishment,[25] which has been conducted for several years. Here again the investigator had to be introduced before he was allowed to enter. The madame owns the property, having paid $20,000 for it some years ago. Like other women of her type, she has what she calls a "protector"— in this case said to be a politician and ex-city official. Ten

[24] X 19.   [25] X 20.

Vice Resorts

years ago this man met her when she was an inmate in Diamond Fanny's house on West 40th Street. Becoming infatuated with her, he took her away and "kept" her. Finally, he "set her up in business," and now he "looks after her." The madame keeps a list of girls whom she calls to the house as occasion requires. She described them as being "short ones," "tall ones," "blondes," "brunettes," "stout ones," "thin ones," and "just kids." "Men," she said, "are very fussy and you have to cater to them if you want to keep their trade." Some of the girls, she said, are employed by day in stores and offices, and take this method of increasing their earnings.

At 11.30 P. M., February 16, 1912, the investigator was taken to a very exclusive house [25a] by a chauffeur who receives a commission on every customer he secures. There were fifteen young and attractive girls in the receiving parlors, in one of which in the rear of the house an orchestra of young men played through the evening. The patron is ushered into the front parlor by colored maids trim and smart in white aprons; here the youngest of the "stock" is shown. The parlors are equipped with gold-trimmed furniture. Rich rugs and pretentious paintings testify to prosperity. Wine and beer are sold at the usual exorbitant prices. The inmates are dressed in elaborate evening gowns of silk and satin. As the investigator started to leave, the madame said, "Every Saturday night is bargain night, and next Saturday I shall have twelve young girls and guarantee them to be not over sixteen years

[25a] X 894.

of age. You must come early and get one of the bargains."

To some of these places customers are admitted only if they come in a cab or a taxi. This was the case at a place in West 46th Street [26] at 2.30 A. M., April 1, 1912. At this hour two men were refused admission because they were not known and did not come in a cab. The investigator, however, fared better: he had been brought to the house by Joe,[27] a cabman who recommended him to the madame.

It might be suggested that the foregoing data prove at most that parlor houses were in operation on the specific dates mentioned, and then only. As a matter of fact, the establishments in question were observed from week to week and from month to month. Notorious though they were, there was for the most part no interruption of business, except, in the latter part of the period of our investigation, as a consequence of a startling event to be described later.[28] A dollar house in Sixth Avenue [29] was visited March 5, March 6, May 25, July 21, and August 25, 1912; another [30] on West 24th Street, was visited February 2, February 19, March 24, May 24, May 25, 1912; twelve visits were paid to another in West 25th Street [31] between February 1 and July 16; the same number between February 8 and July 15 to a house in West 31st Street.[32]

[26] X 21. [27] X 22.
[28] The event alluded to is the murder of a notorious gambler, which shortly resulted in a change of attitude on the subject under discussion. See Chapter VII.
[29] X 25. [30] X 41. [31] X 59. [32] X 16.

Vice Resorts

The above instances are taken almost at random; many more are brought together at the close of this volume.[33] They establish beyond a doubt the systematic, notorious, and well-night undisturbed conduct of a large number of brothels in Manhattan during the period with which this record deals.

[33] Additional data, Parlor Houses, Appendix IX; also Appendix III, "Inmates of Vice Resorts."

CHAPTER II

VICE RESORTS: (b) TENEMENT HOUSES,[1] HOTELS, FURNISHED ROOMS, MASSAGE PARLORS

THE general situation in respect to vice resorts other than parlor houses does not materially differ from the conditions described in the preceding chapter. Tenements, hotels, and massage parlors were found to be openly, flagrantly, and in large numbers utilized for the commercial exploitation of prostitution in the interest, not of the woman herself, but of a promoter who drives her to do her utmost and assists in the work by cunningly angling for victims for her. The resorts to be now described were in many, perhaps in most instances, well known, accessible, and — for the period of this inquiry — usually unmolested.

(1) VICE RESORTS IN TENEMENTS

The tenement house law of 1911 defines a tenement house as a "house or building, or portion thereof, which is rented, leased, let or hired out, to be occupied, or is occupied as the home or residence of three families or more living independently of each other, and doing their cooking upon the premises, or by more than two families upon any floor so living and cooking, but having a common right in the halls, stairways, yards, water-closets or priv-

[1] Including apartment houses.

Vice Resorts

ies, or some of them." Any portion of a house of this description which is habitually used for the business of prostitution is regarded in this volume as a vice resort in a tenement. During the period of this investigation 1172 different vice resorts were found in 575 tenement houses at separate addresses in Manhattan.

The majority of the tenement buildings in which professional prostitutes thus ply their trade are situated between West 59th Street and West 110th Street, from Central Park west to Broadway or the river. A few of the cheaper type are conducted on the East Side in the vicinity of East 127th Street. On the lower East Side these resorts are less numerous than formerly.

The conditions in many of these tenements are scandalous and demoralizing to the last degree. Children grow up in them amid unsanitary conditions, with bad air and light, wearing clothes which do not keep the body warm, eating food which does not nourish, sleeping in crowded rooms,—brothers with sisters, daughters with fathers,— dressing and undressing in the presence of boarders or distant relatives, and witnessing sights never meant for the eyes of innocence. And, as if this were not enough to complete the moral breakdown, the prostitute creeps in like an infectious disease and spreads her degrading influence,— often without the least effort to conceal her vocation.

Examples are all too common: On February 19, about 7:30 P. M., an investigator was told of a disorderly place in a basement near by.[1a] It was suggested that he

[1a] X 112, X 113, X 114.

ring the janitor's bell and ask for the woman. When he did so, a little girl, apparently twelve years of age, came to the door. The child fully understood; going to the basement door, she called for the woman, who, opening the door, carefully scrutinized the investigator and invited him to enter.

A pale little girl, about fourteen years of age, was the companion of the dirty, rum-soaked janitress of a tenement on West 107th Street. The woman declared with vehemence that she would never allow any of these " vile huzzies " to live in her house; but there were plenty of them on the street, she said, turning to the child for confirmation of her statement. And the child told of their haunts in the neighborhood, giving house-number after house-number.

One day on West 108th Street the following scene was enacted: Two small girls and two boys were standing on the stoop as a man came up and rang a certain bell. As he did so the children snickered and spoke in whispers to one another. They knew that the bell rang in the apartment on the second floor rear; that the woman who came to the door in a loose kimono, with a mass of yellow hair and painted cheeks, was a prostitute [2] and that many other men with the same furtive eye, the same hesitating manner, had often passed through that door on other afternoons and nights.

A census was taken in 27 different tenements where immoral conditions were found to exist during the month of February, 1912; 18 of them situated on the East Side, 9 on the West Side. There were 390 families

[2] X 115.

Vice Resorts

living in the 27 tenements, with 425 children under 16 years of age, 214 boys and 211 girls. In addition, there were 92 unmarried men over 16 and 65 unmarried women over 16. The investigator also reported 30 widows living in these houses, with 18 children, the eldest being 12 years of age. In the different apartments 56 women were found who, on the basis of dress, conversation, and general bearing, were classed as "suspicious." While passing through the buildings up flights of stairs, from floor to floor, he noted the bad air, the dim light, the sagging floors, the dirty rooms where the walls were cracking through the paper. At times children were playing in front of doors behind which prostitutes plied their trade.

The prostitute does well for herself to take up her abode among the families of the poor. Her first move is to "get a stand-in" with the janitor or his wife. She "slips" them a dollar to see that the moving man does not injure the furniture. She alone among the tenants gives presents, fruit and candy to the children and pays them to run errands; slowly, but surely, she establishes herself securely under the eye that does not see and the ear that does not hear.

In no essential respect does the conduct of a tenement vice resort differ from that of the parlor house previously described. Prices are of the same range, from fifty cents to ten dollars; occasionally twenty-five dollars may be demanded. The same pretense of medical examination is made. The same advertising devices are employed. A madame who conducts a prosperous business in a tenement in West 58th Street sends a letter to her former cus-

Commercialized Prostitution in New York

tomers announcing the removal of the "library."[3] The use of the word "library" to indicate the resort and of "books" to indicate inmates is a popular one. Another madame urges her former patrons to renew their "membership in the library"; "new books," she asserts, are "on file in our new quarters." Still another enterprising promoter invites men to her place of business by saying, "Please call as I have a *new* member in the lodge." Similarly, business is procured through the same agents utilized by the parlor house — runners, bartenders, cabmen and chauffeurs. Where several establishments are conducted in one apartment building, elevator boys are given liberal tips by rival madames for "steering" callers to their flats. Often the madames or selected inmates go to public places or on the streets to solicit men. Sometimes they visit a large office building and under some pretext seek an interview with the heads of firms or with managers, and leave their cards. One day a young lawyer received a letter asking him to call at a certain address in Harlem on a matter of business. Though he did not recognize the name, he kept the appointment. He was dumfounded to find the supposed client a madame who had four inmates in her resort.

Liquor is more largely sold in tenement resorts than in parlor houses; the prices are usually the same, five dollars for a small bottle of wine, two dollars for a round of beer. In many of the resorts in tenements drugs are used by the inmates and sold to customers. For instance, the investigator of a resort on West 111th Street found several men smoking opium. In another flat, on West 37th

[3] X 117, X 118.

Vice Resorts

Street, one of the colored inmates was snuffing cocaine. In a tenement on West 39th Street there is an opium "joint" on the second floor where prostitutes "smoke." Some of the girls spend five and six dollars a day in this place. A girl who solicits on the street for a vice resort in a tenement on West 38th Street is a "dope fiend," and the madame of a flat on West 43rd Street, where there are four inmates, is addicted to the opium habit.

Not infrequently an apartment is utilized as a callhouse: girls, not living on the premises, are summoned by telephone when customers arrive. Additional recruits are also procured by call, when needed. The "call" is sometimes a half-way stage for the working girl on the road to complete prostitution. One day the madame of a call-house on West 58th Street received a special delivery letter, the number of which was 14.446—9, reading as follows:

"*Dear Madam,—*

"I tried to get you on the wire, but could not get you. Kindly send Miss Viola, the pretty little blonde, over at 2.30, not later if possible, on Monday afternoon (to-morrow) without fail — this is a good engagement.

"Also send me another pretty young girl and accommodating at 1.30 sharp. Now please do not disappoint me.[4]

"Signed (Mrs.) ——

"Sunday, May 28th."

Call-houses are usually cozy and homelike, presided over by a woman who dwells upon her efforts to make

[4] The original copy of this letter is on file. The woman's name and address are X 119, X 120.

Commercialized Prostitution in New York

her customers happy and comfortable. She declares that there are so many " nice respectable men " who are lonely in a big city and who want places where they will feel absolutely safe, where they can meet pretty girls, spend the evening, and get a few drinks. The stock in trade of such a house is usually a collection of photographs of the girls who are " on call." In addition, the madame exhibits a description of them, with measurements to show their physical development; the prices are appended. Her victims are variously procured: sometimes in restaurants frequented by girls who are employed in offices and stores: again, her place of operation may be the ladies' retiring room, where she enters into conversation with girls, inviting them to a meal or to spend an evening in her apartment. If she sees a girl alone at a table, she asks whether she may sit down with her and urges her to have a " little drink." Thus acquaintance springs up and " dates " are made for the theater, the madame paying the bill. At other times she goes to a department store and selects a girl, from whom she makes her purchases. The girl may be flattered by evidences of interest and friendship, or tempted by the prospects of fine clothes, leisure, and opportunities for pleasure. The danger is especially great if she has previously lapsed.

On certain streets on the East Side below 14th Street and in Harlem there are a number of cider " stubes " in the basement of tenement houses. In these " stubes " foreign girls act as waitresses, serving small glasses of cider or other soft drinks to customers. While serving, the girls solicit their customers to enter small rooms in the rear of the basement. The keepers of these " stubes "

Vice Resorts

are constantly advertising in the foreign papers published in New York for waitresses, offering to pay five or six dollars a week for such service. There is no doubt that many ignorant foreign girls are thus lured into lives of prostitution. One keeper who had a waitress about 38 years of age told the investigator that she expected to have two or three young girls in a few days. Another proprietor tried to secure the custom of the investigator by saying that he expected to secure two nice young girls for his " stube." Both were advertising in a German paper for help at the time. Such an advertisement for a very disreputable " stube " on East 4th Street appeared in a German newspaper on March 29, April 6, 8, 12, 13, 14, and 19.

Our records abound in material illustrating the foregoing account. For example, on May 19, 1912, at 7 P. M., and again on May 20, 1912, at 8 P. M., the investigator visited a vice resort in a tenement in West 43rd Street.[5] There were four inmates in the receiving parlor, all claiming to have medical certificates. The madame [6] declared, however, that if none of them suited she would for a larger price call up a young girl who was not " a regular sport." Thereupon she summoned the girl by telephone.[7] The newcomer appeared to be about eighteen years of age. While talking with the investigator, Irene said she had been in the " business " since last September but worked in a department store in Brooklyn.[8] Previously to this she had been employed in a store on Sixth Avenue. About one and a half years ago — so she says — her sweetheart, a shipping clerk, who makes $12 a

[5] X 121.   [6] X 122.   [7] Bryant, X 124.   [8] X 123.

Commercialized Prostitution in New York

week, seduced her, promising marriage: he does not know that Irene is making money " on the side " in this manner. Her aunt, with whom she lives, is very strict with her, requiring her to be home at ten o'clock every night.

The investigator pretended not to be satisfied with Irene; thereupon another girl, Margie, spoke up: she knew a " kid " that would suit, but the price would be ten " bucks " (dollars). From other remarks made, the investigator believes that the " kid " referred to is her sister. Margie leaves the flat at 5.30 P. M., for her home in Brooklyn, where she lives with her parents. They are under the impression that she is employed through the day in a wholesale millinery store downtown. The madame still insisted that if the supposed prospective customer really wanted young and pretty girls she could get them: " but," she added, " these girls come high, five and ten dollars."

On November 6, 1911, a woman who was afterwards employed in this investigation received a letter concerning a cider " stube " in a tenement in East 5th Street.[9] The letter read as follows:

" Reading of your good work in lending your services to assist the unfortunate creatures, I hope you will give your undivided attention, for this certain woman [10] is engaged in this business for the last seven years and is too shrewd to be caught. You will have to watch carefully her movements. She keeps a cider store on East 5th Street, New York. . . . Look up her record and you will

[9] X 125.   [10] X 126.
For further examples, the reader is referred to Appendix X, " Additional Data — Tenements."

32

Vice Resorts

see she was arrested a few times. . . . She just was sentenced four months over the Island. . . . Please I beg you to look into this matter. I would give you my name, but it is impossible for me to do so. I am a citizen of the U. S. A. I know this place ruins many young girls."

At 12.30 P. M., February 22, 1912, the investigator found two women in this place, by both of whom he was solicited to go to a rear room for immoral purposes. When they failed in their efforts, the proprietor said that she could get him a young girl if he preferred. Two days later the resort was visited by another investigator, who found two women acting as waitresses, by one of whom he was similarly solicited.

The various establishments above mentioned were all repeatedly visited in order to show their relatively permanent character and their freedom from interference: one [11] on Broadway was visited nine times in five weeks: another,[12] in West 29th Street, five times between February 8 and August 19; a third,[13] in the same neighborhood, five times in four months.

(2) ASSIGNATION AND DISORDERLY HOTELS

The parlor house and the tenement vice resort are, like shops, fixed places for the carrying on of prostitution as a trade. There is, besides, an enormous amount of itinerant prostitution utilizing mainly disorderly hotels. These places are commonly called " Raines Law " hotels. The history of the creation of the " Raines Law " hotels in New York City is exceedingly interesting. The

[11] X 147. [12] X 164. [13] X 182.

Commercialized Prostitution in New York

primary object of the framer of the law was to minimize the evils connected with saloons. As pointed out in the report of The Research Committee of The Committee of Fourteen, issued in 1910 under the title of " The Social Evil in New York City, a Study of Law Enforcement," [14]

" from the passage of this law dates the immediate growth of one of the most insidious forms of the Social Evil. This growth was due to a heavy increase in the penalties for a violation and the expected increased enforcement of the law by state authorities beyond the reach of local influences. To illustrate, the license tax was raised from $200. to $800., and the penalty of the forfeiture of a bond was also added.[15] To escape these drastic penalties for the selling of liquor on Sunday in saloons, saloon keepers created hotels with the required 10 bedrooms, kitchen and dining-room. The immediate increase was over 10,000 bedrooms. There being no actual demand for such an increase in hotel accommodations, the proprietors in many instances used them for purposes of assignation or prostitution, to meet the additional expense incurred. In 1905 there were 1407 certificated hotels in Manhattan and the Bronx, and of these about 1150 were probably liquor law hotels. In 1906 an important administrative provision was added to the law. This amendment, known as the Prentice Act, provided that hotels must be inspected and passed by the Building Department as complying with the provisions of the law, before a certificate could be issued to them. As a result of this new legislation, 540 alleged hotels were discontinued in Manhattan and the

[14] New York, A. H. Kellogg Co. (1910), p. 38.
[15] This $800 fee was imposed in Manhattan and the Bronx and was the rate established by the Raines Law at the time of its passage. The rate of $200 was the tax for saloons prior to the passage of the Raines Law.

Vice Resorts

Bronx. A large number of these places, however, continued under saloon licenses."

Since that time the fight against these vicious hotels on the part of the Committee of Fourteen has been constant and effectual. As a result, the business of prostitution as formerly carried on in them has been well-nigh suppressed. Very few of the hotels found to be used for "assignation" and "disorderly" purposes during the present investigation are ten-room establishments. In 1912, 400 of the 425 ten-room hotels which now exist were conducted as hotels for men only.[16]

A disorderly hotel, as we use the term, is one which violates Section 1146 of the Penal Law (keeping a disorderly house) by admitting the same woman twice in one night with two different men, or by renting the same room twice in one night to two different couples, or by regularly admitting known and habitual prostitutes. An assignation hotel is one doing business with transient couples, the women not necessarily being habitual prostitutes.

According to the official records, there were 558 hotels in Manhattan in 1912 which were certificated under the Liquor Tax Law. This number includes the legitimate commercial hotels as well as those which were the outgrowth of the Liquor Law. During the period of this investigation in 1912, 103 hotels were found which are classed as being assignation places, disorderly, or suspicious. Evidence was discovered which proved that habitual prostitutes were openly soliciting men on the street

[16] Report of The Committee of Fourteen, 1912.

Commercialized Prostitution in New York

and elsewhere to go to 65 of these hotels for immoral purposes. A woman investigator discovered 25 additional hotels where prostitutes declared they could freely take customers or have them openly visit their apartments or rooms. This gives a total of 90 different hotels in Manhattan which may be classified as "disorderly." In addition to these, seven different hotels were discovered which prostitutes claimed to be able to use for immoral purposes, though admitting that they had to be careful not to frequent them too often. In some of these places prostitutes are not allowed to use a room more than twice during every twenty-four hours, once during the day and again at night. There are six very high-class hotels which prostitutes asserted to a woman investigator they had used, or could use, under certain conditions. It is no uncommon thing for the more prosperous and well-dressed prostitutes to solicit trade in the lobbies of these hotels.

The hotels above referred to are situated in the following sections of Manhattan: Sixth Avenue from West 23rd Street to West 46th Street; Eighth Avenue from West 116th to West 125th Streets; the side streets between Broadway and Sixth Avenue from West 34th to West 53rd Street; Lexington, Third, and Fourth Avenues, and Irving Place. The centers where soliciting for these hotels is most flagrant are as follows: East 14th Street and Third Avenue, and north on Lexington Avenue; Sixth Avenue and West 28th Street; Seventh Avenue and West 35th Street; Longacre Square to the east; Columbus Avenue from West 60th to West

Vice Resorts

62nd Street; Eighth Avenue from West 116th to West 125th Streets.

Of these resorts many are weather-beaten buildings, dirty and unsightly without, unsanitary and filthy within. The small rooms are separated by thin partitions through which even conversations in low tones can be heard. The furniture is cheap and worn with constant use. A dilapidated bureau or dresser occupies one corner; a rickety wash-stand equipped with dirty wash bowl and pitcher stands in another. Cheap chromos hang on the wall, dingy with age. A small, soiled rug partly covers the floor which is seldom, if ever, scrubbed with soap and water. The air is foul and heavy with unpleasant odors, for the windows are rarely opened. The awnings that shut out the light are seldom lifted; they are sign-posts to the initiated, hanging mute and weather-beaten all the year round.

During the fall of 1907 a large number of parlor houses in the Tenderloin were raided and closed through the combined efforts of the Police Commissioner and the District Attorney's office. Some of these houses had been operated by men who subsequently transferred their activities to "hotels," where they continued to practise their former methods. Others took their women with them, lodging them in the "hotels," paying them certain commissions, and treating them in the same manner as in the house. A group of women thus attached to a "hotel" solicit for it on the street or in the rear rooms of saloons.

Between the proprietors of these "hotels" there is

Commercialized Prostitution in New York

great business rivalry. They constantly try to induce prostitutes attached to other resorts to patronize their place of business and become "regulars." They even go so far as to hire young men to make friends with the women and to offer them large commissions and better protection than they can secure elsewhere. At times, saloon keepers who allow prostitutes to solicit in their rear rooms do so on condition that the women take customers secured in their places of business to friendly hotels. For instance, the owner of a notorious saloon in East 14th Street demands that the women in his rear room take their customers to a certain hotel on Third Avenue. If one should break the compact and go to a rival place, she would be thereafter debarred, as if she had violated a code of honor.

Most of the solicitation for "hotels" is nowadays done on the street. Even here the proprietor attempts to keep his women in line. He sets spies at work to see that they take the trade where it belongs. The young men so employed are often the "pimps" of the street walkers, keen to see that their women do not "get away with any money" by going to a strange hotel, from which they cannot collect the commission. A young man of this character stations himself near the entrance of a certain hotel on the Bowery and, as his woman enters with a customer, carefully takes a pin from the right lapel of his coat and puts it on the left lapel. Woe to the woman if she fails to produce the money represented by the accumulation of the pins in the left lapel, when the business of the night is over!

When the street walkers of certain hotels are arrested,

Vice Resorts

the proprietor hastens to court to pay the fines, should such be imposed, or offer bail so that the girls may return to their " duties." In some cases he insists on repayment of the money he has advanced; and the girl is grateful because he has saved her from the Island. If a girl " breaks away " from a hotel and goes to a rival place of business the proprietor will go so far as to have her arrested again and again to teach her the lesson of " loyalty." In some cases she is glad to return to his good graces, especially if she finds herself on the Island.

There are many street walkers who are " free lances," taking their trade to the hotel which offers the best inducements. They realize that they are adrift — with no one but their " pimp " to protect them. And " pimps " are usually admirable protectors, masters of the art of " saving " their women from the hand of the law. They are keen, wise young men, well grounded in the business of exploiting the girls of the street at the least possible expense. Some of them are known as " gun men," " strong arm guys," " guerillas," and do effective work for politicians.

The prostitutes who are attached to certain hotels, as well as those who go from place to place with their trade are often given " rebates " or " commissions " on all the business they bring in. The rebate system was found to exist in 21 of the 65 hotels to which investigators were solicited to go for immoral purposes. If a customer pays $2.00 for a room, the prostitute receives $1.00 as a rebate. If, when in the room, he orders wine or beer, the girl receives another rebate or commission on the amount of the bill. Sometimes it is ten per cent, sometimes

Commercialized Prostitution in New York

twenty-five per cent: this, in addition to her own price, which varies from $1.00 to $5.00, or as much as she is able to persuade the customer to give her. Many hotels have rebate clerks whose duty it is to keep the accounts of the girls and pay them the commissions due them. This is a very important branch of the business; for if the solicitor is satisfied and is making "good money," she feels like continuing her patronage and "hustling" all the harder for her hotel.

Some of the disorderly hotels have two registration books, one of which is used for entering single visits during a period of twenty-four hours, the other to register the number of times different rooms are used during the same period. The first book is the one displayed to inquisitive investigators or inspectors. In some resorts there is a regular office, as in a legitimate hotel, where couples register at the desk; in others, a small window is all that can be seen. The clerk pushes the book through the opening and the man registers, often without seeing the clerk's face. The woman is not seen by the clerk at all, as she stands in the shadow away from the window.

Disorderly hotels offer a comparatively safe place in which to commit crimes of one kind or another. A well-known hotel referred to on another page has been the scene of murder. But the chief crime is stealing. The most successful prostitutes who solicit for these hotels are "gun mols," that is, pickpockets. They use all manner of subterfuges to "lift" the "roll" from the pockets of their customers. When their victim is heavy and sleepy from drink, they usually succeed, getting away before he realizes his loss.

Vice Resorts

But the hotel is utilized not only by the criminal prostitute: it is too often the scene of first seduction. A young, weak, and foolish girl is induced to dine, then to drink, with a comparative stranger who has first taken pains to ingratiate himself with her: without recollection of what has taken place in the interval, she awakens next morning amid the totally strange surroundings of a hotel of this character.

A brief description of a typical assignation and disorderly hotel will illustrate some of the general observations above made:

A Third Avenue hotel [17] has had an interesting and varied history. The ground is owned by citizens who are well known in social and financial circles. The name of the place has been changed since 1906-7, but the same proprietor conducts the establishment. Once he ran a house in the old Eldridge precinct, later another in East 9th Street. When these places were suppressed, he opened the hotel here in question. He and his manager [18] were both members of the Independent Benevolent Association in 1909. For some years this hotel has been on the Police List as under " strict surveillance "; now and then it has been raided. As far back as 1906 one of the agents of an investigation then in progress was told by a prostitute that detectives had informed the girls that if they resorted to this hotel they would not be molested; whether this is true or not, the fact remains that the hotel was still doing business during the period of this investigation.

On January 26, 1912, an investigator was solicited in

[17] X 207. [18] X 208.

Commercialized Prostitution in New York

the rear room of a notorious saloon on East 14th Street by "Pearl," who said she would have to take him to the hotel in question. Knowing the history of the resort, he accompanied the girl to the sitting-room in order to see if conditions were still the same; while there he talked with two other girls who are attached to the place. Thus he ascertained that the proprietor has two relays of solicitors, one group on the street from early morning until night, the other group on duty all night. To see that they attend strictly to business, a young man is employed to watch them at their work. If the girls enter into a dispute with customers over terms, the assistant endeavors to straighten out the difficulty. If they are arrested, he informs his employer, who, in turn, goes to the court and does what he can to secure their release. Mamie and Mary both stated that the rebate clerk gives them all amounts over $1.00 which their customers pay for rooms. In case customers buy wine at $5.00 per bottle, the girls receive $2.00 per bottle as a commission.[19]

(3) FURNISHED ROOM HOUSES

In addition to the more elaborate establishments already described, furnished rooms frequently serve their occupants as vice resorts. During the period of this investigation 112 furnished room assignation houses were discovered. The majority of these are within the following boundaries: First Avenue, Houston Street, the Bowery,

[19] As to this and other hotels, repeated observation at different periods established the notorious character of the places. Corroborative evidence is collected in Appendix XI, "Additional Data, Hotels."

Vice Resorts

and Avenue B; Second Avenue, 27th Street, Seventh Avenue, 31st Street; 33rd Street, Seventh Avenue, 42nd Street; Third Avenue, 27th Street, Seventh Avenue, 31st Street; Eighth Avenue, 33rd Street; Seventh Avenue, 42nd Street. The places are particularly dangerous because a stranger, seeking inexpensive board and lodging, has no way to ascertain their character: an innocent girl may thus unwittingly find herself in the most demoralizing surroundings.

Prostitutes do not necessarily live in the furnished room house. They may simply have an understanding with the madame, who, in reality, conducts an assignation house run on the same principle as a hotel, but without register or clerk. The price of the room is determined by the " privileges " for which the girl stipulates, — usually to the effect that, though not resident, she may bring " friends " there at any hour of the day or night. In some houses the prostitute pays $2.00 per night; elsewhere the landlady demands as much as $3.00 per night, or half of what the prostitute earns. In this way a large weekly rental is secured for very inferior quarters. Once possessing such a room with " privileges," the prostitute solicits or picks up customers on the street, and in public places of all sorts, such as dance halls, restaurants, and the rear rooms of saloons.

The women who use the furnished room houses are divided into three classes. The first are the occasional or clandestine prostitutes, to whom the furnished room offers a more secret place than the hotel for both the woman and the man. The second are regular prostitutes who use hotel and room alternately. They prefer to

Commercialized Prostitution in New York

go to the hotel, as they declare it is safer. "We are protected in the hotel," they say; "the proprietor knows us and you won't be molested." But customers who object to hotels are taken to her furnished room if the girl is not suspicious. The third class, who use the furnished rooms almost exclusively, are women who are nearing the end of their vogue as professional prostitutes. Rejected by hotels because they are dirty, diseased, or in the last stages of drug and liquor habits, these outcasts from the prosperous marts of trade escort their prey to their own miserable quarters.

A few illustrations of the manner in which the furnished room trade works will suffice:

A house of this character in West 31st Street [20] is one of the most notorious in the city. Late at night, August 23rd, 1912, it was entered by a large number of couples from a dance hall near by; subsequently, one of the men, about forty-five years of age, complained to the investigator that he had been robbed there that night. Four evenings later, eight different prostitutes entered with their customers in the course of less than five minutes. Shortly after, a colored maid from the house applied to a saloon near by to change two five-dollar bills. During the conversation she told the bartender, from whom she frequently bought liquor for the guests, that the rooms in the house were nearly all taken.

At 11 P. M. on March 19, 1912, several prostitutes were soliciting on Third and Lexington Avenues for a furnished room house in East 116th Street.[21] They each pay the landlord $2.00 per night for room and "privileges."

[20] X 253. [21] X 261.

Vice Resorts

One of these women appeared to be about twenty-one years of age. " I pay $2.00 per night for my room," she said, "and bring in as many men as I can grab. Whenever I am ready to quit for the night I meet my ' fellow ' and we go there to sleep."

A furnished room house in West 40th Street [22] is surrounded by tenements in which many white and colored families are living. On February 9, 1912, two colored women stood in the doorway, soliciting men as they passed by. As the investigator approached, two white children about ten and twelve years of age respectively, stood a few feet away listening to what was said.

(4) MASSAGE PARLORS

The massage parlor, so-called, is the last of the resorts to be dealt with. It is estimated that there are over 300 so-called massage parlors in Manhattan, a large part of which are believed to be vice resorts: only 75, however, were actually investigated in the course of this study and this is the number used in calculating the number of vice resorts in Manhattan.

Our investigation was thus restricted because of the peculiar difficulties involved in ascertaining the real character of many of these establishments. Some are transparent enough: others can be uncovered only by a customer. Our workers were instructed that it was not desired to attempt an extended investigation of every place. They were told to learn the nature of the massage given, the equipment, prices, the bearing, attire, and general be-

[22] X 262.

Commercialized Prostitution in New York

havior of the operatives. On the basis of these data they were to form an estimate as to whether or not conditions were suspicious. From earlier investigations and reports it was already believed that in nine cases out of ten the practices in these places are immoral and degrading to the last degree.

A large number of massage parlors are located on the upper floors of buildings on Sixth and Columbus Avenues and on the side streets from West 23rd Street to West 80th Street. They are indicated by means of large signs displayed in the windows or tacked on the doors. These places also advertise in a weekly paper published on Saturdays and offered for sale at five cents per copy on news-stands in hotels and other public places.

The rooms are usually equipped with high couches, bureaus displaying comb, brush, alcohol, and powder, and with wash stands. A manicure table is often placed by the window,— on it a set of instruments used in caring for the nails. In these places the operators insist that they give straight massage and that they do not conduct an immoral business. In other parlors, the sign on the window or door is the only evidence that such treatment is given. These are openly disorderly, no apparent effort being made to conceal the fact. The prices charged range from two dollars to five dollars, according to the service demanded.

Not a few former madames of houses of prostitution have established vice resorts under the guise of massage parlors for the purpose of continuing in business after their houses were closed by action of the law. Into these resorts they bring their former inmates,

Vice Resorts

who now pose as experts in the art of scientific massage. In the matter of securing new girls, the keeper of a massage parlor has a great advantage; for she openly advertises in the daily papers for girls to learn the " business of massage," or for those who have had experience in this or that method of massage as practiced in foreign lands. The advertisements state the age of the girl wanted and the weekly salary. As a result, many unsuspecting girls, answering advertisements, come into personal contact with well-dressed and apparently respectable proprietors. If the girl appears to be weak and easily led, the keeper begins by asking her how much money she has been in the habit of making each week; then remarks smilingly that some of her former operatives have made four or five times as much by not " being too particular." She describes in a general way what she means by " too particular." " Her customers," she says, " are often very rich and generous; if a girl is attentive and jolly, these men will give her generous prices and tips, and thus she can ' coin ' money."

It is only just to say that not all massage parlors are of the type described above. Some are legitimate and render scientific service to men and women who are actually ill. If the proprietors of such places would escape the general condemnation of their business, they should voluntarily seek the endorsement of respectable physicians and engage operatives who have *bona fide* certificates showing that they have spent a certain period of time in recognized institutions in preparation for their calling.

A few examples only need be given:

Commercialized Prostitution in New York

Margaret,[23] proprietress of a massage parlor on Sixth Avenue,[24] spent the evening of May 10, 1912, at a café in West 45th Street.[25] She admitted that business had latterly not been brisk: it had become difficult to get suitable operatives. The men who were procuring girls for her were becoming afraid to go after "young girls" and she did not want any "old ones." "Some fools," she said, "are writing stories about young girls being sold into slavery and even country girls are getting wise and think the men are going to put them into prison instead of giving them a chance to make a little money for themselves. That sort of thing only happens in the lower class of places. I have a nice business and nice men and I give the girl one dollar out of every two and three, and two dollars out of five, and half of anything over that. I had two girls; but one left me the other night because I would not let her take 'dope.' There comes a time with these 'dope fiends' when it interferes with business and they have to cut it out."

By way of inducement, Margaret invited the investigator, who was a woman, to work in her massage parlor the following Saturday and Sunday, offering to allow her to keep all she made: she "had to have an operative to help take care of her regular Saturday and Sunday customers"; by the following week she felt sure that her procurer would have a girl for her. The investigator called at the parlor early the following week to ascertain what had happened. She found that the house had been sold and that the new landlord had raised the rent for the "parlor" occupied by Margaret from $60 to $75

[23] X 246. [24] X 248. [25] X 247.

Vice Resorts

per month. Thereupon Margaret had moved out, going to the beach to open a temporary house for the summer.

Massage parlors are not uncommonly found in tenements,— there is one, for instance, in such a building in West 47th Street.[26] Two operatives were employed there with a madame [27] in April, 1912. Different resorts in this tenement have been reported to the Tenement House Department several times by the police, and arrests have been made here as far back as 1909.

A former member of the Chicago Vice Commission was in New York City in April. His experience in studying conditions in the former city had made him watchful and suspicious. One day he noticed a number of working girls, young, and foreign in type, climbing the stairs of a building in West 43rd Street.[28] As the girls came down some appeared to be disappointed, as though they had not been successful in their errand, whatever it might be. His interest was aroused. Observing a massage sign on the second floor, he concluded that the girls had been answering an advertisement to call at this place of business. An investigation thus started resulted in securing the following facts:

On April 3, 1912, a morning newspaper contained the following advertisement under the classification of "Help Wanted—Female." "Girl for light housework, not under 18; $7 to $9 a week. Mrs.[29]——, —— West 43rd Street, 2 flights up."

Later in the day a young woman investigator was sent to the address with a copy of the advertisement. She was

[26] X 250-a. [27] X 250. [28] X 251. [29] X 251-a.

greeted at the door by the woman, who soon disclosed the character of the place. In reply to the inquiries of the investigator, she explained the nature of the business: her customers paid from two to ten dollars, the girls receiving approximately one-half. An inmate had earned $48 in a week: but a girl's usefulness is brief, for frequent changes are necessary in order to retain the trade.

On the same date a morning paper published in the German language printed the following advertisement under the classification, "*Verlangt Weiblich.*"[30] "Girl, neat, German, not under 18 years of age. One who knows how to massage or one who is willing to learn. Wages paid while learning. Inquire Mrs.[31]——, —— West 43rd Street, two flights up." This is the massage parlor described above.

On April 9, 1912, the same investigator received the following letter from the proprietor of the parlor:

"*Dear Mrs.* ——:

"If you have not taken any position yet, would you kindly call on me?

"Respectfully,

(Signed) "——."

A week later the investigator called again, finding the establishment still in operation, with a new assistant, procured through the landlord. With a little prodding, the garrulous madame resumed her confidences, explaining the process of "fixing up" girls so as to appear young, and other details of her nefarious occupation.

In the foregoing pages we have circumstantially described the more prominent forms taken by vice in New York City. It is surely no exaggeration to main-

[30] Wanted — Female. [31] X 251-b.

Vice Resorts

tain that the evidence submitted proves that prostitution in New York City is widely and openly exploited as a business enterprise.[32] The exploiters, the scenes of their operations, their methods, their associations, and their victims are all equally notorious. It is idle to explain away the phenomena on the ground that they are the results of the inevitable weakness of human nature: human weakness would demand far fewer and less horrible sacrifices. Most of the wreckage, and the worst of it, is due to persistent, cunning and unprincipled exploitation: to the banding together in infamous enterprises of madame, pimp, procurer, brothel-keeper, and liquor vender to deliberately carry on a cold-blooded traffic for their joint profit,— a traffic, be it added, from which the girl involved procures at the most, with few exceptions, her bare subsistence, and that, only so long as she has a trade value.

[32] For a statistical summary of vice resorts, see Appendix I.

CHAPTER III

PLACES WHICH CATER TO VICE

PLACES which cater to vice are divided into two groups. The first group, catering directly to vice, includes saloons and their accessories, such as concert halls and cabaret shows; the second group, operating indirectly, comprises public dance halls, burlesque theaters, amusement parks, and boat excursions. The proprietors of these places usually have full knowledge of the demoralizing influence of their establishments, and deliberately encourage such conditions for the purpose of increasing their profits. "The saloons which cater to women," writes Professor Rauschenbusch, "the dance halls that encourage indecent dances and supply long intermissions for the consumption of liquor; pleasure resorts and excursion steamers, theaters, music halls, and moving picture shows that use the ever ready attractiveness of sex interests — are all smoothing the downward road — and they know it."[1]

Nevertheless, it would be unjust to condemn indiscriminately all persons connected with the places which indirectly promote vice. An exception should be made of certain proprietors of dance halls and amusement parks, the commissioners of public parks, and some excursion boat owners.

[1] "Christianizing the Social Order," p. 278.

Places Which Cater to Vice

(1) DISORDERLY SALOONS, CONCERT HALLS, AND CABARET SHOWS.

These places may all be considered under one heading because they are connected with saloons: they differ only in the character and grade of entertainment given in them, this varying with the ingenuity of the proprietor.

A disorderly saloon is one where indecent acts occur, where indecent language is used publicly, where there is open solicitation for immoral purposes, or to which known and habitual prostitutes resort. The records in the office of the State Commissioner of Excise show that up to and including January 28, 1913, 4,583 liquor tax certificates were issued in the Borough of Manhattan under Sub-Division One of the Liquor Tax Law. During the period of this investigation, *i. e.*, from January 24, 1912, to December 15, 1912, the rear rooms of 765 saloons at separate addresses were investigated. Unescorted women, who from their actions and conversation were believed to be prostitutes, were seen in 308 of the 765 rear rooms investigated, and the investigators were openly solicited by prostitutes for immoral purposes in 107 separate rear rooms. In some of these places white men and colored women, in others colored men and white women, mingle freely.

The majority of disorderly saloons are situated on Third Avenue and side streets from East 10th to East 125th Streets; on Sixth Avenue and side streets from West 22nd to West 49th Streets; on Seventh Avenue and side streets from West 23rd to West 52nd Streets; and on Eighth Avenue and side streets from West

Commercialized Prostitution in New York

14th to West 125th Streets. There are other disorderly saloons on the lower East Side, on the Bowery and surrounding streets, on Amsterdam, Columbus, and Lexington Avenues.

Many of these disorderly saloons occupy the ground floor of buildings the upper floors of which are used as assignation and disorderly hotels under the same management. The rear rooms are filled with small tables, where customers are served with drinks from the bar. Some of the rooms are large and clean, others small and exceedingly dirty. The ladies' retiring rooms in the most disorderly places are very unsanitary. A report on one of the rear rooms describes it as being "long and narrow, with a row of tables down the length of two walls and in the center. So narrow and low and dirty is the room that it is as if a stable had been hastily emptied and swept out and turned into a temporary drinking booth."

The managers of these establishments are sometimes sober and industrious men. They have been selected by the brewers to open saloons because of their personal qualities; for they are hail fellows well met, "good mixers," who make and hold friends. But these qualities do not always go hand in hand with business sagacity. The "good mixer" soon finds himself in debt to the brewer who set him up in business. The iron-clad mortgage which the brewer holds on the fixtures hangs over the saloon keeper like a menacing hand. He finds that he cannot make any money in the ordinary business of selling liquor over the bar; sales are increased if women of the street are encouraged to use the rear

Places Which Cater to Vice

room as a "hangout" where they can enter unescorted to meet men. In addition, the proprietor finds that he can still further increase his profits by renting rooms over the saloons to the women and their customers. "We have to evade the law to make any money," [2] remarked the owner [3] of a resort in East 116th Street. Some of the saloon keepers, of course, need no forcing. They started out to exploit prostitution in connection with the liquor business. Their business is organized with that in view. Prostitutes are attached to the rear room, as to the hotels previously described, by certain rules and customs. For example, one woman is not permitted to entice the customers of another; the girl who is unable to hold her customer is gradually forced to saloons that are less exacting. When the prostitute has secured her customer, she must in certain saloons order fancy drinks. This has to be cleverly done so as not to offend. The girl intimates that she loves to drink wine because it makes her jolly and companionable. If she is personally attractive and well dressed, the man does not object. "You know," she murmurs, "I hate a cheap skate who won't treat a girl like a lady." If she is unsuccessful in persuading her customer to buy expensive drinks, the proprietor puts her out as a poor "wine agent," discharges her from his employ, as it were. This is the practice of the manager of a well-known saloon in East 14th Street.[4] On the other hand, the proprietor pro-

[2] Mr. Arthur H. Gleason brought out this point in two articles under the title of "The Saloon in New York," published in *Collier's Weekly*, in the issues of April 25 and May 2, 1908.
[3] X 263.
[4] X 264, X 265.

tects the successful prostitute, just as does the hotel keeper, previously mentioned.

The giving of commissions to prostitutes on the sale of drinks to their customers in the rear rooms of saloons does not appear to obtain as a general practice in Manhattan; but it is understood that women do receive commissions on bottled wine and beer which customers order when occupying with them the rooms upstairs.

Efforts are frequently made to enliven the scene by music and singing. In the ordinary rear room, with cheap furniture, flickering lights, bad air, and filled with rough men, a sallow-faced youth, with a cigarette hanging out of the corner of his mouth, sits at a piano and indifferently bangs out popular airs in wild, discordant notes. This becomes a "concert hall" when the proprietor provides more music and additional singers. After a while a café is established, where food can be obtained as well as drinks. The grade of the entertainment improves a bit further and the place is known as a cabaret show, a poor imitation of the legitimate cabaret show given in respectable restaurants. Besides music, dancing, sometimes of an obscene character, is carried on in the rear room. Dancing is, indeed, cultivated for the express purpose of stimulating the sale of liquor and what goes with it. The dances are frequented by prostitutes, pimps, thieves, and those who want to see the "sights." Young and foolish girls, for whom "social club" dances have become commonplace, are persuaded to visit these saloons. Here they meet men whose sole object is their subsequent exploitation for pleasure or for money. Under this influence and

Places Which Cater to Vice

environment they drift all the more rapidly into lives of professional prostitution.

The prostitutes who frequent certain saloons in Manhattan combine their immoral business with crime, particularly stealing. They boldly seek out a man who appears to be " green," or under the influence of liquor, and " trim him," as they say. The girls use their pimps, or, what may be nearer the truth, the pimps use their girls, to carry out these robberies. A pimp, becoming acquainted with a stranger, " steers " him " up against " his " gun mol " (a prostitute who is a pickpocket), who aids in the " trimming " process. Sometimes, if the hour is late and they are in the right place, the pimps and their women become so bold as openly to go through the pockets of their victims and afterwards throw them into the street. On one such occasion the victim called loudly for the police, and, though an officer stood on the other side of the street, his eyes were withheld and his ears were stopped. The pimp laughed at the stranger and told him to " yell louder " for all the good it would do him.

Of the statements just made abundant confirmation is at hand:

A saloon in East 14th Street,[5] one of the landmarks of this busy street, has been notorious for many years. Its proprietor has a wide reputation. His home life, according to report, is all that it should be; no one has ever seen him intoxicated. Big, jolly, aggressive, he is the embodiment of hospitality as he stands at the bar, greeting those who enter with a kindly shake or a friendly nod. In the

[5] X 265.

Commercialized Prostitution in New York

rear room of his resort disgraceful conditions exist. At one end there is a small platform, on which a young man sits, playing popular airs on a piano through the long hours of the night. White-faced waiters, with their hair carefully cut and plastered down, glide noiselessly about the tables. Carefully trained are these young men in keeping the glasses full. They work quickly. About the tables sit equally well-trained prostitutes. A man who entered at 6.30 P. M., January 26, 1912, and stayed until 8.30 saw the waiters urge the men customers to invite different girls to their tables. Two of the girls were not engaged. As the rule of the place forbade them to go to the table where men were sitting, they enlisted the waiter's aid. Gliding to the table where three men were drinking, he soon succeeded in having the girls invited to join the party. The investigator gained the confidence of the girls with whom he conversed. "A girl must order fancy drinks here when she is treated," said one of them; "if she don't, the manager [6] orders her out and won't let her come in again." Pearl, a girl about twenty years of age, solicited him to go to a hotel [7] not far away. Two months later, at about 11 P. M., there were more than twenty prostitutes and fifteen men in this rear room. The same conditions existed during the evening of April 8, 1912, when a woman entered the rear room alone. She walked to the extreme end of the room and saw eleven prostitutes and four men sitting at tables. If this woman had been a "regular," that is, one who frequented the place night after night, a waiter would have brought her,

[6] X 264.   [7] X 269.

Places Which Cater to Vice

entirely free, a small glass of beer or ginger ale. She learned on inquiry that if a " regular " was " arrested " the manager would " fix it up." Inducements were also offered in the hope that she would enter the service of this house. The " suckers " all come down here, she was told: " We get them before the girls on Sixth Avenue do."

On January 20, 1912, a well known pimp [8] met his woman in the rear room of a saloon on Seventh Avenue.[9] An investigator saw this prostitute give him a ten dollar bill. The pimp upbraided the girl for not having more money and struck her a heavy blow in the face. She fell to the floor. There was some excitement when this occurred. The girl was advised to have the pimp arrested, but she refused to do so although her eyes were swollen and discolored. This same rear room harbors other prostitutes who night after night take their customers to a furnished room house in West 27th Street,[10] where the landlord charges twenty-five cents for the use of a room.[11]

(2) MISCELLANEOUS PLACES

In New York City there are places of a certain type which cater directly to vice in that they are frequented, for the most part, by immoral and dissolute persons who not only solicit on the premises for immoral purposes, but create conditions which stimulate the business of prostitution. The proprietors have a guilty knowledge of the fact that prostitutes and their kind use the

[8] X 274.   [9] X 275.   [10] X 276.
[11] For additional illustrations see Appendix XII —" Additional Data — Saloons."

Commercialized Prostitution in New York

premises as an adjunct to immoral trade. Such places include restaurants, pool rooms, delicatessen stores, candy shops, hair dressing and manicure parlors, barber shops, cigar stores, palmist and clairvoyant parlors, livery stables, and opium dens. The places in question are usually situated in the vicinity of vice resorts. To the ordinary observer their outward appearance is that of any respectable business establishment. The signs are on the windows, goods are displayed, customers may come and go, and there is a general air of activity. From January 24, 1912 to November 15, 1912, 180 reports were made in connection with conditions in 91 such miscellaneous places.

In some of these places, known as "hangouts," respectable trade is neither sought nor encouraged. A stranger is looked upon with a certain amount of suspicion and treated as an intruder. If he asks for a meal, he is told that the hour for serving meals has passed; if he desires to purchase a package of food from the shelves, he is informed that the particular brand he seeks is missing.

The real purpose of the place is to afford a rendezvous where confidences may be exchanged and deals planned — where birds of a feather may flock together and be fed or entertained. It is indeed a varied group that sit about the tables or lounge idly at the entrance: owners of houses of prostitution, madames and inmates, street walkers, pimps, procurers, gamblers, pickpockets, thieves, and crooks of every shade and kind. Young boys of the neighborhood become fascinated with the adventurous lives of the men who frequent these places and soon join their ranks.

Places Which Cater to Vice

One of the most important of these establishments is a delicatessen store on Seventh Avenue,[12] a notorious and popular place. The little room is crowded with things to eat and drink. Small tables are placed about the vacant places and at these tables sit owners of houses, madames and inmates, pimps, runners, and lighthouses. All the forces for the conduct of the business of prostitution in parlor houses are here, scheming, quarreling, discussing profits, selling shares, securing women, and paying out money for favors received. If the walls of this little room could speak, they would reveal many secrets. The value of houses is debated, the income from the business, the expenses of conducting it, the price of shares to-day, or to-morrow, or in the future, if this or that happens. Here is the center of the trade in certain types of houses, — the stock market, where members bid and outbid each other and quarrel over advantage given or taken. The owner of this delicatessen store, a stout and rather handsome man, moves about quietly. Upstairs, his wife, hearty and ample, cares for his home and his children. Now and then the children sit at the tables with wondering eyes and listen. The eldest girl, about seventeen, dressed in white, talks earnestly with a handsome procurer or holds the hand of a madame.

In some of the places here alluded to liquor is sold without a license; in others, gambling is carried on. Poker, stuss, No. 21, pinochle, are played in the rear behind closed doors. For instance, during the month of April, 1912, a stranger entered a " coffee and cake hang-

[12] X 108.

out" in East 114th Street.[13] The usual crowd of pimps, crooks, and gamblers sat about the tables eating and drinking. A man rose from a table and walked to the rear to a little white door. He tapped gently; the door opened and closed behind him. As it did so, the stranger saw in an inner room men seated about a table.

Elsewhere a lucrative business in the sale of drugs is carried on. Blanche, a street walker, crazy for morphine at 2.30 A. M., on May 18, 1912, pleaded with a man in a restaurant on Seventh Avenue [14] to purchase some for her. The stranger with whom she was at the time, moved to pity at her pleading, furnished the money. A bottle of morphine tablets was hastily procured from a well-known pharmacy on Seventh Avenue. Snatching the bottle from his hand, she concealed it in her stocking.[15]

The cigar store, the pool room, the coffee and cake restaurant, are the favorite resorts of the pimps. Here they come to make deals for their women, to receive telephone messages from their girls on the street or in vice resorts, to plan "line ups" [16] when a "young chicken" is about to be broken into the business, and to buy drugs for their girls and themselves. It is common knowledge that here gangs are formed and arrangements

[13] X 295.
[14] X 296.
[15] X 297.
[16] A "line up" is the ruin of a girl who flirts with men and accepts their advances and immoral suggestions. Finally she yields to an invitation to visit a furnished room and the word quickly passes among the "gang." One by one the boys and men, perhaps only two or three, perhaps more, visit this room.

Places Which Cater to Vice

for robberies or other criminal acts made; here the spoils are divided; guns are hidden when officers come to search, and men beaten who make a " squeal."

The prostitute herself frequents the hairdressing and manicure parlors, popular with her for two reasons: first, because here she makes herself " beautiful " under the hands of the proprietor, and second, because through the operator she learns of resorts where she may earn " better money." The imparting of such information is a part of the hairdresser's trade. She is the fount of knowledge on this subject; " swell " madames patronize her place, urging her to send them attractive girls. If the right girls do not come in, she advertises in the papers, using her " parlor " as a decoy. Her husband — if she has one — may be a thrifty man who mingles with his wife's customers, selling them attractive hats or suits, and other things, and finally acting as their bail bondsman if they are arrested and brought to court. At least one such husband has grown wealthy in the business.

Such a hairdressing and manicure parlor, for example, is conducted on Sixth Avenue.[17] The woman caters only to prostitutes; and part of her business is to find out if any of her customers are dissatisfied with their present places or if they are not attached to any resort. In either event, she offers to send them to find a place where they can earn more money. One day a woman having her hair shampooed in this parlor actually heard the proprietor send girls to different vice resorts. She advertises in the daily press for help. For instance, on Saturday, April

[17] By X 298 at X 299.

Commercialized Prostitution in New York

6, 1912, a daily paper contained the following advertisement under " Female Help Wanted " :

" Hairdresser and manicure wanted, experienced. Apply ——, —— Sixth Avenue." [18]

Pool rooms and cigar stores offer peculiar facilities for young boys of the neighborhood to become acquainted with the life of the underworld. Even before leaving school, boys often frequent them; soon some of them join little cliques and gangs formed by the criminal element. They become pickpockets or ordinary crooks. If endowed by nature with large muscles and an instinct for fighting, they become preliminary boxers and gradually develop into the gang members or political guerillas who do such valiant service at the polls on primary or election day. From the ranks of these the pimp is developed. As neighborhood boys they have little difficulty in securing girls who, like themselves, are adventurous, or already immoral. It therefore becomes easy either to trap a girl and ruin her, or to " break in " the already immoral girl to a life of professional prostitution under protection.

It is a strange fact, but it is true, that prostitutes often select young men whom they see in front of pool rooms and cigar stores and actually invite them to become their pimps and share the proceeds of their business. A young boy about eighteen years of age was standing near the entrance of a pool room on Second Avenue one hot afternoon in August, 1912, jauntily puffing a cigarette as a stranger passed with a man who had lived in the neighborhood many years. " See that kid? " said the man. " A

[18] X 298, X 299.

Places Which Cater to Vice

young prostitute on the avenue has picked him out for her pimp. They grew up together and both have gone on the bum. She was 'lined up' about a year ago by a gang that 'hangs out' in a cigar store on East 14th Street. Since then she has been a regular prostitute."

There is another group of miscellaneous places, different from those referred to above, namely, the natural channels through which the varied life of a great city passes. These are freely used by the prostitute. Attention is called to them simply to emphasize the fact that wherever groups of people meet for innocent pleasure or for business, there the prostitute lingers to ply her trade. Such places include subway and railway stations, hotel lobbies, entrances to department stores, ferry slips, and post office buildings. Prostitutes find these crowded thoroughfares excellent centers in which to solicit or to make "dates." Pimps and procurers also frequent such places to "pick up" adventurous girls who are alone or in pairs, out for pleasure or excitement.[19]

(3) THE STREETS

The streets of Manhattan are openly used by prostitutes for soliciting. During the period of this investigation, street walking has been most conspicuous in certain localities which may be roughly described as follows:

Broadway, from West 27th to West 68th, and the side streets from West 26th to West 64th;

Sixth Avenue, from West 16th to West 45th, and the side streets from West 25th to West 31st;

[19] For further illustrations, see Appendix XIII — "Additional Data — Miscellaneous Places."

Commercialized Prostitution in New York

Seventh Avenue, from West 24th to West 42nd;
Columbus Avenue, from West 59th to West 66th;
Columbus and Eighth Avenues, from West 99th to West 125th;
Second Avenue, from East 8th to 9th, and between East 12th and East 14th;
Third Avenue, from East 9th to East 28th, and from East 99th to East 137th, and the side streets to Lexington Avenue;
Irving Place, from East 14th to East 15th;
Houston Street, on the lower East Side around Allen and Forsythe Streets.

Of all these thoroughfares, Broadway is most freely utilized for soliciting. During the nights of March 7, 11, 14, 19, 20, and 21, 1912, at the hours of 8.30 P. M., 9 P. M., 10 P. M., 11 P. M., 11 to 12 P. M., 11.30 P. M., 12 A. M., 12.15 A. M., 12.30 A. M., 12.45 A. M., and 1.55 A. M., eighty-four street walkers were seen accosting men at different places on Broadway from West 34th to West 65th Streets. This number does not take into account prostitutes who were merely promenading or those who were lurking in the shadows of the side streets. Reports of a similar character could be given for the months of April, May, June, July, August, September, and October, 1912, showing that solicitation on Broadway was continuous.

Sixth Avenue is another favorite resort for street walkers. On September 17, 18, 23, 25, 26, and 28, 1912, at such hours as 4 P. M., 4.30 P. M., 6.30 P. M., 7.15 P. M., and 8 to 9 P. M., fifty-five prostitutes were seen soliciting men between West 24th and West 29th Streets.

Places Which Cater to Vice

In most instances the destination of these couples was hotels on two corners of West 28th Street. The same general conditions as described regarding solicitation on Broadway and Sixth Avenue exist in other sections of the city.[20]

(4) PUBLIC DANCE HALLS

No places of amusement are so filled with moral dangers to boys and girls as certain public dance halls in New York City. A conviction to this effect, long held, has been strengthened as a result of a thorough and comprehensive investigation of 85 public dances given in 47 different dance halls in Manhattan from January 24 to June 24, 1912. Ninety-six reports were made of conditions in these dance halls by three investigators, two young men and a young woman, who worked independently. In some instances they reported on the same dance without knowing of the presence of one another, thus removing all doubt regarding the facts as presented. No special dances were selected for observation, the investigators having been sent to those which were publicly advertised from time to time.

Of 75 different dances reported between January 24 and June 24, only 5 are characterized as decent; 11 were more or less objectionable, 59 wholly so. At all but 3, intoxicating liquor was sold; at 61, minors were present; at all but 2, the investigator concluded that the attendance was largely disreputable.

A woman investigator reported 31 dances, at 22

[20] For detailed statistical statements respecting street-conditions, see Appendix VII, p. 291.

of which she was solicited by 53 men; men investigators, reporting 80 dances, were solicited 47 times by 43 different women.

The proprietors of the dance halls in question have "open dates," on which their halls may be rented by social clubs or other organizations for the purpose of giving an "affair" or a "racket," as a ball is sometimes called. There are hundreds of these clubs and organizations in New York City, and the chief feature of the year's activity is the giving of a ball which all the friends of the members are expected to attend. Their membership lists are made up of cliques or gangs of young boys and men who come together because of some mutual interest, sometimes for worthy motives, but very often as a cover for disorderly and even criminal purposes. Between some of these groups there is great rivalry, at times leading to fights and disturbances.

The usual method of advertising dances is by distributing "throw aways" or small colored cards on which are printed, not only the name of the group giving the dance, but also the choruses of popular songs, parodies, or verses. These latter intimate the character of the proposed frolic. They all appeal to the sex interest, some being so suggestive that they are absolutely indecent. During the progress of a dance in St. Mark's Place,[21] a young girl, hardly above seventeen years of age, presented a boy with a printed card advertising a ball soon to be held. When the card is folded, it forms an obscene picture and title.

During the past few years aggressive measures have

[21] X 318.

Places Which Cater to Vice

been taken by different reform organizations aiming to bring about a more wholesome atmosphere in connection with public dances, especially those attended by poorer boys and girls. Proprietors have been induced to employ special officers to attend the dances and keep order, prevent " tough " and " half-time " dancing, and protect innocent girls from the advances of undesirable persons. The duties of the special officer are difficult to perform. If he interferes too much, the dancers go to some other place where they enjoy more freedom. As a result, the honest proprietor who endeavors to conduct a respectable hall loses patronage, while the disreputable owner makes all the profit. Again, the young people who attend these balls know immediately when a person different from themselves appears in the hall. At once the dance becomes modest and sedate and the visitor goes away to report " that while conditions are not what they should be, yet on the whole there is great improvement."

A social club [22] gave a ball on the evening of March 23, 1912, at a hall [23] in East 2nd Street. The dancing was very suggestive. The special officer [24] was entertaining a police sergeant, but neither made any effort to regulate the actions of the dancers. The next afternoon another club [25] occupied the hall at the same address, with the same special officer in attendance. Suddenly, when the dancing was in full swing, the officer hurriedly rushed among the dancers and told them to " cut it out " as three detectives had just come in and he did not want to see the place closed up. A girl, apparently thirteen years of age,

[22] X 319.　　[23] X 320.　　[24] X 321.　　[25] X 322.

Commercialized Prostitution in New York

was dancing at the time and the officer put her off the floor, loudly declaring that the proprietor did not allow young girls to dance in the hall. Things resumed their former aspect, however, as soon as the detectives retired.

Wine, whisky, and beer, freely sold in connection with certain public dances, are responsible for much vulgarity and obscenity. Young girls have been seen to yield themselves in wild abandon to their influence, and have been carried half fainting to dark corners of the hall and there, almost helpless, have been subjected to the most indecent advances.

A political organization gave a ball at a resort [26] in Avenue D, February 16, 1912. Wine, champagne and beer were sold from a bar located on the north side of the hall or served at tables. The waiters were men, while three women acted as bartenders. By actual count, one hundred girls and boys were intoxicated. Many of the drunken girls were sitting in corners of the hall on the laps of their equally intoxicated partners, who were hugging and kissing them. The same conditions, with variations, have been observed in other dance halls where liquor was served and where the intermissions between the dances were extended so as to give all an opportunity to buy drinks.

At a ball given by another organization [27] in an East 2nd Street resort [28] on March 1, 1912, the dancing was exceedingly vulgar and suggestive. A police officer watched the obscene exhibition in company with the proprietor of the hall. After the officer left, a detective in

[26] X 328.   [27] X 330.   [28] X 320, X 320-a.

Places Which Cater to Vice

plain clothes and another officer in uniform came in. The proprietor escorted them to the bar, where they were served. Then the host entertained his guests by pointing out the girls whom he considered to be the most adept; and the three men passed comments upon their cleverness.

A crowd of pimps, gamblers, pickpockets, and "strong arm guys" attended a dance given on March 30, 1912.[29] Here a pimp named Daniel [30] deliberately struck his girl in the face with his fist. She fell to the floor and was carried to the dressing room covered with blood. The woman investigator, who had been a nurse, took charge of the girl and summoned a physician. A doctor [31] with an office in East 4th Street, sewed four stitches in the girl's lip and charged her five dollars, which was to include two future visits. The doctor offered the investigator fifteen dollars to help him with a case that night, and five dollars extra if she would accompany him to his room. Nor was this the only immoral solicitation that the woman investigator was subjected to in order to get the facts.

A man who was shot to death not long ago, a "gun man," gave a dance on March 29, 1912, for his own benefit. It was a great event. "Three of the foremost gamblers were present," a man proudly declared, and, with equal pride further said that several madames of houses of prostitution and their inmates were there also. The program of this dance is a veritable directory of "gamblers," "gun men," "strong arm guys," pimps, doctors, lawyers, and politicians. Some of the names are very familiar. They made a motley crowd — all with

[29] Given by Club X 341.   [30] X 342.   [31] X 343.

Commercialized Prostitution in New York

mutual interests. Many in this remarkable gathering came together and paid large admission fees at the door because they feared the gambler who gave the dance.

The occasions above described are not utilized only by hardened profligates: young girls, some perhaps innocent, others, if not entirely innocent, at any rate not yet wholly depraved, and young men not yet altogether vicious attend the gatherings in search of amusement and change. Some of the girls who frequent these public dance halls reveal their loose morals by their manners and actions, but many are innocent working girls who seek legitimate recreation. The sinister element is the pimp who attends with the coldblooded purpose of finding new subjects of debauchery and of subsequent exploitation for gain. These agents of commercialized vice are usually well-dressed, well-mannered, and introduce themselves politely and easily to strangers. They often pretend love at first sight and exhibit marked devotion, by which girls are deceived and to which they too often yield. Clever subterfuges are sometimes employed: a pretended drummer states that he has " sample shoes " or " sample dresses " at his room: " If they fit, they are yours," he says. When the seduction of the girls is accomplished, they are put on the street, and their ruin is complete. These " powers that prey " are a constant danger in public dance halls and find there easy quarry. The girls who refuse to be inveigled are often so ostracized that they must unbend, if they wish to participate in the fun. Dances and refreshments are withheld until the " wall-flower " comes round. Examples can be cited: a model who earns $18 a week, one-half of which she

Places Which Cater to Vice

gives her father;[32] an embroidery worker,[33] making $10 a week; the head of stock in the shoe department of a Sixth Avenue store;[34] a department store girl earning $6 a week.[35] With these working women, pimps and professional prostitutes freely mingle. Forty professional prostitutes were counted at one dance given on March 10, 1912.[36]

(5) EXCURSION BOATS AND PARKS

In addition to the places already mentioned, the prostitute and her exploiter take advantage of other opportunities to ply their trade. The excursion boats between New York and Albany, Bridgeport, New Haven, Providence, Block Island, etc., are often used for a rendezvous. Occurrences of a highly suspicious character are abundant:

August 25, 1912, three couples left the boat bound for New Haven because they could not secure rooms: this, in spite of the fact that it was a day trip. On an excursion boat bound for Montauk Point on July 28, 1912, two young couples occupied staterooms 19 and 21. The girls appeared to be about eighteen years of age. Two girls, apparently seventeen years of age, rented stateroom No. 11, where they remained all day and were visited by four different men. When the boat returned to New York the girls went ashore and boarded a car on East 23rd Street. One pretty little girl on this excursion was accompanied by a woman who appeared to be her mother. The girl became friendly and offered to make a "date" with the investigator. She lives on De-

[32] X 352.   [34] X 357.   [36] By the X 362 Club.
[33] X 353.   [35] X 358.

Commercialized Prostitution in New York

Kalb Avenue in Brooklyn. There were two others, living in Harlem, evidently working girls, who were also willing to make "dates."

It is indeed a matter of common knowledge that professional prostitutes make a practice of soliciting on excursion boats for immoral purposes. The women make regular trips and have a business understanding with porters and waiters, who aid in securing customers. On July 20, 1912, as the boat for New Haven was about to leave the dock, two prostitutes who solicit in a café on West 44th Street [37] came aboard. A street walker who solicits on Broadway and has a home in the Bronx took the trip to New Haven on August 25, 1912. Six prostitutes were soliciting young men on the trip to Block Island on August 11, 1912, one of them formerly an inmate in a house of prostitution in West 47th Street.[38] Her companion solicits on Broadway. These girls said they had rooms in a Block Island hotel,[39] where they invited the men to meet them.

Some of the waiters and porters on these boats act as solicitors for prostitutes. A colored porter[40] on a boat running to Block Island, August 11, 1912, said there were many couples on board having immoral relations. He offered to introduce two men to two girls. On August 8, 1912, a colored porter on a boat for Providence, Rhode Island, told a man that a "wise young girl" occupied stateroom No. 68, and that she would receive men. Robert,[41] a waiter on one of them, declared

[37] X 368.   [38] X 369.   [39] X 370.   [40] X 374.
[41] X 373.

Places Which Cater to Vice

that immoral conditions were most flagrant on the Sunday trips. He described in detail the actions of couples in the staterooms when he served them drinks.

Amusement parks are similarly abused. Seven such parks in the vicinity of New York City were visited during the summer of 1912, and vicious conditions were found to exist to a greater or less extent in all of them. In the drinking places prostitutes sit on the stage in short skirts and sing and dance for the entertainment of men and boys drinking at the tables. The girls are paid very low salaries, and therefore depend upon making extra money from prostitution. The waiters aid in securing customers and receive commissions from the girls on the stage for this service. In some concert halls the girls have signs which they use to indicate the time they are free to leave the stage or the price they require. If they succeed in persuading a man to buy wine in the balcony of the hall, they receive a commission on the sale. In the winter time some of these prostitutes join burlesque shows or continue to carry on their immoral business otherwise in the city.

An investigator visited a concert hall connected with an amusement park on Long Island, July 23, 1912. There were eighteen girls seated on the stage in short skirts, the majority of them intoxicated; in their wild efforts to entertain the crowd of men and boys they exposed their persons. Twenty-five girls sing and dance in a concert hall at another popular amusement park. They are divided into two shifts, each shift working a stated number of hours during the afternoon and night. One of the singers was recognized by a man who had

Commercialized Prostitution in New York

seen her in a house of prostitution in a city in Pennsylvania; one of her companions solicits for immoral purposes on Broadway. Many of these concert halls and similar places are connected with the hotels to which the entertainers take their customers. A very notorious hotel of this character [42] adjoins a disreputable concert hall in an amusement park on Staten Island.

The conditions in dance halls in connection with certain amusement parks are similar to those described under the heading "Public Dance Halls." Here young and thoughtless working girls and boys often yield themselves to the degrading influence of liquor and suggestive dancing; and here also are found the prostitutes and their pimps.

In reference to public parks, it may be stated that the police force is entirely inadequate to their proper surveillance. Shocking occurrences by the score are reported in Central and other parks by different investigators under the date of July 15, August 5, July 20, July 12, etc. Not infrequently boys and girls of sixteen and seventeen are involved in these affairs,— and cases implicating still younger children are reported. The benches in certain sections of Central Park, between 10 P. M. and 1 A. M., presented a most demoralizing spectacle to the observation of every one who walked through the Park during the months of July and August.[43]

---

[42] X 376.
[43] For Statisticals details as to parks catering to prostitution, see Appendix II, "Summary of Resorts Catering to Vice."

CHAPTER IV

THE EXPLOITERS

THE present investigation has established the fact that the business of prostitution in New York City is exploited and, for the most part, controlled by men, though women are also involved. The names and addresses of over 500 men so engaged have been secured, together with personal descriptions and the records of many of them. Some are owners, others, procurers, the rest mainly cadets or pimps,— younger men who have a single girl, at times a " string " of girls, " working " for them on the street or in houses. The woman exploiter is at times herself a proprietor; usually, however, she is employed by men on a salary to operate a resort.

(1) OWNERS

The men proprietors have reached their present vocation by many paths. They have been wrestlers, prizefighters, gamblers, " politicians," proprietors of " creep houses," [1] fruit venders, pawnbrokers, pickpockets, crooks, peddlers, waiters, saloonkeepers, etc. Some of them pose as "business men," carrying cards and samples, to serve as a subterfuge when they are arrested as vagrants or for living off the proceeds of prosti-

[1] A "creep house" is a place where women take men to rob them.

tution. Not a few, however, without concealment, devote their entire time and energy to managing parlor houses and other resorts of prostitution. Some of the latter own a business outright; others have partners who share in the profits. One man, for instance, conducts a house with from fifteen to twenty-five inmates, and, in addition, has an interest in several other ventures of the same character. In some cases the firm is a family affair, including brothers, brothers-in-law, uncles, and cousins.

For several years thirty one-dollar houses of prostitution in the Tenderloin have been operated as a "combine," under the direct control of fifteen or more men. The individuals in question have been in business for many years in New York City, as well as in other cities both in this country and abroad. They buy and sell shares in these houses among themselves, and it is seldom that an outsider, unless he be a relative, can "break" into the circle and share in the profits. The value of the shares depends upon the ability of the owners to maintain conditions in which the houses, being unmolested, are permitted to make large profits. The man who proves himself capable of achieving this through business sagacity and political pull is called the "king." Upon him falls the responsibility of "seeing" the "right" individuals.

Owners follow the trend of public sentiment with a keenness and foresight truly remarkable. If a new official indicates by orders or by sentiments expressed in public that he is in favor of an "open town," there is great rejoicing among the promoters. Agitation in

The Exploiters

the opposite direction reacts on the value of their properties: prices drop and there is a scramble to "get under cover." If spasmodic efforts at reform are made, the more prominent owners meet in council with their lawyers and solemnly discuss what their policy should be. If their houses are closed, they still keep on paying rent, ready to open again — when a favorable word comes or when the moral outbreak subsides. For the owner has no faith in reformers. "They get tired and quit"; "all this will blow over"; "they are sick of it already";— such are his reflections as he recalls past experiences.

The majority of men exploiters of prostitution in New York City are foreigners by birth. Some of them have been seducers of defenseless women all their lives. In one instance, at least, a whole family is engaged in the business,— the parents [2] conduct a restaurant, which is a "hangout" for pimps, procurers, crooks, and prostitutes; the daughters are prostitutes, the two sons, pimps and procurers. The father and mother are constantly on the lookout for girls whom their sons may ruin and exploit on the street or in houses. Another family [3] has already been referred to as conducting a delicatessen store in Seventh Avenue: they occupy the upper floors as their dwelling; the shop below is the favorite rendezvous of owners, madames, procurers, pimps, and prostitutes. The children of this family, one a girl just reaching womanhood, mingle freely with them. The father keeps an eye on the

[2] X 382.   [3] X 108-a.

Commercialized Prostitution in New York

handsome procurers who talk with his children; though he listens daily to their schemes for securing women and girls he would "cut to pieces" any man among them who attempted to defile his own daughters.

The owners in question did not all come directly to America. Some of them drifted to other parts of Europe with young girls whom they had secured in the small towns or cities of their own countries. South Africa was a favorite destination — especially Johannesburg. Many, going thither during the Boer War, are reputed to have made large profits from their business with soldiers as customers. The authorities, however, beat them with whips and drove them from the cities. They fled to South America and then to North America. Their trail of seduction and corruption may be traced through Argentine, Brazil, Cuba, Canada, Alaska, and the large cities of our own country — San Francisco, Portland, Seattle, Tacoma, Butte, Denver, Omaha, St. Louis, Chicago, Pittsburg, Philadelphia; finally they realize their hopes in New York City. Here they have made a center, and from this center they go back over the old trail from time to time.

If a composite photograph could be made of typical owners of vice resorts, it would show a large, well-fed man about forty years of age and five feet, eight inches, in height. His clothes are the latest cut, loud in design, and carefully pressed. A heavy watch chain adorns his waistcoat, a large diamond sparkles in a flashy necktie, and his fat, chubby fingers are encircled with gold and diamond rings.

On April 6, 1912, a group of owners were parading

The Exploiters

up and down Seventh Avenue in front of the above-mentioned delicatessen store, discussing "business." They were all dressed in their best and looked prosperous. One, a large man with a black mustache, wore a very fine English suit and a hat which was said to have cost eight dollars. A large diamond ring sparkled on his fat hand, a diamond horse shoe pin flashed in his tie, and a charm set with precious stones hung from a heavy gold watch chain. His brother-in-law, part owner with him of a house of prostitution in West 25th Street,[4] was also dressed in the height of fashion,— a smart suit, a black derby hat, and patent leather pumps. A third partner presented an equally dignified appearance. There were eight other owners in the group, making a very imposing appearance as they eagerly waited to talk over matters of "business" with the representative of the "boss,"— a certain official who, as the men claimed, was on this day to send word whether or not the owners could proceed with their nefarious business.

The "king"[5] of this set has the reputation of being able to "see" the right persons; when a member is "in wrong" or wants to open a house, the "king" must first be consulted. The "king" is interested in eleven houses of prostitution — of some of which he is the sole owner; each establishment contains an average of about fifteen inmates. He supports two notorious women,[6] who serve as madames, each jealous of every attention bestowed by him on the other. Many years ago he was a soldier in Russia, where he ruined a young girl whom

[4] X 46.   [5] X 34.   [6] X 86, X 87.

he afterwards took to South Africa. Since that time she has earned thousands of dollars for him. He brought her to this country and traveled with her from city to city until finally he settled in New York, where he has since built up a prosperous business and gained an "influential" position.

Among the others are two brothers who combine the business of exploiting prostitution with that of selling diamonds. They are noted for their ability to outwit the law, for they openly declare that they can buy their way out of any trial. Besides their houses, they have conducted pool parlors and restaurants, and one of them has the reputation of being a "fence," or receiver of stolen goods. The history of these two men illustrates the manner in which pimps develop into proprietors. When they first came to America about twenty years ago, they found employment on a peddler's wagon. Soon after, one of them ruined a fifteen-year old girl who was born on Broome Street, New York City. For seven years subsequently she was his woman, earning money for him on the street and in houses. The other brother, not to be outdone, also secured a girl and became a pimp. Later they were both employed as watch-boys about houses of prostitution. Being ambitious, they were soon operating regular houses on Allen Street, which at that time was part of the old Red Light District in Manhattan. Here they prospered for a number of years, though in the end they were driven from the East Side. With four women they then went to Boston, where they opened a house. Apprehended there, they "jumped their bail" and returned to their former

The Exploiters

haunts in New York. Their old enemy had evidently lost his power; for the brothers were allowed to continue in business. After the closing of the district, the scene of their business ventures was transferred to Buffalo during the Exposition of 1901. Driven thence, they went to St. Louis, where they soon owned houses, saloons, and gambling places. Ex-Governor Folk was District Attorney in St. Louis at that time and the brothers were among those who fell into his net. One brother, known as the "King of White Chapel," that being the Red Light District, was indicted on several counts for felonies and misdemeanors. The other brother and one of his women [7] were also indicted. The enterprising pair secured bail, which they immediately forfeited, and, leaving all their wealth behind, began to roam from place to place with their women. One went to Havana, and one to Pittsburg; driven from Pittsburg, the latter soon joined his brother in Havana. From Havana the two men and their women went to South Africa and settled in Johannesburg. Here once more they made a large sum of money. The authorities seized one of the brothers and sentenced him to jail; on the expiration of his term, he was whipped and ordered out of the city. The brothers then went to Vienna, to London, and from London sailed to New York City. When they returned to the city of their early business success, they opened a house of prostitution on West 34th Street in company with a man who had just returned from South Africa. For a year they prospered.

[7] X 383.

Commercialized Prostitution in New York

When the former District Attorney of St. Louis, who had since become Governor, learned of their presence in this country, he secured their extradition. The brothers took $25,000 to St. Louis with them and not long afterwards returned to New York entirely penniless. No wonder the elder and more crafty of the two brothers declares that the law cannot touch them! No wonder, when he is intoxicated, he strikes his chest and shouts defiance to the law! During all these vicissitudes one of his women [8] remained loyal. She is known among the owners of houses all over the country as the "best money getter" in the world. When her owner was "broke" and in sore distress, she put him on his feet again. She is his woman to-day.

The instances cited are by no means exceptional. Prostitution has become a business, the promoters of which continually scan the field for a location favorable to their operations; and the field is the entire civilized world. No legitimate enterprise is more shrewdly managed from this point of view; no variety of trade adjusts itself more promptly to conditions, transferring its activities from one place to another, as opportunities contract here and expand there. The keeper of a disorderly saloon [9] finds himself hampered in Chicago: he migrates to New York to become part owner of a Sixth Avenue resort.[10] Raided in Philadelphia, another [11] goes first to Pittsburg, thence to this city, where he purchases an interest in a West 25th Street [12] establishment. The

[8] X 384. [10] X 403. [12] X 467.
[9] X 402. [11] X 407.

The Exploiters

former owner [13] of places in St. Louis and Omaha is now part owner in two houses [14] on this same street. Still another [15] was in the business successively in Philadelphia, Chicago, San Francisco, Dallas, and Los Angeles. One of the partners [16] in a resort in West 36th Street [17] has at different times had houses in Portland, Seattle, Brazil, Argentine, and London. Another [18] is simultaneously interested in houses in this city [19] and in Norfolk, Virginia. The part owner [20] of a notorious place on Sixth Avenue [21] has conducted houses of prostitution in St. Louis, Buffalo, and Johannesburg, South Africa, and has traveled all over the world in the business of exploiting prostitution.[22]

(2) PROCURERS

While keepers of houses are also procurers, there is a group of men who devote themselves singly to this work. These are the typical " white slavers," whose trade depends entirely upon the existence of houses of prostitution. To this point we shall in a moment recur in connection with women promoters of prostitution. For the present I desire simply to emphasize the fact that the procurer has practically no chance to ply his trade unless there are houses of prostitution from which he can accept orders and to which he can dispose of " goods."

[13] X 408.
[14] X 258, 409.
[15] X 73.
[16] X 414.
[17] X 416.
[18] X 421.
[19] X 311.
[20] X 68.
[21] X 426.
[22] For further details, see Appendix XIV, "Additional Data — Shipping Women."

Commercialized Prostitution in New York

The successful procurer as well as the pimp, to be next described, boasts that, once a girl comes under his influence, she will do anything for him. No matter how ugly or repulsive outwardly, he holds his women. One of the most active procurers in the city is short, heavy, and humpbacked.[23] He has the reputation of being even more successful than a competitor [24] who is handsome, athletic, and well-dressed. The former has been apprehended in other cities on the charge of procuring, once serving two and a half years in Philadelphia under an assumed name.[25] To-day he walks the streets of New York City, a free man, unmolested.

Procurers frequent entrances to factories and department stores, or walk the streets at night striking up acquaintance with girls who are alone and looking for adventure. They select a girl waiting on a table in a restaurant, or at the cashier's desk, and gradually make her acquaintance. They attend steamboat excursions, are found at the sea shore and amusement parks, in moving picture shows, at the public dance halls,— in fact, wherever girls congregate for business or for pleasure. They choose with almost unerring judgment the type of girl who may be pliable to their will.

At 5 P. M., on March 14, 1912, six procurers [26] stood on the corner of 27th Street and Sixth Avenue waiting for the shop and factory girls to pass by on their way going home from work. For one hour the investigator watched these men and saw them endeavoring to attract

[23] X 385.   [24] X 386.   [25] X 385-a.
[26] X 68, X 386-a, X 386, X 387, X 388, X 389.

The Exploiters

the attention of several girls. At last two of them [27] succeeded in interesting two girls, who accompanied them.

On Sunday, June 23, 1912, a group of procurers [28] went to a certain seashore resort. On the beach they were joined by a notorious procurer, then employed as a life saver.[29] He greeted his comrades with the words: "Ich hob' frisch' Schore" (I have fresh goods.) The group then put on their bathing suits and went into the surf. After a while they missed one of their number,[30] whom they finally found with a young girl apparently eighteen years of age: she was the "fresh goods,"— the object of the "line up," as it afterwards developed.

(3) THE PIMP

The pimp or cadet as he is commonly called, has not yet developed into a professional procurer or keeper of a house of prostitution. While all procurers and owners of houses are in reality pimps, the converse is not always true: all pimps are not procurers, though they may hope to be some day.

The pimp enters the business when he either ruins a young girl for his future profit or becomes the lover and protector of a prostitute already in the business. As the future pimp grows up in a crowded neighborhood, he becomes a member of a gang and, as such, is admired by some reckless girl in the vicinity. Proud of her acquaintance with him, she shares the spoils resulting from his petty thieving and other escapades. Very early in

---

[27] X 386, X 387.
[28] X 88, X 163, X 393, X 74.
[29] X 386.
[30] X 385.

their career the two begin to have immoral relations, not only with each other, but with different boys and girls of their own kind. They have never had moral standards in any proper sense of the term. The large majority of boys who become pimps and seducers of girls and the large majority of girls who become prostitutes were at the start not immoral, but unmoral. Later the boy drifts to the pool parlor or gambling room for his recreation and companionship, the girl to public dance halls and similar places of amusement. Many of these girls are already clandestine prostitutes, secretly carrying on the business of prostitution while at the same time engaged in some legitimate employment " just to keep up a respectable appearance." Under the pimp's influence and suggestion the girl finally " breaks " away from her secret immoral life and becomes a " regular." The pimp shows her the way, provides places for her to solicit or " hustle " on the street or in the vice resort. He attends to the business arrangements, even to the collection of her money, though when she is " well broke," he allows her to collect her own money and give it to him. Some pimps beat their women, on the principle that that is the only way to make them fear and love them. This may seem a paradox; but it is indeed true that many prostitutes do not believe their lovers care for them unless they " beat them up " occasionally.

The psychology of the relation of prostitute to pimp is a complicated one, difficult for the normal individual to understand. In the cases above alluded to, boy and girl have been comrades, the boy lording it over the

The Exploiters

girl until she submits to being his property. But there are prostitutes, apparently quite able to stand alone, who deliberately select a pimp; if they cease to be satisfied with him, he is discharged and a successor taken. Why should a prostitute of either kind desire a pimp? There are many reasons: the pimp is her business agent in dealing with owners, hotel keepers, etc.; he is her " go-between," if she gets into " trouble " with the law; her companion, for she is lonely after the night's business; but — most important of all — her lover — one person who seems to care for her as a human being, whether he does or not, and for whom she does herself really care. A spark of affection lives at the heart of this ghastly relation.

In her relation to the pimp, as well as to the house madame, the prostitute is not infrequently to all intents and purposes a white slave. For the pimp, like the madame, subjects her in many cases completely to his will and command. This does not mean that the girl is necessarily imprisoned behind locked doors and barred windows. But restraint may be thoroughly effective, even though not actually or mainly physical. Uneducated, with little or no comprehension of her legal rights or of the powers which could be invoked to aid her, often an immigrant or at least a stranger, she is soon cowed by the brute to whom she has mistakenly attached herself. Should she make an effort to break away, she is pursued and hemmed in by the concerted efforts of her cadet and his associates. As a rule, however, pimps are skilful enough to play for and to obtain the

Commercialized Prostitution in New York

sentimental loyalty of their women; so that the prostitute herself becomes the greatest obstacle to her own freedom and rehabilitation.

There are hundreds, perhaps thousands, of pimps in New York City. During this investigation scores of their names and personal descriptions have been accumulated, as well as those of their women. One of the best known [31] is a "life-taker" and "strong arm guy," a dangerous fellow, twenty-two years old, who has been repeatedly arrested as a consequence of his quarrels. A "pipe fiend" and gambler, his favorite occupation is "stuss." At elections he has his own "mob" who work at the polls for corrupt politicians. His girl is a slim, bleached blonde, "good for $100 to $150 a week on the street," it is said.

On June 26, 1912, five pimps were playing cards in a restaurant on Seventh Avenue. The day was very hot. During the afternoon the girl [32] who is "hustling" for one of them [33] came into the restaurant wearing a heavy velvet suit. The wife of the proprietor asked: "What are you doing, wearing a suit like that in this kind of weather?" She replied that though she was bringing home eight, ten, and twelve dollars every night, she could not afford a new dress. "He needs it for gambling," she said, pointing to her pimp. Leaving the table in anger he deliberately slapped her in the face: "Didn't you pay $32 for that suit?" he said. "What more do you want?"

[31] X 340.
[32] X 396.   [33] X 393

The Exploiters

Another [34] frequents a restaurant in Second Avenue.[35] He is twenty-nine years of age, smooth shaven, with a scar on his face. Before he became a pimp he was known as a "pool room shark." He smokes opium, snuffs cocaine, and plays stud poker. With men of his kind he is not very popular: they declare that he cannot tell the truth, that for a "shell of hop" he would kill a dozen Chinamen, and for a nickel would "frame up" his best friend. "Just an ordinary, every day, common pimp," they say,— "can't borrow a dollar and lives on nothing but the money his woman earns."

Hearing of places where business is better, owners and pimps ship their "goods" about in hope of larger profits. The women remit their earnings, even if separated hundreds of miles. For example, Fanny, a woman belonging to a notorious pimp,[36] formerly solicited on Third Avenue. A year or more ago Fanny was brought into court, charged with street walking. She was sentenced to not less than three months nor more than five; after a month she was released, according to her pimp, who declared that it had cost him $500 in lawyers' fees, etc. Thereupon he sent Fanny to Butte, Montana, whence at the end of one week she sent him $150. On June 21, 1912, the pimp complained that Fanny was then sending him only $150 per month. He was sure that she was "holding out on him," for he knew that she made at least $100 a week.

Sophia, belonging to an equally well-known cadet,[37] whose own parents try to secure women for him, reached

[34] X 399.
[35] X 400.
[36] X 427.
[37] X 382-a.

Commercialized Prostitution in New York

New York from New Orleans late in June, 1912. Her pimp and her brother met her at the station. To the former's utter surprise she declared that she was "through" with him. A quarrel ensued; the pimp was worsted and had to abandon his claim to the girl,— one of the occasional cases, already referred to, in which the girl throws over her pimp.

(4) MADAMES

The women who run houses have as a rule risen from the ranks. They were once street walkers or parlor house inmates who possess unusual business talents. They have learned the secrets of the trade; they know the kind of inmates to get, and where to get them. They know how to deal with customers and how to make them spend money.

It takes a woman of tact and force to operate a house with from fifteen to twenty-five inmates competing with one another on a commission basis. She must keep them contented, prevent quarrels, and stifle petty jealousies. She must attach as many of them to the house as she can and keep them loyal. To do this the madame seeks to become the adviser and friend of the girls, while at the same time she drives them to the utmost to earn larger profits for the house. It is not uncommon for the girls as well as the customers to call her "mother." Strange as it may seem, some men marry these women and find them devoted wives.

All of the thirty cheap resorts referred to in a previous chapter as belonging to men are managed by madames and housekeepers who are either their wives or

The Exploiters

their women. These women attend to all the details connected with the business. They receive customers, "show off the girls," urge visitors to spend money, collect money, punch checks, sell liquor, keep the books, and settle up with the boss: when the houses are raided or an arrest has to be made they are the ones to go to jail. The large majority of them were born in foreign countries. They have had years of experience in operating houses in many cities of North and South America, as well as in foreign lands, especially South Africa. The loyalty displayed by them toward the men who employ them has become a tradition. Year after year, through adversity and prosperity they have followed their masters and obeyed their will. Beaten, exploited, infected, jailed, they still remain steadfast. Very rarely can one of them be persuaded to testify in a court of law against her master. A striking example is furnished by a woman [38] who came under the influence of her master [39] when she was a child of fifteen and was living with her parents in a distant country, where he had seduced her. At 9 P. M., on June 27, 1912, she came into a restaurant where her man was playing cards and upbraided him because he had purchased an automobile and placed it at the disposal of another one of his madames, neglecting her. She called him vile names and declared that she would go to the police and "squeal" on him. She told how for fifteen years she had earned money for him, and all she had to show for it was a furnished room to sleep in and a diamond ring, while he put his other woman in a "swell" apartment. "I've been cut to pieces for you,"

[38] X 87.   [39] X 34.

she wailed, " I've been your slave for fifteen years and now you turn me down for that wench." She had hardly concluded her tirade when her man rose from his chair and struck her brutally in the face with his fist. She reeled as though about to fall, then cowering before him left the place weeping. She did not " squeal " to the police.

When a man owner employs either his wife, woman or a housekeeper to operate his house, it is understood that she shall be the one to suffer punishment in case of arrest. In order to avoid punishment, men who rent houses for these purposes sub-let them to the women, who are then held as the responsible parties. When arrest or eviction comes, and the madame is sent to jail or dispossssed, the real proprietor again sub-lets his house to another woman. This fact explains why the arrests for conducting houses of prostitution do not result in diminishing to any extent the number of such resorts. On June 24, 1912, a keeper had a sub-lease drawn up for a house and inserted the name of Anna,[40] the prospective madame who was to " stand for " the arrest or eviction notice, should there be one. On March 31, 1912, " Joe "[41] said that he was paying $85 per month to his landlord and $25 per month as a bonus to the agent for his house of prostitution in West 28th Street.[42] The landlord[43] is reputed to be a wealthy business man,—" a fine fellow," said Joe, " he is now fighting a dispossession notice for me. It is understood between us that if I can't beat it, I can sub-let the house to

[40] X 501.
[41] X 260.
[42] X 183.
[43] X 463.

The Exploiters

another woman and charge her a bigger rent. Later, when we get another notice, I can say, ' All right, I will dispossess this woman.' Then I can get another. It's no joke to run a house, believe me. The women are sent to jail. My wife got sixty days for running this house the other day. That arrest will cost me $300 for her alone. Now the women have started a new game. In case one gets three months, we have to give her $500 to keep her mouth shut." On March 11, 1912, a partner [44] in a house of prostitution in West 24th Street [45] was describing his fortunes as a keeper of houses in New York City during the past fifteen years. Among other things he said, " My housekeeper got three months last week, and I am paying her $5 a day for every day she is in jail."

Not a few of these madames have been arrested in different countries and cities as " gun mols " (pickpockets). That is part of their training, and the robberies they commit add many dollars to the incomes of the men who have put them in the business. A customer who enters their houses in an intoxicated condition is often robbed of everything of value. If he remonstrates he is told by the police to swear out a warrant for the woman he suspects and appear as a witness against her. It is not often a man will do this under the circumstances.

The women who operate houses on their own account belong to a rather different type: their establishments are almost always pretentious. Born, as a rule, in this country or in France, they make a show of elegance and refinement. Their houses are elaborately furnished and

[44] X 44.   [45] X 502.

they and their "boarders" appear in stylish gowns, and endeavor to interest their guests by affecting a knowledge of art or music or literature. Many of them openly boast of influential and prominent friends, on whose good offices they can rely in emergencies.

In either case the housekeeper earns money not only from the customers of the house, but from the inmates. Theoretically the inmates receive one-half of all the money they take in. This is not actually the case. They are indeed fortunate if they receive any money at all after weeks of service. At most, they obtain from fifteen to twenty per cent instead of fifty per cent. Sometimes, as the first step in the process of exploitation, the madame tries to induce the girl to give up her pimp, in order that she may have her more directly under control. Having attached the girl to herself, she sells her all sorts of things: coats, suits, dresses, kimonos, chemises, underwear, hosiery, shoes, hats, gloves, feathers, plumes, combs, hairpins, toilet articles, silver meshbags, watches and rings. Hundreds of girls are thus preyed upon. Not infrequently, however, it happens that madames prefer that their girls keep their pimps, because such girls are made to work harder by the aid of the latter. As the madames and pimps divide the gains of the unfortunate creatures, their interests usually agree and they unite to exploit their common property.

The articles mentioned in the preceding paragraph are not infrequently described as stolen goods, brought to the houses by peddlers who are hired to dispose of them by crooks and shoplifters. A pimp and procurer [46] was in a

[46] X 518.

The Exploiters

resort [47] on the third floor of a house on West 58th Street [48] on June 15, 1912, trying to sell the madame several pairs of silk hose, to be sold in turn to the inmates. The stockings were frankly admitted to be stolen goods which had been turned over to him by a shoplifter [49] who is a member of a 14th Street gang and is known as a " strong arm guy." On March 28, 1912, about 8 P. M., a young crook [50] came into a restaurant in Seventh Avenue [51] and exhibited a dress which he declared he had stolen from a prominent store.[52] The dress was marked $18.29. It did not fit any of the madames who were in the restaurant at the time. Finally he sold the dress to the madame [53] of a house in West 25th Street [54] for $10. She in turn disposed of it to one of her inmates for $35. The notorious madame [55] of a house in West 25th Street [56] had fifty chemises on March 25, 1912, which she had purchased from a peddler,[57] giving him $31 for the lot. "I am selling these to the girls for $6, $7, and $8 apiece," she said. "If I bought them in a store they would cost $2.75 apiece; but what is the difference whether I get it or the pimp gets it?"

"I never allow a girl to get down to owing me less than $5," said another madame. "When she is as nearly out of debt as that, I send for Sam the peddler and suggest that she buy some clothes and toilet articles. There's Ruth,— just watch her when she comes in. I

[47] Kept by Madame X 519.
[48] X 116.
[49] X 520.
[50] X 50.
[51] X 108.
[52] X 540.
[53] X 51.
[54] X 46.
[55] X 17.
[56] X 59.
[57] Named X 522.

dressed her up the way you will see her; the dress cost me $20. She paid me $70 for it."

The procuress may be dealt with in this same connection. Like the madame she has, as a rule, become too old to find prostitution itself any longer a profitable business; but native shrewdness and plausibility enable her to turn her experience to account as a pandar. I have already spoken of men procurers; but the woman procurer is even more insidious. She meets young girls in private rooms, talks to them in public places, invites them to her home without arousing suspicion. As a woman she knows many avenues of approach closed to men, and is quick to sympathize with discouraged or vain girls.

One of the best procuresses in New York City operates as a sort of employment agent, receiving a commission from immoral girls for finding profitable houses for them to work in. In this way she supplies the cheaper grade of houses, the girls paying her from $2 to $5 commission, according to the character of the house to which she sends them. Another,[58] also the madame of a house in West 38th Street,[59] goes to France to secure girls for her exclusive $5 and $10 house. On June 6, 1912, eight inmates were counted in her establishment, several of whom were young French girls who could speak little or no English. One of them told a stranger that she had not been in this country very long. On July 17, 1912, at about 7 P. M., a madame was asked [60] whether she could use three girls just

[58] X 507.
[59] X 493.
[60] By X 508.

The Exploiters

brought from Vancouver, British Columbia. Betsy, the madame, said she could not, but pointed with her finger to two men owners [61] of a house in West 28th Street.[62] One of them asked the woman what the girls looked like. The procuress indicated that they were well built, young, and pretty. The man cautiously advised the woman to take the girls somewhere and "green them out." [63]

The close and essential connection between the white slave traffic and houses of prostitution is clearly exhibited by the foregoing instances. Houses of prostitution cannot exist except through trafficking in women. Prostitutes who live scattered through the city may earn money for their pimps; but traffic in scattered prostitutes is practically impossible. As soon as houses are set up, an opportunity for trade is created. The proprietors give specific orders to the procurer — for young girls, for innocent girls, for blondes, for brunettes, for slender women, for stout women. And the procurer fills the order, resorting to every possible device in the effort to do so,— to deceit, misrepresentation, intoxication, "doping," or what not. The white slave traffic is thus not only a hideous reality, but a reality almost wholly dependent on the existence of houses of prostitution.

[61] X 418, X 509.
[62] X 419.
[63] This expression means that the girls should be broken into the business in some private place, until they were fitted for the public houses.

CHAPTER V

PROSTITUTE AND CUSTOMER

(a) THE PROSTITUTE

THE professional prostitute, in the sense in which the term is here used, is the woman or girl who sells herself for money, whether for her own pecuniary benefit, or under the direction or control of owners of vice resorts, of madames, procurers, or pimps. There has been much speculation as to the number of such women in New York City. Various estimates have been made from time to time, ranging from 25,000 to 100,000. A recent estimate places the number at 30,000.

At the beginning of this investigation, it was determined to count all women who were believed to be professional prostitutes seen in connection with resorts of all kinds in Manhattan, as well as those who used the streets for solicitation. Although these resorts were visited two or more times, only one count made on one visit is included in the total. As a result of this method, adhered to throughout the entire period of the study, *i. e.*, from January 24th, 1912, to November 15th, 1912, the number of professional prostitutes actually counted was 14,926. Of this number, 6,759 were found on the streets in different localities in Manhattan; 8,167 prostitutes were seen and counted in parlor houses, resorts in

Prostitute and Customer

tenement apartments, disorderly massage parlors, hotels, saloons, concert halls, and miscellaneous places.[1] Not all the vice resorts operating in Manhattan were visited; nor were all the women in these resorts seen during the visits: a certain number of repetitions would thus probably be more than offset. On the basis of the foregoing figures, it is safe to say that a total in round numbers of 15,000 does not overstate the number of professional prostitutes in Manhattan. This estimate does not include occasional or clandestine prostitutes; it includes those only who publicly offer themselves for sale in the open marts.

An effort was made to ascertain the salient facts in the personal history of 1,106 prostitutes — mostly street walkers. The approximate accuracy or truthfulness of the facts stated may be inferred from the extent to which they are confirmed by Miss Davis's intensive study of the inmates of Bedford Reformatory.[1a] Our investigator was a woman who was regarded as extraordinarily successful in winning the confidence of the girls, with whom she associated on easy and familiar terms, and by whom she was regarded as one of themselves. Of the 1,106 women thus interrogated, 762 gave America as their native land; 347 gave New York State as their birthplace; 95 were born in Pennsylvania, 63 in New Jersey, 35 in Ohio, 26 in Connecticut. Of the 344 born in foreign countries, 107 came from Russia, 72 from Germany, 35 from Austria-Hungary, and 32 from England and Scot-

[1] For statistical details, see Appendix III, "Inmates of Vice Resorts."
[1a] See Chapter VIII.

Commercialized Prostitution in New York

land. Their previous occupations include domestic service, trade, industry, commerce, stenography, school teaching. Those who are arrested come mainly from the class first named, thus confirming the results obtained by Miss Mary Conyngton, an investigator for the Department of Labor at Washington, who declares that out of 3,229 women arrested for offenses against the law, 2,606, or 80.71 per cent claim to have followed the ordinary pursuits of women " within and outside the home." [2] But, it must be added, the majority of those now engaged in prostitution seldom reach the Night Court or rescue homes. They are too well-dressed, too clever, and have long since learned the art of escaping the hand of the law. Of the women at large interrogated, 487 gave their occupational history; of these, it is not surprising to find that the percentage of domestic servants is lower than among 168 girls found in rescue homes, refuges and asylums. Of the 487, there were 117 who stated that they had been or were employed in department stores; 28 were clerks in smaller stores; 72 had worked in factories; 25 gave office work; 31 said they had been or were then stenographers; 9 telephone operators; 72 had been on the stage, and 16 of

[2] See Report on " Relation between Occupation and Criminality of Women," page 29, being Vol. XV of Report on Conditions of Women and Child Wage-Earners in the United States.

It is further to be remembered, in accounting for the disproportionate number of servants among those arrested, that, as Miss Jane Addams has pointed out, many of these girls have had such brief periods of domestic employment that they cannot fairly be reckoned in the servant class. They describe themselves as such merely in default of any other convenient term; they may have served for a few days here or there, but, strictly speaking, they **have no calling at all.**

Prostitute and Customer

these still remained in this occupation during the theatrical season; 13 declared they had been milliners; 8 were school teachers; 4 were trained nurses; 5 had sold books on commission; 4 were artists; 2 artists' models; and 1 was a translator. Seventy-nine of the 487 gave home pursuits as their former occupation; 27 of these said they had been domestic servants; 8 were nurse girls, 17 were dressmakers, 18 were waitresses and 9 chambermaids. Five hundred and eighteen (over half) represented themselves as without regular employment, either before or after they became prostitutes and 101 refused to say what their employment had been.

The types of employment appear to be much more varied than the types of girl. With few exceptions, the girls are characterized as weak, vain and ignorant, fond of pleasure,— not, of course, at the beginning, necessarily vicious pleasure,— easily led,— now by natural emotion, again by cunning design. The explanation of her present plight as given by the girl is almost invariably complicated. No single reason can usually be assigned. Roughly speaking, four kinds of causes are mentioned:

    First.   In connection with family life.
    Second. In connection with married life.
    Third.   Personal reasons.
    Fourth. Economic reasons.

The great difficulties in their family life seem to have been neglect and abuse by parents, sternness and lack of understanding, immorality of different members of the family, and poverty in the home. In connection with marriage, it was usually alleged that the husband persuaded the wife to go into the business: he was

Commercialized Prostitution in New York

practically a pimp. Sometimes, cruelty or criminality on his part is assigned,— again, incompatibility, failure to provide, or desertion where the wife stated that she had no other recourse, never having learned to support herself. Of personal reasons, there are usually several, no one of which can be regarded as paramount. Sometimes a girl's lover puts her into the life or deserts her after seduction, leaving her without hope for the future: " I was ruined anyway," she would say, " and I did not care what became of me." Again, " I loved the excitement and a good time, easy money and good clothes." Another one remarks, " I was born bad and actually enjoy the life." " I was tired of drudgery as a servant," said another, " I'd rather do this than be kicked around like a dog in a kitchen by some woman who calls herself a lady." Few girls ever admit that they have been forced into the life as " white slaves." Some were lonely and wanted company, some were demoralized by the environment of the stage; others fell into bad company, and did not have the moral courage or the opportunity to desist. Generally speaking, of girls and women who are either ignorant, lonely, giddy, sub-normal, loveless, childless, rebellious, weak of will, discouraged of heart, unhappy or poverty-stricken, the prostitutes are those who at critical periods have given way to such an extent that they drift or plunge into immoral lives, professional or otherwise.

The same sort of explanation is given regardless of former occupation: " I was glad to get away from drudgery," says a former servant, " father drank and I was put out to work too young "; " my folks were poor, father died from drink, mother is a heavy drinker," says a fac-

Prostitute and Customer

tory girl; " I had never had anything for myself, father drank heavily," says a saleswoman. Or, again,— a factory worker, " there is more money and pleasure in being a sport." A shop-girl, " I wanted nice clothes and a good time "; a stenographer, " I wanted good times, money and clothes." Seduction, too, is alleged at all levels,— base men taking advantage of natural craving for interest and affection. " I was 17 when I went with my sweetheart," said a shop-girl; " I never intended to make it a business, I was in love with the first fellow," declared a former stenographer. The point should also be emphasized that victims of this kind do not succumb merely to man's impulse; often they are conquered by deliberate design. Undoubtedly responsible for part of the supply is, therefore, the thoughtless, intelligent, independent man, who seeks out a vain, unhappy, emotional girl as his victim. I refer to the employer who takes advantage of his stenographer or telephone girl, taking her to luncheons in private dining-rooms in expensive restaurants in the business districts. In department stores, certain floorwalkers, salesmen, buyers, managers, foremen, and even proprietors are constantly placing temptations before the weak and yielding girls who come under their direction.[2a]

How far direct economic pressure is responsible for prostitution, it is difficult to state. A calculation of the wages previously received reveals great discrepancies. Seventeen former domestics averaged $5.55 a week, plus board and lodging; 18 factory workers received from $3

[2a] This statement is substantiated by the findings of a private investigation made in New York City during 1912.

Commercialized Prostitution in New York

to $7.50, 20 received from $8 to $14 a week; 110 shop-girls averaged $8.24 a week. The above salaries range, however, from $3 to $15 weekly, the majority receiving $6, $7, and $8. Eleven receive $10; eleven, $12 apiece; and three, $15 each. Twenty former stenographers earned on the average $11.25 a week; of the eight women who claimed to have been school-teachers, one had earned $80 a month, and one $90. One hundred and thirty-nine girls (12 per cent) declared that they went into the life for economic reasons. Thirty-three put it this way, " I could not support myself "; fifty-five declared that they could not support themselves and their babies, sometimes their parents; forty-five said they were out of work and could not get it; nine were in ill health or had some defect keeping them out of work. Many more cited in explanation of their conduct the deprivations to which they would otherwise have to submit. Their alleged earnings as prostitutes, even if exaggerated, suggest a startling contrast: former servants claim that their receipts from soliciting vary from $26 to $68 per week; thirty former factory workers claim average weekly returns of $24; 40 more profess an average of $76 a week; a group of stenographers (17) average $55 per week.

The critical period when the first sexual offense of these women was committed appears to belong between the 14th and 21st years of life; the average of 1,106 such girls is 17 years. Twenty-five servants first erred between the 9th and 26th years; their average age was 16; 40 factory workers, first erring between 14 and 22, averaged a little over 17; 110 salesgirls give the same result. Occasionally they declare that they never knew the time

Prostitute and Customer

when they were virtuous. "When I was a kid of 6, I used to kiss sailors and other men for candy and do other things," said one. Naturally the age is highest in case of the former teachers, of whom one reports her first offense at 21, another at 20; one or two report their fall in their 18th year. The average time which elapsed before the girls finally drifted into professional prostitution was two years, *i. e.*, when they were 19 years of age. The life of the professional prostitute has been estimated at five years, on the ground that she dies, withdraws, or is incapacitated after she has been in the business on the average for that length of time. But a study of more than a thousand prostitutes, all now actively engaged in the business in New York City, does not sustain this view. The majority of these girls, though entering the life before 18, are at 24 still active and aggressive in seeking trade. There is a sudden drop, however, at 25, fluctuating more or less until the age of 30 is reached. Of the 1,097 professional women whose histories were carefully compiled on this point, 15 were exceedingly active at 32, 13 at 34, 11 at 40, 3 at 44, and 3 at 50. The average age of the 1,097 who are at present inmates of vice resorts, solicitors in saloons, and on the streets, is 25 years.

It is curious to note that prostitution is definitely stratified. Women divide themselves into three distinct classes and recognize the subdivisions. To the upper class belong the inmates of $5 and $10 houses. The middle class is formed by girls in one dollar and fifty cent establishments. The street girls are, generally speaking, at the bottom. As in the upper, so in the underworld, social status changes with prosperity or adversity, though the tendency — by reason of the progressive demoralization of the life — is definitely downwards. Under the influence of age, dissipation and disease, physical deterioration rapidly sets in. Those who are at the top fall into the lower classes, except in the cases in which they become madames, managers or mistresses, or abandon the life. Those in the middle class usually end on the streets.

(b) THE CUSTOMER

The necessary counterpart to the prostitute is her customer: she is the concrete answer to his demand. There are prostitutes at different economic levels, because their customers are derived from all social classes. The careless, unkempt woman at the bottom is adjusted to the requirements of the least exacting; a somewhat better type meets the demands of men of moderate means; the showy woman at the top corresponds to the fastidiousness of the spendthrift.

The customers found in the fifty-cent vice resorts already described are usually longshoremen, truck drivers, street cleaners, coal heavers, soldiers and sailors, recently landed immigrants of low moral standards, and laborers of all kinds. Their treatment of the women is not infrequently brutal,— usually perhaps in consequence of intoxication. To one- and two-dollar houses resort men and boys who earn ten, twenty, twenty-five or more dollars per week. They are proprietors of small business enterprises, clerks, bookkeepers, bartenders, barbers, tailors, waiters, soldiers, sailors, messengers in banks, members of social and political clubs or of bene-

Prostitute and Customer

fit organizations. Saturday and Sunday are the popular nights with men of this type. The owners and madames provide extra " goods " to " take care of the trade " on such occasions. This fact was brought out many times during the investigation as the workers went from one house to the other counting the inmates. A house that early in the week contained only ten or twelve inmates would on Saturday and Sunday have its numbers increased to fifteen and twenty-five. This was especially true in resorts like those on Sixth Avenue.[3]

I have in mind one prominent organization [4] whose members are regular customers in houses of this grade. Many of the rank and file are themselves owners and pimps, who joined the club in order to advertise their houses and women to their associates. Another organization [5] of similar character has a membership of about 500 young men whose ages range from twenty-one to thirty. They are fond of attending boxing contests, wrestling bouts, athletic meets and public dances. After such exhibitions or " affairs " they go in groups of five or ten to the houses, spending long hours in promiscuous orgies. Owners make a specialty of catering to clubs of this character. When they give public balls, " rackets," " chowder parties," or other outings, the madames, buying tickets liberally, attend with their best looking inmates or with runners to drum up trade. After the ball or outing is over, groups of men and boys follow them back to their quarters.

The proprietors of the highest priced houses are very

[3] X 33 and X 9.
[4] X 541. [5] X 545.

cautious in the conduct of their business. There is no promiscuous intermingling of customers in a common receiving parlor where the men huddle on a bench awaiting their turn, or sit in chairs gaping at each other unashamed. Separate parlors are used for display; privacy is carefully guarded. In order to make doubly sure that their visits will not be known, prominent customers occasionally hire an entire establishment. An instance is cited in which a well-to-do patron remained three days in such a resort. At times, however, men are utterly reckless: they have been known to leave their business cards behind them, or their signatures in books or on presents given to the inmates or the madame. One such individual is the New York agent for a famous automobile concern; another is the manager of a company which manufactures a well-known typewriter; another travels about from city to city selling hats; while still a fourth is connected with a celebrated watch company.

A numerous but pathetic group is that made up of young clerks who, living alone in unattractive quarters, find in professional prostitutes companions in the company of whom a night's revel offsets the dullness of their lives at other times. There are thousands of these men in New York. No home ties restrain them; no home associations fill their time or thought. Their rooms are fit only to sleep in; close friends they have few or none. You can watch them on the streets any evening. Hour after hour they gaze at the passing throng; at length they fling themselves into the current,— no longer silent and alone.

No small part of the business is the so-called "out

Prostitute and Customer

of town" trade. It has been conservatively estimated that over 250,000 visitors enter this city every day in the year for business or for pleasure. This great host visit the theaters, parks, seashore resorts, museums; they trade in stores and shops, and some of them, before they return to their homes, become customers in vice resorts. They, too, include all social classes: soldiers and sailors, traveling men and buyers, men in attendance on business, political or fraternal gatherings and conventions, and mere pleasure seekers.

It is impossible to estimate the number of men and boys who become customers in vice resorts in Manhattan during the course of one year. On the basis of data actually on file, it may be assumed that inmates of resorts and women on the street trade with between ten and fifteen men per day. This statement is corroborated by data secured by the Vice Commission in Chicago, where the average was found to be 15 per day for 18 inmates in one house covering a period of 22 months,[6] as well as by data obtained in Syracuse, New York, where the average number of customers entertained by one inmate during a period of 6 months was 12.[7] Taking the lower figures as the basis of calculation, if the 15,000 professional prostitutes of Manhattan entertain ten guests apiece, the customers total at least 150,000 persons every day.

[6] See "The Social Evil in Chicago, Report of the Chicago Vice Commission," page 101.
[7] See "The Social Evil in Syracuse, N. Y., Report of the Morals Survey Committee," page 95.

CHAPTER VI

THE BUSINESS OF PROSTITUTION; ITS COST

THE present chapter deals mainly with the business of prostitution as conducted in parlor houses and brothels. Our investigators were fortunate in being able to mingle freely with promoters and their assistants during a period of many months, listening to their conversations, consulting with them about business deals, helping them "make up their books" after the day's business was over, and writing letters for them; they were, in fact, treated as members of the inner circle and thus obtained first-hand information. Copies of leases for property are on our files; records of expenses and receipts in the handwriting of the promoters were secured; conversations carried on between promoters and bearing on their business dealings, have been recorded. It is commonly believed that men who live upon the proceeds of prostitution are untruthful, that no dependence can be put upon their statements. This doubtless holds as to their utterances on the witness stand or before an investigating body. But among themselves they talk about their business dealings with great freedom, and probably with more or less general accuracy. They eat and drink, buy and sell, plan and scheme like other business men; and under such circumstances the

The Business of Prostitution; Its Cost

facts and conversations presented herewith were obtained. On the other hand, it must be distinctly stated that our agents were not authorized or permitted to " frame up " cases in order to secure facts. They did not operate houses of prostitution in the effort to obtain direct evidence, although opportunities of this kind frequently presented themselves. They could have leased property for immoral purposes, bought shares in houses of prostitution, or have become active agents in arranging the details essential to the safe and successful conduct of the business. Their instructions forbade anything of the kind: it was their part merely to observe without arousing suspicion on the one hand, and without actual participation on the other.

(1) LEASING PROPERTY

In order to secure houses to be used for immoral purposes, " go-betweens " called " mecklers " are employed. The " meckler " is paid a fee, never less than $30 and sometimes as much as $100. Occasionally he receives a small percentage of the receipts.

A man of this character [1] lives in East 139th Street.[2] During the period of this investigation, he selected a building on Sixth Avenue [3] as suitable for the business of prostitution. Several promoters had previously tried unsuccessfully to secure a lease on this property. Through the pawnbroker who occupies the first floor, the " meckler " in question ultimately succeeded in securing the owner's [4] consent: the rental was $300 a month,

[1] X 428. [3] X 423.
[2] X 428-a. [4] X 548.

despite the wretched conditions of the premises. He therefore rented the upper floors to three others,[5] who shared with him on a 20 per cent basis. The enterprise was not successful; not long after the "meckler" sold his share[6] for $450. The house closed in March, 1912, because of poor management. Later three other men purchased the lease and re-opened the place.

On June 26th, 1912, two owners[7] of a house of prostitution[8] in West 28th Street, sought to rent a house[9] on West 29th Street. The go-between was instructed to secure a lease on the house for one year if possible, and was told to give the agent to understand for what purpose they wanted the property. If objection was made, he was to tell the agent that in case of dispossession proceedings, the tenant could be evicted and a new lease issued under a different name. This was said to be the usual plan when the police made an arrest or issued an eviction notice. The go-between carried out his instructions literally. The house agents candidly admitted that "the owner knows that the only thing we can let the house for is for a cat-house" (meaning a house of prostitution). They stipulated that the place was not to be conducted as a gambling house or pool room; otherwise they did not care. The rental finally agreed upon was $2,000 a year. It was also agreed to insert in the lease a clause permitting the lessee to sublet the house to some other tenant in case of arrest and subsequent dispossession proceedings. A deposit of

[5] X 111, X 549, X 550.
[6] To X 110.
[7] X 47-a, X 408.
[8] X 12.
[9] X 554.

The Business of Prostitution; Its Cost

$30 was made and a receipt was given in the name of the supposed broker, or "meckler."

In the renting of premises for purposes of prostitution various devices are employed to protect agent and owner, despite the fact that there is an overwhelming probability that in most cases both possess from the outset guilty knowledge of the facts. In some places, direct responsibility is avoided through renting empty apartments to janitors for a rental ranging from $40 to $50 a month. The janitor furnishes these apartments on the instalment plan and sublets them to prostitutes at the rate of $15 to $18 per week. Then, in addition, he often receives from $3 to $5 per week to "look away," as he terms it. If the respectable families do not like it, they may move; and many of them do move.

The method of subletting furnished apartments by the janitor, with the consent of the agent (who probably shares in the extra profits) is employed in a tenement building on West 109th Street. In other places, the agents rent apartments by the week, demanding payment in advance. After a day or two, they may inform the occupants that a complaint has been made and that they will have to move. They do not return any of the advanced rental, but proceed to repeat the performance. This has happened in connection with furnished apartments on such streets as West 107th and West 108th.

During the month of February, 1912, a woman investigator visited 122 real estate agents for the alleged purpose of renting an apartment for immoral purposes. In each case the investigator endeavored to convey to the agent the object for which the apartment was ostensibly desired. Of the 122 agents visited, only 17 refused outright to be parties to the transaction. A few of these were indignant, others said they had to be careful, and still others said the owners of the property were exceedingly strict. Sixty-seven agents agreed to rent certain apartments for this purpose and gave the investigator the addresses of 98 separate apartments where she could conduct the proposed business. Many of these addresses proved to be places where the present investigation had already discovered disorderly conditions. The remaining 38 agents were classified as doubtful. Some of them were annoyed because the investigator openly hinted her purpose; they suggested that they did not care, but would not knowingly rent the property in their charge for such a business. Others pretended to ignore the questions of the investigator and gave her 65 separate addresses where apartments could be rented. They were willing to rent apartments of this character, but did not want to appear to do so. A young man in a real estate office on Eighth Avenue stated that they "never ask people for their marriage certificates; they require only that tenants conduct themselves quietly." One well-known agent [10] betrayed and indeed confessed embarrassment when frankly told the purpose for which it was desired to rent a house. He remarked: "I know what you wanted the house for, but I had much rather you had not told me. If I don't know it, I don't know it. Now suppose you people are dispossessed and get on the witness stand and squeal, how would I look?" At

[10] X 552.

The Business of Prostitution; Its Cost

a further conference, the agent refused to agree to a new lease in case of an eviction. "The only trouble," he said to the stranger, "is that you talked too much. I knew what you wanted the house for, but I very much rather you had not told me. What I don't know don't bother me. I tell you what I'll do. You send somebody else up here in a week or so and I will give you the house and don't talk too much about it."

In some of the buildings mentioned in the course of the negotiations here in question, practically every apartment is a vice resort. As many as 16 such resorts were found in one 7-story building. In another, every apartment except one was a vice resort, the one exception being the home of a butcher who supplied meat to the other tenants.

Whatever the lease may indicate to the contrary, property rented for immoral purposes produces extraordinarily large returns. Not infrequently a high rental is thus produced by houses and apartments that are so dilapidated that they cannot be rented at all to decent human beings. Again, there is a tacit understanding that the rental named in the lease is merely a blind. The agent receives an additional sum, which he may pocket or divide with the landlord. The lease of a house [11] of prostitution in West 26th Street places the rental at $100 a month; the keeper [12] pays $150. On October 5th, 1912, three men were negotiating with a real estate agent [13] in West 30th Street, who agreed to rent them two houses [14] in West 38th Street at extortionate rates.

[11] X 462.   [12] X 387.   [13] X 463.   [14] X 465, 466.

Commercialized Prostitution in New York

On the same day, an Eighth Avenue agent [15] was promised a bonus of $50 per month for a house [16] in West 28th Street. Occasionally the increased charge appears in the lease. When the madame [17] of a West 40th Street establishment undertook to rent this house, she was told by the agent [18] that the rent would be $110 per month, and that he would lease the building to her for one year with a three months' clause. Then he added, " Now be frank; I will find out anyway. Do you intend to do anything up there?"

" Well, I might take a chance," she said.

" If you do," he replied, " the rent will be $125 per month."

On March 9th, 1912, at 11.30 P. M., a man was solicited by two colored girls to enter a vice resort in West 40th Street.[19] The agents [20] of this building have offices in West 42nd Street. The building is 5 stories high and four families live on each floor, paying a monthly rental of from $20 to $25. The street walkers, however, pay as much as $40 per month for their rooms. Their neighbors [21] declare that the agent has knowledge of the character of these tenants. A public school is next door, and on the opposite side of the street is a church.

(2) TRADING IN SHARES

A group consisting of 38 men own and operate 28 one-dollar houses of prostitution in a certain section of

[15] X 467, 468.
[16] X 469.
[17] X 109.
[18] X 562.
[19] X 563.
[20] X 564.
[21] X 565.

The Business of Prostitution; Its Cost

Manhattan.[22] Among themselves they trade actively in shares. One of them [23] — already referred to as the "King" by reason of the scope of his enterprises and influence — is said to own shares in 10 houses, and his brother and nephew each have a sixth interest in another resort which he gave them as a present. His one-dollar resorts are located on the following streets: — three on Sixth Avenue, two each in West 25th Street and West 24th Street, and one each in West 28th Street,[24] West 31st Street,[25] and West 40th Street.[26] He is also the proprietor of a $5 house located in West 49th Street.[27] In some houses there are three partners who are said also to own shares in other places of the same character; in one instance, two brothers are partners in two houses — one in Sixth Avenue, and one in West 27th Street. Four partners were formerly interested in a business conducted in West 24th Street.

The group of men who operate these 28 houses of prostitution are very careful in disposing of their shares. The purchaser must either be one of their own number or some relative or friend. Sales are made for different reasons, sometimes to effect economies in management. For example, on June 7th, 1912, an owner [28] sold a half interest in a Sixth Avenue resort to a man from the West, for $2,200. Thereupon he bought a one-third interest in another house on Sixth Avenue for $900, being admitted to the firm that he might serve as lighthouse

---

[22] The other two houses, making the 30 resorts later referred to under "Receipts," are operated by women.
[23] X 34.   [25] X 16.   [27] X 585.
[24] X 419.   [26] X 583.   [28] X 568.

and procurer. A half-partner [29] was taken into another Sixth Avenue house [30] for $1500. The low price was subsequently accounted for by the owner as follows: "Do you suppose if the new partner had not had a good woman, I would have taken him in for that sum? I would have to take a woman in anyway and give her at least 20 per cent of the profits, without getting anything for it except her labor. To start with, I am getting $1,500 and a good woman; I save $25 per week on a procurer, and besides get a partner who is interested in the house and not a total stranger who does not care whether the house does business or not; the place is running straight now." While these two men were discussing this economical move, the madame [31] of a house in West 40th Street [32] approached, to remark that she had a good house in the 26th police precinct, and wanted to have one of them come with her as a partner, so that she could use his influence in making some very necessary arrangements looking toward the success of the business. In reply to this offer, the person addressed replied: "They (meaning the police authorities) will not stand for a one-dollar house of prostitution on that street and besides I have enough, my hands are full." Thereupon one of the partners in another resort on Sixth Avenue,[33] remarked that if she wanted to pay him $2,000 for his one-third interest, he would sell it.

"Why do you want to sell?" asked the woman.

"My woman is very sick," he replied, "and she has

[29] X 575.
[30] X 423.
[31] X 110.
[32] X 109.
[33] X 403.

The Business of Prostitution; Its Cost

to go to the mountains; also her sister is very sick and I am ' broke.' "

" How heavy is business? " she asked.

He replied that the house was " working " between $1,000 and $1,200 per week. She regarded $2,000 as too much for a one-third interest, as the hot months were coming on and business would probably be very dull; however, she would give $1,500.

" No," he answered, " you cannot buy my share for $1,999."

Buyers are of course wary. They must be convinced that they are getting what they pay for; occasionally, therefore, tentative arrangements are made. A madame is installed until actual experience proves that the property is worth the price asked.

The following transactions were actually witnessed by our investigators: On March 3rd, 1912, sale of three one-third interests in a Sixth Avenue resort for $650 apiece; March 11th, 1912, sale of a half interest in another Sixth Avenue resort for $2,200; March 19th, a sale of a one-third interest in a West 40th Street resort for $1,500,— a poor investment, for the house was shortly closed; in July, 1912, a one-third interest in another resort in West 40th Street was purchased for $3,000 by an owner, who transferred his women thither from a place in 28th Street. Occasionally pressure is brought to force a part owner out. On one such transaction, a profit of $500 was made; in another a share was bought for $500,— far below its market value.[34]

[34] The houses and individuals involved in all the above transactions are identified in our records.

Commercialized Prostitution in New York

Quarrels and disputes between shareholders are of frequent occurrence. Such disputes are deplored among the more intelligent promoters because they fear exposure of one sort or another. A dissatisfied shareholder may " squeal " to the police; or his woman may sit on the steps of a rival's resort, calling the attention of the police to a particular house. The policy of the business is to keep everybody satisfied and contented. Nevertheless, misunderstandings occur; on April 8th, 1912, two shareholders were engaged in a hot dispute; one of them had been a silent partner who never " came to the front " when extra demands were made on the finances of the firm, but left the other to pay the bills. It was claimed that, as a result of his neglect, the house was closed and an officer was ordered to stay inside. The business was ruined. Finally the officer was removed, whereupon the " silent " partner wished to be recognized as owning a share. As the complainant had borne the brunt of the difficulties with the police, as well as the subsequent losses, he refused; besides, he had taken in two other men as partners. The delinquent partner became very angry and threatened to send his woman to the house and to make all sorts of trouble. The two new partners advised that he receive $150 and be declared " out for good." But the silent partner was not satisfied when he heard that one of the new partners had sold his share for $1,700. So he demanded $600 more for his share, claiming that he was still a partner, which sum he subsequently received. [35]

The precarious nature of such investments, depending,

[35] The parties involved were X 72, X 586, X 69, X 415.

The Business of Prostitution; Its Cost

as it does, for its value on variations in public opinion and municipal policy, can be illustrated from former as well as current history:

During the fall of 1907, the Commissioner of Police, as well as the District Attorney, became very active in closing houses of prostitution in Manhattan. An owner who was put out of business at that time made the following statement, in substance, in the presence of two witnesses:

"At the time I was put out of business by Police Commissioner Bingham in 1907, I left New York with $4,800 and bought a farm in Jersey. After things had cooled down, or in February, 1911, I came back to New York to look the ground over. Finally things looked all right and I bought a one-third interest in a place in West 25th Street for the sum of $1,200. Three days later, "bing," I get a raid and a cop in front of the door for a whole month. Then the cop was taken away and I opened again for a few days, when, "bing," another $300 raid with a cop inside. I was tipped off that my partner did not suit, so I bought her interest for $600 while the cop was still inside. I then "doubled up" with a friend. We opened very slowly; I would not let the women solicit at the windows. The weather was very hot. In August I bought my friend out for $1,200 which made me even. From February to April, I paid $100 a month in rent and other expenses and did n't make a cent until August. Since that time up till now I have saved only $9,000. The house stands me $4,000 after paying rent, the cost of the raids, and the purchase price."

As already pointed out, any change in the political

Commercialized Prostitution in New York

situation or in the attitude toward the business on the part of the authorities of the city, or a reform movement, reacts immediately upon the value of the shares in vice resorts. Just before the murder of the gambler Rosenthal last summer, the shares in houses of prostitution were very valuable, and it was practically impossible to secure them except at large prices. On June 4th, a part owner in a house in West 25th Street declared: "It is impossible to get something decent unless you pay a prohibitive price. I had to pay $1,700 for a one-third interest in this place and only to-day I paid $1,000 for a year's lease on three houses in the same street. These buildings have changed hands seven or eight times during the past year and it is rumored that they are going to be torn down."[36] On June 19th, 1912, the owner of a share in a Sixth Avenue house told a man that the "stocks are awful high." He offered to sell his one-third share, costing $500 originally, for $2,000.

The Rosenthal murder took place July 15, 1912, and shares in houses of prostitution at once declined. Some of the promoters were very pessimistic over the situation and declared that the houses would be closed and their business ruined. On August 6th, 1912, while discussing the situation, one of them[37] declared that it was all over with them. His partner[38] remonstrated with him, holding that the authorities would not close the houses. To this the former replied:

"Well, I show you how much I think of it — I will sell my interest and get out."

[36] The persons and places are X 407, X 67, X 59, X 72-a.
[37] X 73.   [38] X 72.

The Business of Prostitution; Its Cost

"It's a go," said the other, "I've been a gambler all my life; I'll buy it." The price paid for this share several months before was $1,700, and the same sum was demanded and refused. After some arguing, the bargain was closed at $1,000 and $100 was paid on account.

Prior to the murder in question, a one-third interest in a Sixth Avenue place was worth $2,000. On August 8th, 1912, the owner offered to sell his interest for $1,000.

"No," said the prospective buyer, "I will give you $500, and I am taking a gambler's chance in giving you that much." [39]

The decline in values has continued since the date of the above conversations. At this moment an interest in certain places can be purchased for the amount of a night's profit.

(3) BUSINESS DETAILS, ETC.

It is impossible to give even an approximate estimate of the receipts from the business of prostitution in Manhattan during a stated period. We could not secure access to the books of the owners, even if they kept accounts, which none do in a systematic way. But bits of direct evidence, absolutely accurate and reliable, in the shape of records for a day, a week, or month were obtained here and there; we can also report what owners and inmates say regarding their incomes. Whatever allowances are made for overstatements and misstatements, intentional or accidental, the total is sufficiently staggering.

The most eloquent and significant exhibits obtained

[39] Persons and places: X 417, X 403, X 69.

Commercialized Prostitution in New York

were the cards on which the night's business of the inmate is punched. These casual bits of information are in no wise exceptional. One shrinks from multiplying them by the number of women engaged, and the number of days in the year.

Lillie, inmate in a vice resort in Sixth Avenue [40] showed the investigator a white card in which were punched 7 holes, each representing one customer or service at $1 apiece, or $7. It was the record of her earnings during a period of six hours ending at one A. M. on March 14th, 1912. Of the $7, Lillie received $3.50 as her share, from which amount $1.50 was deducted by the madame to pay her board for the day.

The account of 6 inmates in a West 58th Street resort showed that on Sunday, April 21st, Alma had earned $7; Pauline, $15; Pansy, $14; Rose, $17; Bella, $16; and Ruth, $15: a total of $86, or an average of $14 per day for each inmate. The price in this house ranged from $2 to $5, according to the customer. The receipts of 3 inmates for another day in April were, Rose, $49; Alma, $16; and Ruth, $30: a total of $95, or an average for the day of $31 per inmate. The receipts on May 3rd, 1912, were as follows: Rose, $28; Bella, $21; Alma, $13; Pansy, $4: a total of $66, or an average of over $16 per day per inmate. For the week April 22-28 inclusive the receipts from 4 to 6 inmates were as follows:

        Monday,   April 22nd, 1912, $50
        Tuesday,   April 23rd, 1912, 38
        Wednesday, April 24th, 1912, 34

[40] X 751.

The Business of Prostitution; Its Cost

Thursday, April 25th, 1912, $39
Friday, April 26th, 1912, 54
Saturday, April 27th, 1912, 53
Sunday, April 28th, 1912, 57

This gives a total of $325 or an average of about $46 per day.

Sixteen white cards were obtained from a dollar house in West 28th Street showing the earnings per inmate on July 9th, 1912. "Babie" is credited with $27; Buster, $30; a girl whose name is not readable, $27; Charlotte, $23; Dolly, $20; Dorothy, $11; Minnie, $15; Eva, $16; one whose name is not given, $15; another, name not given, $14; another, $10; others whose names are omitted, $14, $14, $9, $8, $11 respectively. The total is $264 or an average of about $16 per inmate for the day. The madame when paying the inmates the one-half due them for their day's work always deducted the sum of $1.50 for board.

In the figures above given, there is no element of doubt whatsoever: they are taken from the actual records of the day's business,— the cards in the possession of every inmate. Whether they can be regarded as fairly representative is another question, which it would be futile to discuss. We possess, however, certain totals, the precise reliability of which the reader must judge for himself. It has been stated that our investigators succeeded in establishing themselves on an intimate footing with those most prominently concerned in the commercial exploitation of prostitution. They took part in conferences, and could discuss business and its prospects without suspicion. From time to time these agents

Commercialized Prostitution in New York

found themselves in position to canvass freely the question of returns, past, present and future. The approximate estimates of the value of the various properties prior to the Rosenthal murder; and the main items of expense incurred in their conduct were set down as thus obtained. In regard to the general credibility of the figures it is to be remembered that these men are decidedly communicative among themselves and that any exaggerated departure from probability would have drawn forth expressions of skepticism or disbelief; on the other hand, it is not pretended that the figures are more than roughly significant of the scope and profits of a fluctuating trade; they are given for what they are worth.

TABLE SHOWING APPROXIMATE MONTHLY RECEIPTS FROM INMATES, MONTHLY EXPENSES, NUMBER OF INMATES, NUMBER OF MADAMES, ETC., IN 30 ONE-DOLLAR HOUSES.

Location of house	House receipts[41] (½ fees)	House expenses[42]	No. inmates	No. madames	No. maids	No. lighthouses	No. owners	Value of business S=sale B=bid.
No. — W. 18	$3,600	$814	18	2	4	1	3	....
" " " 24	3,200	735	17	2	3	1	2	....
" " " 25	3,200	606	16	1	3	1	2	....
" " " 25	4,000	839	24	3	4	1	2	....
" " " 25	3,227	705	20	1	3	1	1	$5,100 S.
" " " 25	3,000	571	9	2	3	..	3	....
" " " 28	2,800	729	17	2	4	1	2	....
" " " 28	3,000	821	16	4	3	1	3	....
" " " 31	2,800	516	12	..	3	..	3	2,000 S.
" " " 35	2,400	788	14	3	3	1	2	....
" " " 40	1,200	275	4	..	2	..	2	....
" " " 40	1,000	293	6	..	2	..	1	....
" " " 40	2,000	628	12	2	3	1	2	....
" " " 56	3,200	797	20	3	4	1	2	....
" Sixth Ave.[43]	2,400	691	14	1	2	1	2	....
" " "	3,600	689	19	2	4	1	2	4,400 S.

[41] The girl gets one-half, the house one-half.

[42] The effort is made to meet these expenses by the charge made for board—a charge paid by the inmates out of their " half."

[43] From this point to the end of the table, shops occupy the first floors of the buildings named.

The Business of Prostitution; Its Cost

Location of house			House receipts (½ fees)	House expenses	No. inmates	No. madames	No. maids	No. lighthouses	No. owners	Value of business S=sale B=bid.	
No.	Sixth	Ave.	2,400	733	14	2	3	1	3	....	
"	"	"	2,000	593	12	1	2	..	2	....	
"	"	"	3,200	555	12	2	2	..	3	6,000	S.
"	"	"	1,200	437	5	1	2	1	1	....	
"	"	"	3,200	667	15	2	2	1	2	3,750	S.
"	"	"	3,600	847	20	2	4	1	1	....	
"	"	"	2,800	627	15	1	2	1	4	10,000	B.
No. — W. 24			2,000	674	10	1	3	2	4	{2,500 / 3,200	S. / S.
" " " 26			3,700	819	20	2	4	1	2	....	
" " " 27			3,000	570	16	1	2	1	2	....	
" " " 28			3,000	741	16	1	3	1	3	....	
" " " 28			1,200	441	8	1	2	..	1	....	
" " " 36			3,000	748	16	2	3	1	2	3,000	S.
" " " 36			2,800	706	15	3	3	1	1	....	
Total			$81,727	$19,655	432	50	87	24	65		

Similar data were also procured — and in substantially the same manner — for eight five-dollar houses.[44]

TABLE SHOWING APPROXIMATE MONTHLY RECEIPTS OF HOUSES FROM INMATES, MONTHLY EXPENSES, NUMBER INMATES, NUMBER MADAMES, ETC., IN 8 FIVE-DOLLAR HOUSES.

Location of house	St.	House receipts (½ fees)	House expenses	No. inmates	No. madames	No. maids	Lowest price of service
No.—W.	38	$ 2,400	$ 871	12	2	4	$3
" "	41	1,800	924	10	2	3	5
" "	46	2,800	938	14	2	3	5
" "	46	3,200	952	16	2	5	5
" "	46	1,800	760	12	1	4	5
" "	47	3,000	871	15	2	3	5
" "	49	1,800	878	12	2	3	{2 / 5
" "	52	1,600	885	9	2	3	5
Total		$18,400	$7,079	100	15	28	

Ten disorderly tenements were studied in the same way, with the following results:[45]

[44] For itemized account of certain expenses, see Appendix VI, p. 280.

[45] For itemized account of certain expenses, see Appendix V, p. 279.

Commercialized Prostitution in New York

TABLE SHOWING APPROXIMATE MONTHLY RECEIPTS FROM INMATES, MONTHLY EXPENSES, NUMBER INMATES AND NUMBER MAIDS IN 10 DISORDERLY APARTMENTS.

Location St.	House receipts (½ fees)	House expenses	No. inmates	No. maids
No.—W. 43	$ 500	$ 189	3	1
" " 45	600	235	3	1
" " 49	700	259	4	2
" " 50	700	264	4	2
" " 55	600	261	4	2
" " 58	800	143	4	2
" " 58	800	175	4	2
" " 58	1,000	440	5	2
" " 60	500	208	3	2
" " 65	600	144	3	1
Total	$6,800	$2,318	37	17

We have deliberately refrained from attempting to make even an approximate calculation on the basis of the foregoing tables of the profits annually derived from commercialized prostitution in New York City. But a moment's reflection will suggest the enormous sums involved. If, for example, the table dealing with thirty parlor houses, *i. e.*, less than one-half of those investigated, even roughly represents the monthly volume of business, over $2,000,000 a year are paid to their inmates, one-half of which is at once paid over to the houses; the running expenses of the houses are about one-quarter of a million; but the profits are not reduced by this sum, for the payments of the inmates for board and lodging are supposed to be equal to the expense of conducting the establishment. Moreover, the estimates above given entirely omit certain very important indirect sources of revenue,— for large profits are derived from the sale of liquor, tobacco, lewd pictures, booklets, verse and other reading matter.

The Business of Prostitution; Its Cost

Finally, patrons often tip lavishly, leaving "gift" or "luck" money, and in innumerable other ways add to the revenue of the resorts. The total expenditure incurred and the net profit to the exploiters, therefore, run high up into the millions annually.[46]

A partial confirmation of the scale of the estimates above given is furnished by the following incident:

During the evening of May 3, 1912, one of the owners of a house of prostitution in West 25th Street was trying to sell a one-third interest in his one-dollar resort. He had written on a sheet of brown wrapping paper the receipts and expenses for one month in connection with the business in this house. This document is in our possession. The items which interest us in this connection are receipts for four weeks and two days, or 30 days in all: First week's receipts, $1,735; second week, $1,612; third week, $1,463; fourth week, $1,401; two days, $243; making a total of $6,454 for the thirty days, or an average of about $215 per day. The average number of inmates in this house is 15. In that case, each inmate earned $15, that is, received 15 men each day.

The income of the street walker is probably subjected to greater fluctuations than that of the house or flat inmate, weather and other conditions greatly affecting her earnings. It is therefore impossible to gain any conception of the volume of money that changes hands in consequence of street business. Samples are, however, available; the account book which was secured from a young prostitute, neither very aggressive nor very at-

[46] For itemized statement of certain expenses, similarly obtained, see Appendix IV, p. 288.

Commercialized Prostitution in New York

tractive, who solicits on East 14th Street and receives usually one dollar for her services, runs as follows:

Wednesday	$7.50
Thursday	7.00
Friday	9.00
Saturday	9.50
Sunday	4.50
Monday	7.50
Tuesday	8.00

a total of $53.

The items for the next seven days are as follows:

Wednesday	$ 6.50
Thursday	6.50
Friday	7.00
Saturday	12.00
Sunday	10.00
Monday	9.00
Tuesday	6.00

a total of $57.

The following six days' receipts were as follows:

Wednesday	$6.00
Thursday	6.00
Friday	3.50
Saturday	8.00
Sunday	5.50
Monday	5.00

a total of $34.

The following seven days' receipts are:

Wednesday	$6.00
Thursday	5.00
Friday	3.00

The Business of Prostitution; Its Cost

Saturday 7.00
Sunday 8.00
Monday 6.00
Tuesday 6.00

$41 in all.

There were only five more days accounted for, when the girl ceased to keep any record of her receipts:

Wednesday 3.50
Thursday 2.00
Friday 5.50
Saturday 4.50
Sunday 10.50

the total of these five days being $26.

Thus in 32 days, this poorly dressed, rather ignorant and unsophisticated street walker, earned $211, an average of between $6 and $7 per day.

Practically all the figures in the above concern profits derived from the sale of the bodies of women. In addition, the exploiters — owners and madames mainly — derive further gain (by no means inconsiderable in amount) from such items as the sale to their women, at exorbitant prices, of clothing and other feminine requirements. Huge as these immediate profits of exploitation are, they are enormously increased by the vast sums made from the sale of intoxicating drinks, which business has been shown to be so closely allied with prostitution, and by abnormal rentals received for the use of all kinds of property for purposes of prostitution. Even then, the stupendous although unknown figure involved in the maintenance of this army of upwards of 15,000 women in New York City fails to indicate what prostitution costs society. For perhaps the greatest cost of all is yet to be mentioned, namely, disease. Wherever prostitution exists, there venereal disease flourishes,— maiming, incapacitating the participants surely, and not infrequently innocent ones in close association with them.

Reliable and complete statistics as to the prevalence of venereal disease, its consequences immediate and remote, are not to be had. In the absence of compulsory reporting, it is impossible to estimate the number of cases under treatment by physicians; in addition to these, large numbers endeavor to conceal the truth by foolishly resorting to quacks, advertised nostrums, etc. Figures obtainable from hospitals represent, therefore, only a fraction, probably an inconsiderable fraction, of those afflicted; as far as they go, a careful study elicits the following facts:

During the year 1911, 522,722 cases of all kinds were treated in 17 dispensaries in New York City; 15,781, or 3.01 percent of these cases, were venereally affected. The hospitals of the city possess few beds for the reception of venereal patients; nevertheless, 5,380 persons — 6.33 per cent of all cases treated in 13 different hospitals — were venereally affected, about two-thirds male, one-third female. These infections occur at any time from the first to the seventieth year,— the period of greatest frequency being between 16 and 30 years of age: between 16 and 20, 796 were males and 369 females; between 21 and 25, 1,182 and 454, respectively; between 26 and 30, 692 and 268.

For several reasons these figures are far from suggesting the actual extent of venereal infection,— in the first place, because, as above stated, the hospitals receive but a

The Business of Prostitution; Its Cost

fraction of the sufferers; in the second, because accurate diagnosis has only recently become feasible. The percentages increase heavily as soon as the more delicate and reliable tests devised by Wassermann and others are applied. For example, 308 adults were admitted to the medical wards of a certain New York hospital during the months of January, February, and March, 1913; though the Wassermann test for syphilis was made in the case of only 166 of these, 38, *i. e.*, 23 percent of those examined, gave positive results; this is equivalent to 12.3 percent of the entire 308. Had the test been applied to all adults admitted, undoubtedly the ratio of syphilitic infection would have been higher still. As a matter of fact, the test as usually performed does not disclose all cases of infection; so that the prevalence of disease is actually greater than the tests indicate.

The civil state of the patients in the cases first mentioned is shown in the following table:

Males			Females		
single	married	widowers	single	married	widows
640	2950	57	589	802	90

From the standpoint of occupation, every social class is represented,— necessarily so, inasmuch as every social class figures in the phenomena of prostitution. The occupations given by male patients were as follows: professional, 52; clerical and official, 307; mercantile and trading, 250; public entertainment, 120; personal service, police and military, 186; laboring and servant, 1,181; manufacturing and mechanical industry, 932; agricultural, transportation, and other outdoor employments, 645; no occupations, 58; classified as unknown, 8; children, 11; congenital origin, 31; schoolboys, 10; students, 10. The occupations of female patients are as follows: professional, 46; domestic and personal 1,144; trade and transportation, 109; manufacturing and mechanical, 86; no occupations, 72; unknown, 9; schoolgirls, 21; children, 76.

In respect to the disease with which they were afflicted, 413 of the 1,563 females suffered from syphilis; 1,036 from gonorrhœa; 9 from chancroids, and 105 from complications. Eight hundred and eighty-three of the men were suffering from syphilis; 1,445 from gonorrhœa; 203 from chancroids, and 1,276 from complications.

It needs no argument to show that the cost of prostitution is enormously augmented even by the amount of disease accounted for in the preceding discussion; as this represents but a small part of the whole, the totals thus reached require to be multiplied by a large factor. But the reckoning would still be incomplete, even if we knew the actual volume of syphilis, gonorrhœa and chancre; for there would remain to be included the remote effects, not less certainly due to venereal affection, and even more fateful and costly than the immediate manifestations,— paralysis, sterility, miscarriage, deformity, degeneracy, insanity,— curses that stretch even "unto the third and fourth generations." From the effort to translate such losses into dollars and cents, the boldest calculator may well shrink: yet they are a part,— a certain, inevitable part — of the cost of prostitution.

CHAPTER VII

PROSTITUTION, THE POLICE, AND THE LAW

IN respect to vice and vice resorts, the police rules require that each police captain must report to the Commissioner all places in his precinct where disorderly, degraded or lawless people congregate, and also give notice in writing to the owner, lessee or occupant, that such room or building is so used, and that such use constitutes a misdemeanor. If the owner, lessee, or occupant does not abate the nuisance, the captain is empowered to obtain a warrant for his arrest and to prosecute him as required by law. In addition, each captain is required to make charges of neglect of duty against any patrolman who fails to discover a serious breach of peace on his post, or fails to arrest any person guilty of such offense. If a house is under suspicion of being disorderly or is so in fact, the officer on the beat is required to restrain acts of disorder, prevent soliciting from windows, doors, or on the streets, and to arrest all persons so doing. He must also carefully observe all other places of suspicious nature, obtain evidence as to the character and ownership of such houses and report the same to his commanding officer.[1]

Between January 1 and August 1, 1912, police captains

[1] For Rules and Regulations made pursuant to charter provisions, see Appendix VIII, p. 293.

Commercialized Prostitution in New York

in Manhattan reported to the department 112 separate places as suspicious or disorderly; against these, they made 542 complaints. Seven complaints were made against one place in the 5th precinct, 46 against 9 places in the 16th precinct, 180 against 35 places in the 23rd. The police activities are tabulated in the following table: [2]

Precinct	POLICE REPORTS No. Reports	No. of Places Involved
5	7	1
6	8	4
12	5	3
15	46	9
16	9	3
18	81	15
21	20	6
22	34	10
23	180	35
26	105	15
28	5	1
36	3	3
39	21	3
43	18	4
Totals	542	112

The following table distributes the places reported according to the character of the resort and the precinct:

POLICE REPORTS

Precincts	Prostitution Places	Assignation Houses	Disorderly Places	Total
1	..	..	..	..
2	..	..	..	..
5	1	..	..	1
6	..	..	4	4
7	..	..	..	..
8	..	..	..	..
10	..	..	..	..
12	3	..	..	3

[2] This table was compiled for the Aldermanic Committee appointed to investigate the police department, which fact explains why the period does not coincide with that of our own investigations. The table is a matter of public record.

Prostitution, Police, and Law

POLICE REPORTS—*Continued*

Precincts	Prostitution Places	Assignation Houses	Disorderly Places	Total
13	..	..	..	..
14	..	..	..	..
15	..	..	9	9
16	3	..	..	3
17	..	..	..	..
18	..	..	15	15
21	1	5	..	6
22	9	1	..	10
23	25	5	5	35
25	..	..	..	..
26	15	..	..	15
28	..	..	1	1
29	..	..	..	..
31	..	..	..	..
32	..	..	..	..
33	..	..	..	..
35	..	..	..	..
36	..	3	..	3
39	3	..	..	3
40	..	..	..	..
43	4	..	..	4
Totals	64	14	34	112

On the basis of both months and precincts these reports are distributed thus:

POLICE REPORTS

Precincts	Jan.	Feb.	Mar.	Apr.	May	June	July	Total	Separate Places—Total
1	..	..	..	..	..	..	..	..	..
2	..	..	..	..	..	..	..	..	..
5	1	1	1	1	1	1	1	7	1
6	4	4	..	..	..	..	..	8	4
7	..	..	..	..	..	..	..	..	..
8	..	..	..	..	..	..	..	..	..
10	..	..	..	..	..	..	..	..	..
12	1	2	1	1	..	..	..	5	3
13	..	..	..	..	..	..	..	..	..
14	..	..	..	..	..	..	..	..	..
15	9	9	8	6	6	4	4	46	9
16	3	3	3	..	..	..	..	9	3
18	15	11	11	11	11	11	11	81	15
21	6	5	5	1	1	1	1	20	6

Commercialized Prostitution in New York

POLICE REPORTS—*Continued*

Precincts	Jan.	Feb.	Mar.	Apr.	May	June	July	Total	Separate Places—Total
22	2	3	3	3	6	9	8	34	10
23	27	29	28	22	24	24	26	180	35
25	..	..	..	..	..	..	..	..	..
26	15	15	15	15	15	15	15	105	15
28	..	1	1	1	1	1	..	5	1
29	..	..	..	..	..	..	..	..	..
31	..	..	..	..	..	..	..	..	..
32	..	..	..	..	..	..	..	..	..
33	..	..	..	..	..	..	..	..	..
35	..	..	..	..	..	..	..	..	..
36	3	..	..	..	..	..	..	3	3
39	3	3	3	3	3	3	3	21	3
40	..	..	..	..	..	..	..	..	..
43	4	4	2	2	2	2	2	18	4
Totals	93	90	81	66	70	71	71	542	112

It would appear thus that in the fifth precinct the same house is reported month after month; in the 18th, 11 houses are reported during five of the 6 months; in the 26th precinct, 15 houses are systematically and regularly denounced.

Our own investigation began approximately three weeks later than the above tables and ran three months longer. In its course, our investigators reported 429 parlor houses, massage parlors, furnished room houses and hotels; and 379 saloons and miscellaneous places allied with prostitution. The 429 resorts first mentioned are distributed as follows:

INVESTIGATORS' REPORTS

Precincts	Parlor houses	Massage parlors	Furnished rooms	Hotels	Total investigation Addresses
1	..	..	..	..	..
2	..	..	..	..	..
5	3	..	..	..	3
6	6	..	..	1	7
7	..	..	..	..	..

Prostitution, Police, and Law

INVESTIGATOR'S REPORTS—*Continued*

Precincts	Parlor houses	Massage parlors	Furnished rooms	Hotels	Total investigation Addresses
8	..	..	..	..	..
10	..	..	..	..	..
12	3	..	..	..	3
13	..	..	1	2	3
14	..	..	2	..	2
15	11	..	19	9	39
16	..	..	..	1	1
17	1	..	2	..	3
18	21	8	10	8	47
21	3	..	5	12	20
22	22	3	41	7	73
23	35	23	14	21	93
25	1	1	1	2	5
26	29	17	10	16	72
28	1	8	2	5	16
29	..	9	..	3	12
32	..	1	..	1	2
33	..	..	..	..	..
36	..	..	..	10	10
39	5	..	2	1	8
40	..	..	..	..	..
43	1	..	3	6	10
Totals	142	70	112	105	429

The 379 saloons and miscellaneous places allied with prostitution were discovered in the following precincts:

Precincts	Saloons, etc., and miscellaneous places allied with prostitution	Precincts	Saloons, etc., and miscellaneous places allied with prostitution
1	2	13	4
2		14	2
5		15	26
6	11	16	7
7		17	
8		18	26
10		21	17
12		22	45

Commercialized Prostitution in New York

Precincts	Saloons, etc., and miscellaneous places allied with prostitution	Precincts	Saloons, etc., and miscellaneous places allied with prostitution
23	39	33	1
25	14	36	26
26	61	39	29
28	16	40	4
29	2	43	24
32	23		
Total			379

Comparison of the police reports with those made by our investigators shows marked differences. For example: in the sixth precinct, the police report 4 addresses, our agents 18, of which 11 were saloons, etc.; in the 15th, the police found 9, our agents 65, twenty-six of them saloons, etc.; in the 21st, the police gave 6, our agents 37, seventeen of them saloons, etc.; in the 22nd, the police report 10, our agents 118, forty-five of them saloons; in the 26th, 15 and 133 respectively, 61 of the latter being saloons, etc.; in the 28th, one place is noted by the police, 32 by our agents, 16 of them saloons, etc.; in the 32nd, none by the police, 25 by our agents, 23 of them saloons, etc.; in the 33rd precinct none is reported by police, one by our agents.

In the following table, both sets of reports are arranged side by side in tabular form, all forms of disorderly resorts being grouped together:

Precinct	No. disorderly places reported by police Jan. 1—Aug. 1, 1912.	No. disorderly places found by our investigators from Jan. 24—Nov. 15, 1912.
1	0	2
5	1	3
6	4	18

Prostitution, Police, and Law

	No. disorderly places reported by police Jan. 1—Aug. 1, 1912	No. disorderly places found by our investigators from Jan. 24—Nov. 15, 1912
12	3	3
13	0	7
14	0	4
15	9	65
16	3	8
17	0	3
18	15	73
21	6	37
22	10	118
23	35	132
25	0	19
26	15	133
28	1	32
29	0	14
32	0	25
33	0	1
36	3	36
39	3	37
40	0	4
43	4	34
Totals	112	808

Tenement resorts are not included in the preceding data. In the year 1912, the police reported to the Tenement House Department as vicious 138 separate addresses, in which they had made 153 arrests,— 65 of these arrests in two precincts, the 13th and the 15th; from 247 other sources, the department learned of 211 addresses: in all, 349 separate places were reported.[3] Our own agents discovered 1,172 separate disorderly apartments in tenements at 578 separate addresses between January 24th and November 15th.

In the following table, both sets of reports are com-

[3] In 40 of these cases, the complaint was dismissed as having "No basis." In 194 cases, the cause of complaint was removed, and in 8 cases no action was necessary. In 6 cases, a violation was held. Police made arrests in 153 of these cases.

Commercialized Prostitution in New York

bined, according to precincts; the tenement house reports cover the entire year (January-December 31, 1912), ours only the period of investigation (January 24-November 15, 1912):

TENEMENT HOUSE DEPARTMENT RECORDS

Precincts	Police Reports		Complaints from all sources including police		Investigation Reports	
	No. reports	No. separate buildings involved	No. complaints	No. separate bldgs. involved	No. separate addresses (Bldgs.)	No. separate disorderly apartments
1	..	..	..	..	..	..
2	..	..	..	..	..	..
5	1	1	2	2	1	1
6	2	2	4	4	5	9
7	1	1	2	2	1	1
8	..	..	..	..	..	..
10	2	2	2	2	..	..
12	5	5	6	5	1	1
13	27	23	38	28	10	10
14	1	1	1	1	1	3
15	38	35	46	42	58	69
16	1	1	4	4	2	2
17	4	4	15	14	5	5
18	..	..	3	1	25	26
21	3	2	7	4	6	6
22	4	4	18	15	75	123
23	3	3	8	7	28	44
25	..	..	..	..	1	2
26	12	10	13	11	102	396
28	14	12	17	13	95	164
29	..	..	..	..	..	..
31	1	1	3	3	3	3
32	16	14	22	18	85	206
33	..	..	..	..	..	..
35	..	..	2	2	2	5
36	12	11	14	13	58	81
39	..	..	3	3	4	4
40	..	..	1	1	..	..
43	6	6	16	16	10	11
Totals	153	138	247	211	578	1172

Prostitution, Police, and Law

During the same period, 794 separate saloons and concert halls were investigated, of which almost one-half, — 308 — were found disorderly; in addition to which, 91 miscellaneous places of a disorderly character were reported. The distribution of such disorderly places by precincts was as follows:

Precincts	Separate disorderly saloons, concert halls, etc.	Miscellaneous Places — Allied with prostitution	Miscellaneous Places — Semi-public used by prostitutes	Total disorderly saloons, etc. and miscellaneous places
1	..	2	..	2
2	..	..	1	1
5	..	..	..	..
6	11	..	..	11
7	..	..	..	..
8	..	..	..	..
10	..	..	..	..
12	..	..	..	..
13	4	..	..	4
14	2	..	..	2
15	11	15	..	26
16	7	..	..	7
17	..	..	..	..
18	18	8	..	26
21	13	4	..	17
22	38	7	1	46
23	26	13	5	44
25	12	2	..	14
26	50	11	3	64
28	15	1	3	19
29	2	..	1	3
31	..	..	..	..
32	20	3	5	28
33	1	..	..	1
35	..	..	..	..
36	26	..	1	27
39	26	3	..	29
40	3	1	..	4
43	23	1	..	24
Totals	308	71	20	399

The total number of actual vice resorts of all kinds

Commercialized Prostitution in New York

discovered in Manhattan was 1,606, situated at 1,007 different addresses; in the 26th precinct, 174 were found, — 29 parlor houses, 17 massage parlors, 102 tenement resorts, 10 furnished room houses, 16 hotels; in the 22nd precinct, 148 disorderly places were located, 22 parlor houses, 3 massage rooms, 75 tenement resorts, 41 furnished room houses, 7 hotels.

The investigator who succeeds in establishing himself on a footing of unsuspected familiarity in the underworld is soon admitted to confidences which show how the underworld accounts to itself for the comparative statistics above given. The credibility of the confidences in question each reader must decide for himself. Among themselves, as has already been pointed out, owners, madames and women talk freely. The conversations overheard are not staged, nor are they exceptional in character. Our agents participated in and reported in the form of affidavits frequent conversations and discussions, in which the relations between police and promoters formed the main or sole topic. Whether the details are literally accurate or not these conversations, reported from all sections of the city, and by different observers, working independently of one another, at least portray the state of feeling and opinion of the participants and their like.

On March 7, 1912, a group of men [4] interested in a West 26th Street house [5] were discussing prospects. "Profits are not what they used to be," complained one of them. "I used to be able to bank $600 or more every week. To-day my receipts are $1,500 a week,

[4] X 387, X 387-a, X 424-a, X 596.   [5] X 462.

Prostitution, Police, and Law

but see,— thirteen plain clothes men [6] get $10 a month each; one of them, a tough proposition, gets $25; two patrolmen get $2 each a day; the lieutenant and sergeant get $5 a month; besides, regular protection costs $100 a month, paid to a go-between,[7] once a wardman. And then I've got to buy tickets and contribute to funds for strong arm guys in trouble."

Mysteriously rapid communication of inside information as to police policy and movements is a frequent theme. A well-known owner was in conference with his mates on March 21, 1912. "They are all transferred, not one of them is here," he announced in reference to the plain clothes men. It subsequently developed that at the time the statement was made, the men transferred had themselves not yet learned that such a step was contemplated.[8]

On May 2, 1912, a card game and drinking-bout was in progress at a well-known establishment. The following dialogue took place:

"How is business?" asked one of the men, as he was shuffling the cards.

"Well, we run pretty strong," replied the other. "Let us hope that it will keep up. There's a new style nowadays. The 'coppers' don't call us out any more; we deal with an outsider."

"Who is it?" asked the questioner (our agent).

"What do you care?" was the reply. "Do I ask you who you gave-up to, uptown?"

[6] Among them X 598, X 599, X 600, X 601, X 602.
[7] X 603-604.
[8] The persons and places involved are: X 34, X 108, X 608, X 609, X 610, X 611, X 600, X 598, X 613.

Commercialized Prostitution in New York

After the Rosenthal murder, however, the aspect of affairs changed. About six o'clock in the evening of July 18 the "king" was consulted by several anxious associates to ascertain whether he had "seen" anybody. He replied that he had, and that everything was all right, unless something unforeseen should happen, as the "squeal" thus far involved only the gamblers. Suspense was thereby relieved and great was the merriment thereon. "It might be better if we had a grocery store," suggested one of the wits present. A week later, however, the situation was more squally. It had begun to be whispered that "the police would take no protection money on the first of the coming month." It was recalled that on a previous occasion 12 houses in a certain block had each paid $500 on Monday and that on the following Saturday, the houses were smashed up. "The same thing might happen here," remarked an anxious proprietor. On the day that payment was to be made, August 1, to be precise, a well-known owner entered a West 26th Street resort with a big roll of bills, as to the destination of which he was in doubt. One of his pals had left town, the other was in jail. He "did n't know whether the police would take it or not." Suddenly a brilliant idea struck him; he turned to our agent who was supposed to be conducting an uptown flat and to be in position to secure protection, offering him the money. "You take it," he suggested, "see what you can do. Maybe you can connect."

To the same effect is the testimony of a memorandum procured under somewhat dramatic conditions. On May

Prostitution, Police, and Law

3, 1912, a large group of owners [9] were engaged in playing cards at a well-known establishment. Two of the group stopped their game in order to engage in calculations involving the sale of a third-interest in a house in West 25th Street. The memorandum was subsequently obtained by our agent. Six different accounts figured in the calculation of income, expenses, profits, etc. In the matter of expenses, $631 appear as paid out for the following items: "Buttons" (*i. e.*, uniformed police) $166; sergeant, $30; "gang" (perhaps plain clothes men) $104; club (meaning unknown), $200; boss, $25; smaller items absorb the remainder.

Personal conversations between police officers, owners of disorderly places and our investigator, supposed to be one of themselves, pointing to intimate dealings and relations, were likewise frequently reported with additional data identifying those concerned. On March 18th, 1912, it was reported that a uniformed officer [10] called at a well-known disorderly house [11] asking for a notorious owner; [12] he explained his errand in these words, written down from memory shortly afterwards: "I'm broke. He hasn't seen me for a few nights and I would like to have some 'sugar.'" Two days before, two plain clothes men, in passing a well-known hangout, beckoned one of the owners to come outside; shortly after he returned, remarking to his comrades, "The 'dogs' are outside."

About two o'clock one afternoon, three men, two of

[9] Persons and places involved: X 108, X 44, X 502, X 659, X 415, X 416, X 414, X 542, X 11, X 663, X 664, X 407, X 73, X 67.
[10] X 662.   [11] X 108.   [12] X 34.

Commercialized Prostitution in New York

them well-known owners of a place in West 35th Street,[13] were standing in West 30th Street, 100 feet from the station house; when a few moments later the plain clothes men started to go on duty, one [14] of them beckoned to two of the officers [15] and engaged them in prolonged conversation. Its purport was subsequently summarized to his friends: "Don't worry!"

At times a " collector " is said to be the intermediary in transactions similar to those implied in the foregoing incidents. Among the best known of these is a saloon-keeper [16] once enjoying the reputation of protecting the entire Red Light district, at that time situated in Allen Street. His saloon [17] is now a hangout for thieves, gamblers and the like. Two patrolmen and an officer [18] are named as coming to his resort to "fix" pimp cases. The "lookout" [19] for a Sixth Avenue [20] establishment remarked, in describing the financial operations of the place, that he receives 10 percent of the profits monthly, that $200 a month go to inspector and captain, and that the patrolman [21] is paid nightly. An individual who has been publicly accused of being a vice graft collector [22] entered a disorderly flat in West 58th Street [23] on June 15, 1912, for the purpose of perfecting arrangements in regard to protection. The madame [24] expressed herself as satisfied with the way in which she was being treated.[25] She stated, however, that her neighbor down-

[13] X 500.
[14] X 572.
[15] X 665, 666.
[16] X 670.
[17] X 671.
[18] X 672, X 673, X 674.
[19] X 26.
[20] X 9.
[21] X 685.
[22] X 691.
[23] X 116.
[24] X 519.
[25] The commander of the inspection district, X 653.

Prostitution, Police, and Law

stairs "had a scrap with the collector for the police [26] over protection and that he had refused to take her money any more. The result is that every one of the 'underdogs' (*i. e.,* plain clothes men) comes running to her every night with a different complaint and you know what that means. She has 'to see them' every time they come. In the long run, it costs three or four times as much; and she got a 'collar' (*i. e.,* arrest) in the bargain." One of our agents witnessed, on the evening of June 1, 1912, a settlement between a well-known collector for the police in New York City and the owners of 15 different establishments, situated between West 18th Street and West 36th Street. At one o'clock in the morning, they sat around a large table [27] on which four piles of money, the smallest denomination being $5 bills, were heaped up. It had been paid to the police collector, who carried it away in a violin case.

The foregoing incidents explain why a district such as Seventh Avenue is called a "money post." [28]

The employment of pressure, in order to bring about a certain kind of differentiation of neighborhoods, is exemplified in the following instance: A notorious madame informed our agent that she was going to open a house in West 40th Street,[29] but admitted that she would have to be careful, because cheaper resorts would

[26] X 691.
[27] X 108.
[28] Our investigators made frequent reports showing that street walkers and others repeatedly prosecuted their business under the eyes of police officers without interference.
[29] X 109.

not be permitted in that vicinity. Through the good
graces of a high official [30] whom she named, she claimed
that she had succeeded in maintaining and quietly conducting a low grade establishment there.

The peaceful operation of disorderly resorts is disturbed from time to time by raids, as in the instance
above noted, in which one madame "got a collar," while
her competitor on the floor above remained unmolested.
Raids are variously accounted for by those who suffer:
now on the score of punishment or revenge, as in the
case last mentioned; again, for the purpose of "covering
the captain on the blotter," *i. e.*, that he may make a
good showing in his report to the Inspector; sometimes
— so it is alleged — in order to keep the owners and their
madames in line so that they will be sure to pay the protection money. The police know who the owner or
madame is without even entering the house, and warrants
are declared to be sworn out in many instances without
any evidence at all. It is understood between operators
and real estate agents that when a house is opened the
owner must "stand for" an occasional "collar," though
the latter sometimes protests vehemently. For instance,
March 14, 1912, the indignant owner [31] of a place on
Sixth Avenue [32] declared his house had been raided the
night before for no reason. "If they don't stop that,
I'll holler," he added; "they have to discharge that
case or I'll know the reason why." Usually when
houses are raided, the real culprits escape arrest. It
was reported on August 15th that 18 disorderly resorts

[30] X 610.   [31] X 68.   [32] X 9.

Prostitution, Police, and Law

had been entered by the authorities. Only a few housekeepers and colored maid servants were arrested.

Frequent reports deal with the presence of police officers in and about disorderly saloons and hotels. On January 25, an officer was drinking in the rear room of a disorderly saloon on St. Nicholas Avenue.[33] On February 1 two officers were served with beer and cigars in the rear room of a similar resort on Columbus Avenue.[34] On March 9 a man, accompanied by a street walker, entered a hotel in West 35th Street.[35] In the hall, a police officer [36] in full uniform, was standing with a bottle of beer in his hand. His number is in our possession. On March 4, a street walker was arrested in Sixth Avenue in front of a well-known café.[37] Thereupon a lighthouse called the owner of his establishment [38] who induced the plain clothes man [39] to release the woman.

The entire situation as respecting alleged police relations was described by all our investigators as radically altered by the events following the Rosenthal murder. Thirty houses were reported as closed in September. In one case closure was so sudden that the girls were not paid off.[40] They exhibited their punched cards and threatened vengeance unless reimbursed — one to the extent of $5.50, another to the extent of $4. The madame [41] of a house in West 28th Street [42] described herself on September 29 as "down and out." In early October,

[33] X 706.
[34] X 707.
[35] X 230.
[36] X 708.
[37] X 729.
[38] X 556, X 557.
[39] X 626.
[40] X 426.
[41] X 741.
[42] Owner X 34.

the proprietor was himself more optimistic: "It's only a question of two or three days," he declared, "and we've got to expect these things." The owners therefore continued in many instances to pay rent for their now empty houses. Early in October, the impression got abroad that conditions were once more propitious: About 2 P. M., October 4, a group of owners held a meeting on Second Avenue,[43] later adjourning to Sixth Avenue,[44] where they again went into "executive session." Several important persons were present.[45] On the strength of a report that the houses could open slowly it was decided at this meeting that certain houses would commence "business" at 8 o'clock that evening, a few more the next day, and a few the next. Accordingly, at the appointed hour, the owners turned on the lights in eight houses situated in West 24th Street,[46] Sixth Avenue,[47] West 31st Street,[48] and West 28th Street.[49] Things however miscarried and the houses were again closed. The chief owner[50] was indignant: on November 10, 1912, he admitted[51] that it was a "lousy tip" he had got, though it "looked good" at the time. He named the source — a practicing lawyer.[52]

Since the close of this investigation on November 15, 1912, in consequence of the activity of the police grow-

[43] X 311.
[44] X 658.
[45] X 34, 47, 413-a, 44, 705, 418, 387-a and 746.
[46] X 502, X 570, X 459.
[47] X 33, X 11, X 403.
[48] X 16.
[49] X 419.
[50] X 34.
[51] At X 108.
[52] X 587.

Prostitution, Police, and Law

ing out of the Rosenthal murder, and the investigations conducted by the Aldermanic and Legislative Committees, the method of conducting the business of prostitution in houses has changed materially. For instance, in the more expensive houses, the $5 and $10 resorts, madames do not allow actual violations of the law on the premises, but have the women sit in the parlor awaiting calls. One such resort is located in an apartment in West 43rd Street,[53] where twenty women were found sitting in the parlor on March 10, 1913. The madame, who has a large personal acquaintance with patrons of a better class, simply awaits telephone calls requesting a lady companion. Knowing the tastes of her customers, she sends one of the women to an appointed place. Thus there is no violation of the law on the premises, and the police are unable to " cover " the situation. But a number of low-priced houses have opened in the old way on a smaller scale: March 12, 1913, three resorts, one each in Sixth Avenue,[54] West 28th Street [55] and West 40th [56] were operating with two or three inmates each, all wearing street clothes. The third inspection district was at this time declared to be free from police molestation. Current talk in the district explains this immunity on the ground that police and owners were so involved with each other, that effective action on the part of the former was prevented by fear that the latter would turn on the light. " They are all opening up," remarked one owner, while chatting with sympathizers in a cigar store [57] in West 116th Street, as recently as March 15, 1913. One

[53] X 778. [55] X 419. [57] X 781.
[54] X 33.   [56] X 93.

owner [58] then had six houses going. "God pity the police if they interfere!" Of a well-known inspector,[59] it has been said, that "having taken money, he can't well step on anybody's corns." A former wardman,[60] now wearing a uniform in the service of the West 125th Street station house, remarked hardly a fortnight ago to two men, one an owner, the other a former associate: "Sit tight; you're getting a little; you're making expenses; squealing seems to be a fad nowadays." Among places now quietly running under changed ownership may be mentioned one each in West 26th Street, West 28th, West 29th, West 31st, West 34th; two in Sixth Avenue and three in West 40th Street.[61]

Confidence is strong in the underworld that "hard times" will not last; the police who are reputed to have worked in collusion with the exploiters of prostitution share the same view. "It will all blow over"—that is the refrain to every discussion. History is quoted to

[58] X 34.
[59] X 610.
[60] X 598.
[61] These are indexed in our records as follows:
X 791 W. 26th Street, owners X 17 and X 34.
X 78 W. 27th Street, owners X 68 and X 69.
X 419 W. 28th Street, owners X 418, X 509, and X 34.
X 792 W. 29th Street, owners X 15.
X 16 W. 31st Street, owners X 34, and a woman.
X 254 W. 34th Street, owners X 793.
X 33 Sixth Avenue, owners X 34.
X 11 Sixth Avenue, owners X 542, X 705, and X 34's nephew and brother.
X 659 W. 40th Street, owners X 103 and X 44.
X 93 W. 40th Street, owners X 34.
X 582 W. 40th Street, owners X 408.

Prostitution, Police, and Law

support this hopeful interpretation of present conditions. A similar repressive policy was instituted in 1907. Houses were closed; some owners with their madames and girls left the city and others betook themselves to flats and hotels. For three years, the business was timid, quiet, unobtrusive, gradually feeling its way back. By January, 1911, the promoters had all returned, keen to recoup; by the succeeding year, they had restored their former prosperity. Now once more their schemes have been disorganized. The tide is turning against them. But they have seen that happen before and they are confident that, as in the past, the " good old days " will return. A prominent madame [62] was on September 18 still paying rent for two houses, one in West 25th Street,[63] one in West 31st Street.[64] " We outlive all those dogs," declared an old-timer,[65] who had lived through all the spasmodic efforts at suppression undertaken in the last fifteen or twenty years.

Talk in the underworld does not stop with the police department: it involves the judiciary and prosecutors as well. There is no misunderstanding the prevalent feeling: these men and women are hurt,— wounded to the quick — because, as they constantly assert, having kept their part of the bargain by paying for protection, the officials do not so regularly " deliver the goods." Our investigators report many interviews to this effect. The owner of a house in West 35th Street has been keenly worried by a three-months' sentence meted out to his madame.[66] " He had understood that judges were not

[62] X 17.
[63] X 59.
[64] X 16.
[65] X 415-a.
[66] X 804.

giving 'prison,' as several such cases had been lately discharged." He instanced one from West 28th Street,[67] another from West 25th Street.[68] "You know what it costs to discharge a case," he added feelingly. On August 30, 1912, three men met at Eighth Avenue and 28th Street; one of them bitterly reviled an official in the criminal court building. "He has no right to do this. Why, did n't we once pay him $4,000,— $150 for each house, to keep out of the district? There were no more raids then,— but now!"[69] On the 17th of October, 1912, several disorderly house cases from the Tenderloin were tried in special sessions: the places were notorious,— involving among others the madames of houses in West 31st and West 36th Streets. The disposition made of them represents the characteristic uncertainty of the action of the court of special sessions. Two of the defendants were acquitted, two were convicted, but received suspended sentences, two were fined fifty dollars apiece, and one pleaded guilty, receiving a penalty of imprisonment for thirty days.

There are a number of lawyers in New York City who are being constantly employed by the owners of disorderly houses to defend their cases in the courts. Their fees vary according to their standing. A former magistrate, who has an office on Broadway, charges $100 for appearing in Special Sessions. He has latterly succeeded in securing the acquittal of the madame of a West 28th Street[70] house. Another lawyer[71] with an office on

---

[67] X 12.   [68] X 67.
[69] X 415-a, X 34, X 633 were concerned in this alleged deal.
[70] X 608.   [71] X 587.

Prostitution, Police, and Law

Park Row, charges from $15 to $25 for his appearance in the police court, and $50 altogether if he has to appear in a higher court.

A few weeks ago one of the madames was sentenced to the penitentiary for three months. During the evening of the day on which she was sentenced, the lawyer who had appeared for her came to a resort [72] where a number of owners had gathered. They upbraided him for pleading " Guilty, your Honors."

" Why did n't you show fight? " demanded one.

" Well," he replied, " there was a time when I used to walk into the court room and make a bargain with the judges when there were three or four charges pending against one woman. I used to say, ' Your Honors, we will make this bargain day. There are four charges against this woman. What will you do? Unless you are lenient, I will fight you and take up your time.' The fine as a rule was no more than $100 for three or four charges. At that time, the coppers used to break in a house and raid it just to get the money for the fine. But times have changed."

As some street walkers are picked up by the plain clothes men and brought into court, they hire by preference a lawyer [73] who lives on West 10th Street.[74] This man agrees to procure their discharge for $50, distributed as follows :

$10 for the bondsman to bail her out, if necessary;
$15 for his, the lawyer's services, and
$25 to go to the arresting officer for his testimony.

It is alleged that the lawyer in question has agents

[72] X 108.   [73] X 832.   [74] X 833.

Commercialized Prostitution in New York

on Sixth Avenue keeping tab on the street walkers. When the girl is "picked up," these agents are on the ground and see that he gets the case; he guarantees to turn her out for $50 or more, whatever he can get, but under no conditions accepts less than $35. If the girl has no ready money and has jewelry, that is taken as security. The first thing he does is to have the case adjourned for two days, which means no less than $15 for bail. During the two-days' adjournment, the lawyer "feels out" the plain clothes man who "picked up" the girl. If the detective falls, he usually gets $15 from the lawyer's fee. If the detective insists on prosecuting, the lawyer has a man ready to swear that it was he who was in conversation with the woman at the time she was arrested, though this is not usually necessary. If the plain clothes man has made an affidavit prior to the granting of the adjournment and is ready to "fall," he will permit the lawyer to entangle him in his cross-examination and to bring it out that he, the plain clothes man, approached the girl, and, in other ways, will contradict himself "safely." This is resorted to when the affidavit is unfavorable to the girl.

Despite the enormous volume of prostitution in Manhattan, the actual number of convictions is small, and the main culprits go scot-free.

During a period of nine months, ending September 30, 1912, 143 disorderly house cases were tried in Special Sessions. Twenty-five pleas of guilty were entered, 82 were convicted, 32 acquitted, and other disposition was made of 4.

The total number of disorderly house cases received in

Prostitution, Police, and Law

this court from January 1, 1912, to October 1, 1912, was 180, and on September 30, 1912, there were 62 actions still pending.

Of the 107 cases in which the defendants were found guilty or pleaded guilty, the following dispositions were made:

Jail sentences	80	
Average term being		3 months and 27 days
Fines	18	
The total amount being		$2,325.00
or an average fine of		129.00
Suspended sentences	9	

In general, the convictions secured were those of employees, the prevailing rules of evidence making it almost impossible to reach the principals.

In the matter of saloons, for the year ending September 30, 1912, the Excise Commission in New York County brought revocation proceedings which resulted in the denial of the privilege of traffic in liquor for one year in only 6 cases. During the same period, the Commissioner brought 143 actions to recover the penalty under bond, of which 18 were cash bond places. These cases, we understand, refer particularly to disorderly hotels.[75]

From October, 1911, to September, 1912, 159 arrests were made for prostitution in tenement houses under Section 150 of the Tenement House Law. Of these, 36 were discharged and 123 convicted. Eighty-four of those convicted were sent to the workhouse for six months, 27 were put on probation, and other dispositions were made of 12.

---

[75] The above data are derived from the report made by the Committee of Fourteen for 1912.

Commercialized Prostitution in New York

Between January 1, 1912, and December 31, 1912, or approximately during the period of this investigation, the Tenement House Department recorded 247 prostitution complaints at 211 separate addresses in Manhattan. The time which elapsed between the receipt of the complaint and the report of the inspector was: returned the same day, 5 cases; from 1 to 5 days, 55 cases; 6 days to 2 weeks, 139 cases; 15 days to 1 month, 38 cases; and over 1 month, 9 cases and one unknown. The average number of days which elapsed between the receipt of the complaint and the final report of the Tenement House Inspector is 10.75, which represents prompter action than was previously obtained. In the period from August 1, 1902, to October, 1908, the average length of time which elapsed between the receipt of a prostitution complaint and the final report of the inspector was 11.28 days.

In conclusion, it is proper to state that the purpose of the foregoing chapter is to picture a situation and not by implication to indicate the responsibility for it. Whether the discrepancies between our reports and official records are due to bad laws impossible of enforcement, to the instructions emanating from superior officials, to inefficiency, to corruption, to the existence of evils with which no official machinery can cope, or finally to all these causes operating together, we do not undertake to say or to imply. The facts are as stated above; the situation portrayed by them actually exists. It is for the community to consider their significance, and to devise such measures as careful reflection may approve.

CHAPTER VIII

A COMPARISON OF CONDITIONS IN 1912 WITH CONDITIONS IN 1915 AND 1916

(1) PARLOR HOUSES

Conditions in 1912: — In 1912, 142 parlor houses were in operation in Manhattan, with 1686 inmates. The majority of these inmates lived in the houses and were under the direct control of the men owners and madams. Some lived with their pimps and came to the houses at regular hours, remaining until closing time.

Conditions November 1, 1915: — On November 1, 1915, only 23 houses were in active operation. In ten of these resorts, 21 regular inmates were counted. In five of the houses, 36 women were "on call." In six houses, no inmates were seen, but it was estimated that they contained 16 women. That is, with the term "parlor house" construed even more broadly than was the case during the previous investigation, the number was cut down from 142 to 23; the inmates, from 1686 to hardly more than 50.

Conditions November 1, 1916: — Not one of the 23 houses reported in 1915 was running. Police activity had suppressed them all, together with 56 others which in the course of the year led a brief, furtive existence. We were able to locate 22 houses in operation as of November 1, 1916, although it is probable that by the time the report reached the public, some of them, at least, had been closed. Eight of these 22 houses were "call houses." Twelve of the houses had an average of from one to two inmates, and in the remaining two nothing was learned as to the number of inmates.

The change in the method of operating these houses was equally significant. In the majority of them, the inmates remained in their rooms, dressed in respectable attire, pretending to be legitimate boarders. In fact, these resorts were to all appearances furnished-room houses.

The contrast between the volume of business transacted by these resorts in 1912 and in 1916 was very striking. In 1912, the houses were in active operation, with a full quota of inmates. In 1916 the few houses with one or two inmates each, were, according to their own testimony, hardly making expenses. They were merely "holding on," speculating as to how long the condition would continue, and eagerly watching for a termination of police activity. "We have weathered all reforms," they said, "from the Lexow Investigation and the Low administration down to the one now in power, and the reformers always got tired and quit. But this one still keeps up after three years. We can't understand it."

(2) TENEMENT HOUSES

Conditions in 1912: — In 1912, 1172 vice resorts were reported in 575 different tenement houses in Manhattan.

A Comparison of Conditions

The number of inmates counted in these resorts was 2294.

Conditions November 1, 1915: — In the course of this investigation, 484 vice resorts in tenements were located, with 771 inmates. It was claimed by the madams that 140 women were "on call." A very great reduction in number had, therefore, been effected. But the actual reduction was greater, for the volume of business was more than correspondingly reduced.

Conditions November 1, 1916: — As of November 1, 1916, 238 vice resorts in tenements were found in operation. On hundred and fifty-eight others, to our personal knowledge, were suppressed by the police during the year. The most significant change in the operation of these flats over previous years was that a large number, in comparison, had become "call" places. Certain madams did not dare to have inmates on the premises, and those who kept inmates had reduced the number, as shown above, to two or three.

It was practically impossible in 1916 for men to enter these resorts without a personal introduction to the madam from some one actually known to her. Even after the admission was gained, the prospective customer was often called on to prove his identity by displaying a personal letter or a business card; or he had to submit to an examination of his hat and clothes to show whether he had purchased these articles in New York or elsewhere.

Because of the small number of inmates and the difficulty of gaining entrance, it was evident that the volume of business in vice resorts of this type had been reduced to a minimum.

Commercialized Prostitution in New York

(3) ASSIGNATION AND DISORDERLY HOTELS

Conditions in 1912: — During 1912, 103 hotels were discovered in Manhattan which were classified as being disorderly or suspicious. The number classified as disorderly was 90.

Conditions November 1, 1915: — In the course of this investigation, 56 such hotels were reported in Manhattan. Investigators one or more times were actually solicited by prostitutes on the streets and in rear rooms of saloons to enter 51 of these resorts.

Conditions November 1, 1916: — There was a decided gain over the previous year in respect to disorderly hotels. A considerable number had been suppressed by the police, and the business in others had been greatly reduced by means of constant raids and arrests. In some cases officers had been stationed, with fairly satisfactory results, in front of persistently vicious hotels. This method had led to some petty grafting, which had been minimized, however, by frequent transfers of the men on post.

During the investigation in 1916, 41 hotels were discovered to be disorderly or suspicious; 1347 men were seen to enter these establishments with known prostitutes. Investigators were solicited to go to 27 of these resorts for immoral purposes.

A marked change took place in the operation of disorderly hotels. Except in the one precinct where conditions were far from satisfactory, the proprietors of most of these 41 resorts would not allow a prostitute to enter with a customer more than once in twenty-four hours.

A Comparison of Conditions

(4) FURNISHED ROOM HOUSES

Conditions in 1912: — In 1912, 112 disorderly furnished-room houses were found in Manhattan.

Conditions November 1, 1915: — During this study no exhaustive effort was made to ascertain the number of disorderly furnished-room houses. They were reported whenever a prostitute soliciting on the street, or in the rear rooms of saloons, invited the investigator to accompany her to such a place. Seventy-eight disorderly resorts of this character were located in this manner. Much the same conditions as those which obtained in 1912 prevailed in 1915 in connection with these resorts, and the situation needed the continued attention of the police.

Conditions November 1, 1916: — The results of the study in 1916 showed that the situation needed the continued attention of the police. When vice is suppressed to any extent in houses, flats, and hotels, it is inevitable that it will at first betake itself to furnished-room houses. This had happened in New York City, and in 1916 it was the most serious problem confronting the police.

During the investigation, 142 furnished-room houses were found. The investigators were actually solicited to go to 60 of these resorts for immoral purposes. They counted 389 prostitutes connected with the houses, and estimated 58 more. To our knowledge 16 houses of this type had been suppressed by the police during the year.

It should be remembered that not all of the 142 furnished-room houses reported were given over entirely to this business. Many of them had respectable roomers also. The landladies were, however, not averse to taking in prostitutes, because roomers of this type are eager and willing to pay a larger rental for "privileges."

(5) MASSAGE PARLORS

Conditions in 1912: — It was estimated that there were 300 illegitimate massage parlors in Manhattan; 75 were actually reported.

Conditions November 1, 1915: — No estimate of the number of these illegal places was attempted during this investigation, but 90 disorderly resorts masquerading as "massage" parlors were reported. Undoubtedly, conditions in respect to these places were better than they were in 1912. The resorts were run far less openly. Indeed, they were so cautiously conducted that evidence to sustain a prosecution could not easily be obtained.

Conditions November 1, 1916: — During the year the police were especially active against "massage parlors." A systematic and persistent effort was directed against all such resorts of an illegal character, particularly where signs were ostentatiously displayed.

An investigation was made of the 90 disorderly resorts where massage signs were displayed at the time of our investigation in 1915. In 41 such places, legitimate businesses of entirely different character are now being conducted. At 31 other places no signs were shown, nor did any of the names of former operators appear in letter boxes or under the vestibule bells. At 9 former disorderly addresses the premises were vacant. The remaining 9 places displayed signs, such as "Massage," "Masseuse." Presumably these resorts were still disorderly.

From 1908 to 1915 a weekly paper, which carried from

A Comparison of Conditions

one to two, and sometimes three, pages of massage parlor advertisements, was sold on the news stands. In the majority of instances these related to disorderly resorts. During the latter part of 1916 these advertisements gradually decreased, until one issue contained only four such notices. Soon afterward this paper disappeared from the news stands.

(6) DISORDERLY SALOONS

Conditions in 1912: — In 1912, 765 saloons were investigated. Unescorted women believed to be prostitutes were seen in 308 of these. The investigators were openly solicited for immoral purposes in 107 of the 308 resorts.

Conditions November 1, 1915: — While this investigation of disorderly saloons was less exhaustive than the preceding one, it was sufficiently extensive to indicate distinct improvement. Out of the 346 saloons investigated, only 84 could be classified as being disorderly, on the ground that prostitutes habitually frequented them for the purpose of soliciting customers.

Conditions November 1, 1916: — Probably at no time in the history of New York City had the conditions in saloons shown such improvement as in 1916. In former years, and especially in 1912, a large number of saloons served as hangouts and soliciting places for prostitutes, but in 1916 this condition had largely been done away with.

During the investigation conditions were observed in 492 saloons. In 34 of these resorts, 109 prostitutes solicited investigators for immoral purposes; but their advances were made with the utmost secrecy, in direct con-

Commercialized Prostitution in New York

trast with the open and flagrant practice in similar resorts in 1912.

(7) THE STREETS

Conditions in 1912: — Street walking was conspicuous on Broadway from Twenty-seventh to Sixty-eighth Street, Sixth Avenue, etc.

Conditions November 1, 1915: — Street walkers were found in reduced numbers on prominent thoroughfares; but their tactics had altogether changed. Open solicitation had been almost entirely stopped. Women conducted themselves inoffensively, leaving the initiative to the customer. In consequence, the traffic was less voluminous, less profitable, and therefore less attractive than formerly. On the other hand, any relaxation on the part of the police was quickly followed by a recrudescence. There was also somewhat more active solicitation in out of the way places where the police were less numerous. On the whole, a very great improvement was reported.

Conditions November 1, 1916: — The improvement in respect to street walking in 1915 was maintained, and further progress was made. Old-time street prostitutes declared that they had never made so little money. They were satisfied to earn a bare existence; whereas, in previous years, notably in 1912, receipts from street soliciting were large.

The police were so aggressive against all types of vice resorts and soliciting on the streets that, as has been stated above, madams and prostitutes demanded introductions and marks of identification before they would recognize a customer. Cabmen and chauffeurs, who formerly

A Comparison of Conditions

had lists of houses and flats to which they conducted customers, declared that they knew of very few resorts. The evidence collected abounded in references to the fear of the police and to the reducetion of the business during the past two years.

Broadway and Sixth Avenue had always been the chief districts for street walkers, but this condition had been changed. Prostitutes could still be found in these sections, but men were seldom solicited unless they made the first advance. The most flagrant street solicitations were made in the 21st police precinct.

(8) THE EXPLOITERS

Conditions in 1912: — The investigation during 1912 established the fact that the business of prostitution in New York City was exploited and, for the most part, controlled by men, though women were involved. Personal descriptions and histories of over 600 men exploiters, including owners, procurers, and pimps, were obtained.

Conditions November 1, 1915: — The vice ring was completely disorganized. After the exposure of their activities in 1912, the owners of vice resorts went into hiding or left the city. Indictments were secured against several, who forfeited their bonds and disappeared.

Notable among those who fled was the man who was designated as " The King of the Vice Trust." He first went to a city in a near-by state, but afterwards sailed for South America. During December, 1914, he returned to New York City, only to find the business of prostitution in a demoralized condition, with practically all the former resorts closed, and those that were open making very little money. When the police department learned of his return, the indictment on the charge of maintaining houses of prostitution, previously found against him, was taken out of the pigeonhole and he was rearrested. Another indictment, this time on a white slave charge, was returned by the Grand Jury. He was released on $2500 bond. Forfeiting this bond, he again fled from the city.

Conditions November 1, 1916: — The vice ring in the old sense of the word no longer existed in this city. In fact, former promoters of commercialized prostitution in this city seemed to have come to the conclusion that " the banner years of prosperity " would never return. It was a known fact that more than 75 former men owners and their agents, such as procurers and pimps, had left the city with their women for more open markets. Twenty of these men moved to a near-by city, where they became the head and front of a string of houses which opened after a recent municipal election. The so-called " King of the Vice Trust," with others indicted with him in 1912, was still a fugitive from justice. During the year 1916 the district attorney's office successfully prosecuted five notorious procurers, most of whom were in active business in New York in 1912. The five men received prison sentences ranging from five and a half years to nineteen years, eleven months, and fines ranging from $1000 to $5000. While some degree of exploitation undoubtedly existed in 1916, it was greatly below the level of the 1912 figures.

CHAPTER IX

A STUDY OF PROSTITUTES COMMITTED FROM NEW YORK CITY TO THE STATE REFORMATORY FOR WOMEN AT BEDFORD HILLS

By Katharine Bement Davis, Superintendent.

Sources: — The materials for this study are found in the records of 647 prostitutes committed from New York City to the State Reformatory for Women at Bedford Hills.[1] Of these, 279 were in the institution at the time the study was made. The remainder were either on parole or had been discharged on completion of sentence. The data are gathered from the girls' own stories supplemented by information from their families, from correspondence with previous employers, interviews with officials of other institutions, letters received and sent by the women themselves; from the officers who chaperone all visits to the girls while in the institution and from personal acquaintance extending in every case from three months to several years. The difficulties inherent in the compilation of such statistics are obvious. Certain data, such as birthplace, age, size of family, education, religion and previous occupation, are probably very nearly accurate. When we leave the domain of facts easily verifiable and come to the question of causes of prostitution, earnings of prostitution, reasons for coming to New York

[1] For purposes of comparison studies were also made of 610 girls in 7 other New York city and state institutions and of 1106 street walkers. See pp. 207 etc.

Commercialized Prostitution in New York

City, past institution records, conjugal condition, there is always a possibility of error. But we believe the study is, on the whole, a fair picture of the New York City prostitute who is convicted in the New York City courts. It may be said that the women convicted in the courts are not a fair sample of New York prostitutes as a class, for the reason that the more prosperous ones are so protected as not to suffer molestation from the police. A comparison, however, of the tables of the institution cases with the cases of women on the streets which include all grades from those who frequent the more expensive hotels down, will not show wide variations.

Birthplace and Parentage: — New York's population is composed of as heterogeneous elements as any city on the continent. It is the meeting place of the nations. What effect has this on the composition of a body of New York prostitutes? Does the native-born American who has enjoyed the economic and social advantages of this country contribute a greater or less percentage than the various groups of foreign-born? Interesting from the point of view of our immigration problem is the proportionate number contributed by each of the chief races in New York City.

An analysis of the 647 Bedford cases shows that American-born whites contribute 62.75 percent of the entire number; American-born colored women furnish 13.14 percent while the foreign-born women are 24.11 percent of the total. (See Table 1.) A preliminary bulletin issued by the United States Census Bureau for the Census of 1910, places the native white population of New York City at 57.3 percent, while the foreign population is

A Study of Prostitutes at Bedford

estimated at 40.4 percent of the entire population. According to this, the American-born contribute more and the foreign-born less than their proportion to the Bedford prostitutes. But 647 cases are a very small number on which to base any judgment. We have at hand, however, some other statistics. The histories of 610 prostitutes in other institutions have been analyzed.[1a] Of these, 168 or 27.2 percent were white foreign-born and 68.5 percent were white American-born. In the study of 1,106 street cases, all white women, made in connection with this report, we find 31 percent foreign-born and 68.9 percent American-born.[2] The percentage of foreign-born is here somewhat higher than in the institution cases because practically no colored women were included among the street cases and few in the institutions other than Bedford. Combining the three sets of records, or 2,363 cases, we have 67 percent American-born white as against 28 percent foreign-born; a poor showing for the American-born. (See page 250, Table XLIX, columns III and IV.)

Taking up a comparison of the different nationalities, we find that in the Bedford cases the countries in the order of their numerical contributions stood as follows: Russia, Austria-Hungary, Germany, Ireland, England-Scotland, France, and Italy. (See Table XLIX, column II.) Ranking the contributions to the 610 cases in the other institutions in the same way, the first five places on the list were identical. Canada comes sixth and France is relegated to eighth place. (Table, column III.) Examining the street cases in the same way, Russia comes first, Germany and Austria-Hungary exchange places as do

[1a] See Page 229.   [2] See Page No. 243.

Commercialized Prostitution in New York

Ireland and England-Scotland, France and Italy occupying sixth and seventh places. (Table, column IV.) Combining all records, the order is the same as for the street cases with the exception that Ireland and England-Scotland are reversed. (Table, column V.) Ranking the foreign-born population of New York City in point of numbers, we have Russia, Germany, Ireland, Austria-Hungary, England-Scotland, and France. (Table, column IV.) Dropping out Italy, the order remains as in column V.

Table L shows numbers and percentages. From this, it would seem that, with the exception of Italy, the various foreign groups contribute prostitutes in numbers proportioned to their numerical rank but not in proportion to their percentage of the total population; thus, Russia forming a trifle over 10 percent of the population contributes only about 8.3 percent of prostitutes; Germany and Austria-Hungary come very near to contributing their full quota; Ireland only about half, while England-Scotland send us a very few more and France a good many more than their proper proportion. It is a well-known fact that Italy sends to the United States every year, many hundred unmarried men or men without their families. This probably accounts for the small proportion of Italy's contribution. It may be argued that this is not a fair rating as we have no complete census of New York prostitutes, but owing to the methods employed in securing our material both in and out of institutions, we probably have here as representative a group of prostitutes as can be found, and a fair cross section of the entire number. It might be a more

A Study of Prostitutes at Bedford

just comparison if we had the figures for the female population of the various national groups within the age limits of the women studied, but that is not attainable. With the exception of the Italian and possibly some of the component parts of the Russian and Hungarian groups, the figures used here are believed to be fairly comparable.

Unfortunately, we have not the data for the parentage of any group except that of the Bedford cases. Table II shows the nationality of parents in detail with the greatest possible attainable accuracy. Table III gives the summary. The graph accompanying Table II represents the same thing to the eye.

We find that the native-born of foreign parentage is about 51 percent. The native-born of American parentage is 18.5 percent. Mixed parentage means one native-born and one foreign-born parent.

Table IV compares these percentages with the parentage of the native population of New York City. The Tribune Almanac for 1912 gives the native white of native parents as 19.3 percent of the total population while the native white of foreign parents is 38.2 percent. Comparing, we see that the native parents contribute about their proportionate quota; the foreign-born of foreign parents contribute less than their quota, while the group that contributes out of proportion to its percentage in the population, is that of the native-born of foreign parents. This is not surprising when we remember that here we have a group in which the fathers and mothers belong to a civilization with speech, tradition and habits different from those of the country in which they are living. The children, native-born Americans with American companions and American schooling, adopt American ideals often not of the highest and are very apt, even when quite young, to feel that they know more than their parents. Lacking in any feeling of reverence, they early refuse to listen to the counsels of their parents. On the other hand, the parents often stand in awe of the superior cleverness, usually superficial, of their American-born children. An observation extending over twelve years of the relations between foreign-born fathers and mothers and their American-born daughters, leads me to feel that right here lies one of the important points of attack in preventive work.

Status of Family: — Occupation of father. Before we are in a position to deal fairly with any problem, we must know all the elements which enter into it. The most important factor in the study of any individual is the kind of family from which he comes. The occupation of a man has very little to do with his moral worth or his good citizenship; but it enables us in a general way, to place him as to his position in society. By his earning capacity we can judge something of the kind of home he can make and the opportunities he can give his children. We have, accordingly, included in our Bedford study, the occupation of the girls' fathers. It will be observed from Table V that the largest single group is that of unskilled labor which forms 21.3 percent of the whole. Men engaged in the mechanical trades form the next largest group, or 18.6 percent; the professions stretched to their limit furnish only 15 individuals or 2.4 percent.

A Study of Prostitutes at Bedford

Size of Family:—It has sometimes been claimed that the number of children in a family has a direct bearing on prostitution. One theory suggested is that prostitutes are apt to be members of a large family where economic pressure is great, where a girl is either driven out by want or has failed to receive proper education and training as a result of insufficient means. In individual cases, undoubtedly, this is true. We have a young woman of German parentage, nineteen years of age, at Bedford at the present time, who was the eldest of ten children. She has never been to school a day in her life, nor to church or Sunday School. She is as much of a heathen as if she had been born in Central Africa. As a child, she had to stay at home to "mind the baby" and there was always one. As she grew older, she became tired of the over-crowded home, had never received any training which would fit her for any occupation, fell an easy prey to a young man who took her fancy; and it was but another step into prostitution as a means of livelihood. We could tell a number of such stories where we feel confident that a very large family on very small means is largely to blame for the downfall of the older daughters.

On the other hand, it is held by some that only daughters are more apt to go wrong than those who have brothers and sisters to hold them up to family standards. It is claimed that an only daughter is apt to be pampered and spoiled, never learns obedience and is often discouraged from earning her own livelihood by her parents with the idea that her social position is thus bettered and she will be more likely to make a good marriage. One very marked case of this kind we have at this present moment at Bedford. The girl's father and mother are small shopkeepers, perfectly respectable but very injudicious people. The girl was allowed to believe all through her girlhood that she could have anything she wanted; and when her wants exceeded the possibility of gratification by her parents, she gratified them in any way she could.

Table VI, which gives the size of the families from which our 647 cases come, shows that in the largest number of cases our girls were one of three brothers and sisters. The next largest group is that of four in the family, two and five brothers and sisters having the same number of representatives. The average number of children is 3.99, not greatly above the average number of children per family in the general community which is given in the census of 1910 as 2.7 percent for New York City. Our figures, therefore, so far as they go, would seem to prove nothing special except that girls go wrong in families of all sizes.

Occupation of Mother: — Probably of more importance than the size of the family is the economic position of the mother, particularly during the years of the daughter's adolescence. It is a vital loss if a girl's mother is away from home all day, leaving her after school hours to associates of whom the mother knows nothing and who may be most questionable in their influence on her developing character. In 145 instances, or in 22.4 percent of the total number of cases studied, the mother worked outside the home. Table VII gives a list of the occupations of working mothers, with the

A Study of Prostitutes at Bedford

number in each group. It will be seen that the women who went out for day's work are much the largest group. They went out to wash, to clean, to scrub offices and for other unskilled labor. The laundresses were employed partly in steam laundries and partly in private families and came home at night. Of the 145 mothers who worked, there were 94 who were widows; one mother was divorced; the husband and father in one case was an inmate of a sanitarium for tuberculosis; in one case the father was in an insane asylum; in 8 cases the father had deserted his family; in 40 cases the husband and father was alive and working. The necessity for earning a livelihood explains simply the leaving of children alone in the group of widows. In the 40 cases where the husband was working, no special necessity for the mother's occupation is shown by our data. The 40 husbands and fathers whose wives went out to work, were engaged in thirty-one different occupations, no one group numbering more than four men. These were the day laborers. Three were colored cooks; three were teamsters; two were carpenters; others include a stationary engineer, a walking delegate, an insurance agent, a market man, an elevator man, etc.

Neither did the size of the family afford a special excuse, as in these forty families there was an average of four children. One family contained ten children; two families each had seven and eight respectively, while the greatest number in any one group was ten families with three children each. It may be that the father was inefficient or irregular in his occupation or the family standards of living were higher. It would be necessary to know all of these details in each family to offer any opinion as to reasons and we have not these data.

But the 94 cases of working widows do not cover all the cases where the father was dead. Of these there were 170. Thirty of the mothers had remarried; two received pensions; in three cases the mothers' whereabouts were unknown and in 41 cases she was supported by her older children or by relatives. Of the total group of fatherless girls there were 154 who had lost their fathers before they had reached an age where they could receive their working papers; 73 were over fourteen; 36 did not know the date of their fathers' death. Among these were some of the orphans and probably some girls who were not willing to tell all they knew. Of the 94 girls whose widowed mothers were employed, 61, or 64 percent lost their fathers before they had reached a working age. One hundred and two girls whose fathers were living had lost their mothers previous to their admission to Bedford. In 42 instances the father had remarried and in 20 instances the fathers' whereabouts were unknown, but they were believed to be living. One hundred and fifteen out of 195 girls in the motherless group had lost their mothers when under fourteen years of age. Of the 93 orphans, 43 had been brought up by relatives, 10 by strangers and 20 in orphan asylums; twenty were old enough to earn their living at the time of their father's death. To summarize, only 282, or 43.5 percent of the women studied, had both parents living.

Until very recently, the Reformatory has had no

A Study of Prostitutes at Bedford

field worker. Our knowledge of the families of our girls has been obtained as stated in the first section. Accordingly, much that would have a bearing on the conditions which have made our girls what they are, is unknown to us. But we do know that out of the 647 cases studied, in 130 different families there were known degenerate strains. This is shown in the following table:

HEREDITY; KNOWN DEGENERATE STRAINS

		Total	Percent
1. Alcoholism in family	35		
2. Criminality in family	5		
3. Epilepsy in family	7		
4. Feeble-minded (very marked) parents	2		
5. General ill health of parents	9		
6. Insanity	16		
7. Parents sex offenders	21		
8. Syphilitic parents	10		
9. Tubercular	25	130	20.09

It is probable on the face of it that syphilis, tuberculosis and alcoholism are likely to be much more generally present than is shown by our figures.

Before we are prepared to say just how many of these factors affecting home life are directly responsible for a girl's entering a life of prostitution, we should be able to say that these factors were or were not present to the same extent in affecting the lives of a group of girls of about the same age, education, industrial efficiency and social status who have not " gone wrong." Would there be as many orphans, as many motherless girls, as many or more working mothers in any such group taken at random? Until we can make such a study, it is not fair to consider the facts given in these sections on the family as anything more than

Commercialized Prostitution in New York

a picture of the conditions from which our girls come.

Education and Occupation: — A girl's education and occupation are very closely connected. We have data with reference to education so far as the Bedford cases go, based on the actual examination of the girls. Table VIII has something to say for compulsory education in New York City, especially when taken in connection with the data from other institutions and from the street cases. The table shows that 50 individuals, or 7.72 percent cannot read or write any language. Of these, 15 are American-born. Thirty-two can read and write a foreign language; 45.3 percent have never finished the primary grades, while an additional 39.72 percent never finished the grammar grades. Of the whole number, only 7.24 percent finished the grammar grades. Thirteen individuals had entered but not finished high school; only four individuals had graduated from high school; three had had one year at a normal school and one out of 647 cases had entered college. The institution cases other than Bedford make a slightly better showing, but here, in a large percentage of cases, we have nothing to go on but the girl's own statement. According to this, only 12 percent finished grammar grades and, according to their own admission, 11.4 percent of the street prostitutes cannot read or write in any language and only 4 percent had finished the grammar grades. (See Tables.)

So far as the Bedford cases go, the industrial efficiency of the women is about on a par with their education. Table X shows the occupation of these girls before entering a life of prostitution. It will be noted that 243

A Study of Prostitutes at Bedford

or the largest group are general houseworkers, forming 37.5 percent of the total number.

Almost all the studies of prostitution heretofore made have noted the high percentage of women who were engaged in domestic service previous to entering the life. So far as my observation goes, I do not believe that this indicates any greater danger from domestic service itself as an occupation than from any other in which unskilled girls engage. Domestic service for women under existing economic conditions corresponds to casual labor for men. It is the job where training and experience are unnecessary in order to find work. Such services would not be desired by families where efficiency is demanded and paid for. A very large proportion of our girls were not competent workers but were girls employed in the lowest stratum of families that employ domestic help at all and where standards of service do not exist. This group includes almost all the colored girls and a considerable number of the foreign-born white girls. The factory operatives form the next largest group; clerks in department stores come third. Ninety-two individuals, or 14 percent, had never engaged in any occupation previous to having entered a life of prostitution. These were either girls whose parents were fairly comfortably off and who preferred to have their daughters at home pending matrimony, or girls who married almost immediately upon leaving school and kept house until matrimony became too much for them. A large proportion of all our young women were not fit to fill any more responsible positions than those they held.

Commercialized Prostitution in New York

Comparing the occupations of the institution cases other than Bedford with those shown in the Bedford table, we find that the factory operatives form the largest group or 32.46 percent, domestic service and department stores coming second and third. (See Table XXX.) The table of occupations of street cases makes quite a different showing, which may or may not be due to the desire of the girls to put the best foot foremost in giving their histories to the investigator. Here the department store clerks form the largest group. Nearly half of the histories, however, say that the girls have never had any occupation previous to entering the life and in 101 cases, no statistics were given. (See Table XLVI). So far as education goes, however, this group is no better equipped for filling more remunerative positions than are the girls in the institutions. Their racial distribution is about the same. There is not much reason to believe that they were greatly different from the institution cases in industrial efficiency.

For comparison with the occupational groups of women wage earners in New York City in the population at large, the latest statistics available are those of the United States Census of 1900. This gives the total number of wage-earning women as 329,489. The groups which run into five figures are as follows:

1. Servants and waitresses ...... 94,789 or 28.7%
2. Factory operatives .... 36,458 " 11.06%
3. Dressmakers .... 34,306 " 10.04%
4. Saleswomen .... 20,578 " 6.2%
5. Seamstresses .... 15,845 " 4.8%
6. Laundresses .... 15,085 " 4.5%

It will be noted that the third group, which is a skilled

A Study of Prostitutes at Bedford

trade, has very few representatives among the prostitutes.

Earnings:—Until recently in our Bedford records, we have not systematically recorded wages earned before entering prostitution. With the beginning of this study, we endeavored to obtain the data from the prostitutes now in the institution. We find, however, that the girls are very hazy as to the exact amounts earned. They "don't remember" because "they always gave all their earnings to their mother" is a frequent statement. In 162 cases, however, they appeared to be sufficiently accurate as to the maxima and minima of earnings to furnish reasonable proof of the truth of their statements; particularly when taken in connection with our knowledge of the girls' ability. The average minimum is $4 and the average maximum is $8. It will be noted that even the average maximum is below $9, an amount generally conceded to be the minimum on which a girl can live decently in New York City. See Table IX. By far, the largest number earned less than this, the average being pulled up by the few girls who were more competent. In this connection we made an inquiry of 194 young women who were at Bedford at the time the study was made, as to whether they were living at home and as to the disposition of their earnings at the time they entered prostitution as a business. Out of 194, one hundred and twenty-two claim to have been living at home. Of these, 32 were supported by their parents or husbands and did not work outside of their home; 53 were working and giving all they made to their mothers; 39 were giving part of what they earned;

24 were living with relatives and of these, 15 gave all they earned to their relatives, while 9 gave a part as board; 20 young women were working and boarding with strangers. They claim they paid board ranging from $1.50 a week in one case to one case which claims to have been paying $13.50. The greatest number paid $4.00 per week. Twenty-six of the girls were domestics living where they worked. See Table XI.

It is interesting to compare the statements in regard to wages made by the girls in Bedford with the statements of those in other institutions and especially with the statements made by the street cases. Table LI presents this comparison. It will be noted that of the 420 cases considered, the average maxima and minima varied between $9 and $13, a much higher point than is reached by girls in the institutions. The total shows data for 238 girls who were domestic servants and 907 engaged in other occupations. In the cases of institution girls, the knowledge that the statement which they give can be checked up and verified by the institution officials, will, in most instances, deter them from going wide of the mark. As this was impossible in the majority of cases interviewed on the street, I feel that not as much reliance can be placed on data as to salary. Granted, however, that the data are reliable, there would seem to be no indication of real economic pressure as a reason for entering an immoral life.

Social Relations: — Statistics with regard to social relations must be taken with several grains of salt. A girl confined in an institution is very anxious to maintain re-

A Study of Prostitutes at Bedford

lations with men outside and sometimes represents a man as her husband who is simply the man she has been supporting by her wages of prostitution. Usually we find this out sooner or later; but as we include in these statistics a considerable percentage of girls whom we have known only for a few months, we cannot be certain. According to present knowledge, out of 647 cases there are 193 married women or 29.8 percent of the whole. (See Table XII.) In this connection it may be said that marriages are apparently entered into with as little consideration as one would give to the purchase of a new hat, and a husband who has ceased to please is thrown aside as easily as an old garment. New connections are entered into with very little regard to the legal aspects of the case. Many a girl has said to me when arguing the matter of a new relationship and the lack of legal separation from the first, " But, Miss Davis, he did not deserve any consideration!" One girl who has committed bigamy by marrying the second man, gave as her excuse, which I think was perfectly genuine, that she wished to be respectable! In a large proportion of cases of girls sent here for prostitution, one or more men and sometimes as many as six stand ready to marry each as a means of securing her release. These are not always the men with whom the girls have been living nor the men whom they have been supporting. The most extreme case that has come to my attention is that of one of our girls who stopped a man on the street as she was being taken to the train by our officer saying: " She is taking me to prison. Will you marry me to save me?" He said " Yes," and actually wrote me asking to be allowed to do so. It should be said in connection with married women, that we have record of comparatively few husbands who are in good and regular standing, as the tables in our annual reports will show.

It is equally difficult to get at the actual truth as to the number of children that the unmarried women have had. The table shows the admissions of 219 women on this point. There are 73 unmarried women who admitted having had children; 16 were pregnant at the time of entering the institution and 18 had previously been pregnant; 428 claim to have had no children. In this connection it may not be amiss to note the fact that an unmarried woman who has had a child is more apt to belong to the mentally defective class discussed later on. The cleverer women know how to prevent conceptions.

Religion: — Table XIII shows the religious affiliation of the Bedford girls. At Bedford, separate services are held for Catholic, Protestant and for Jewish women. On entrance they are asked to state their previous religious connection or preference. They are advised, if they have no definite religious preference, to attend the church to which their parents belonged. They are also told that they may not change after once having declared themselves. The table shows that 41.1 percent are Catholics, 38.9 percent are Protestants and 19 percent are Jews. The colored girls are almost all included in the Protestant section.

The warden of the Jefferson Market District prison states in regard to the religious affiliations of the 7,408

A Study of Prostitutes at Bedford

women sentenced from Jefferson Market Day and Night Court in 1912, that there were 3,533 Catholics or 47.6 percent, 2,525 Protestants or 34.08 percent and 1,301 Jews or 17.4 percent.

The religion of the women committed for all offenses from all the courts of Manhattan and the Bronx in 1912 is as follows:

Catholic	4,630 or	44.4%
Protestants	3,677 "	35.2%
Jewish	1,880 "	18.03%
Total	10,424	

A comparison of these figures with the percentage of Catholics, Protestants and Jews in the population of New York City would be interesting. These latter figures are very hard to get at except in the most general way. The latest authoritative study with which I am familiar is that made by the United States Census Bureau in 1906. It gives the church membership as reported by the various denominations as 1,838,482. On a basis of a regular growth in population from 1900 to 1910, the population of New York City in 1906 was about 4,235,010. On this basis, only 43.4 percent of the population have church connections. Only the heads of Jewish families are reported in this census. They are placed at 30,414. The World Almanac for 1913 is responsible for the statement quoted from "Christian Work and Evangelist" that there are 905,000 Jews in New York. This means racially as well as religiously Jewish. This would be about 19 percent of the entire population. The Census for 1906 gives to the Catholics 1,413,775, or 33.38 percent of the entire population and to the various Protestant denominations only 327,690, or 8.8 percent of the population. This would leave about 38 percent of the population without direct church connection to be distributed as to original affiliations between Catholic and Protestants. I should expect that here the Protestants would outnumber the Catholics.

Bedford's quota of Protestant girls is high, among other reasons because the House of the Good Shepherd, whose inmates are chiefly Catholics, is much the largest of the private institutions to which delinquent women are committed. I should personally believe that if we had the necessary data we should find that, as in the case of the Jewish women, the Protestants and Catholics would contribute in about their proportion in the community at large to the whole group of prostitutes.

Age: — Table XIV shows in column 1 the ages of 647 prostitutes on their commitment to Bedford. In column 2 it shows the age of the girl when she says she committed her first sexual offense. We have the data only in 300 cases. Of these, 279 are cases still in the institution. The age on entering prostitution is also only known for the cases in the institution, as we did not attempt to secure this special data until the beginning of the present study. It will be noted that about 7 percent of the whole number committed their first offense before they were fourteen, and that an additional 9 percent were fourteen at the time. There is, however, only the difference of a year in the average time in committing the first offense and in entering a life of prostitution. The graph which illustrates this was made by using percentages in order to have comparable curves.

A Study of Prostitutes at Bedford

Various Other Contributing Factors: — There has been considerable discussion as to the relative influence of country and city life in the production of character which leads to an irregular sexual life. We have registered the birthplace of all the women included in this study. We find that out of the 491 American-born women, 404 were born in cities while only 85 are known to have been country-born. Of the city-born, 290 or 59.2 percent of the total number of American-born were born in New York City. So far as this goes, it does not support the contention that the ranks of prostitution are recruited from country girls brought to the city for the purpose of immorality. We inquired of 139 girls in the institution at the time the study was made who were born outside of New York City but practised prostitution there, why they had come to New York. Seventy-eight of these claim to have come to the city with their families, who moved there for economic reasons. Only 9 admit having come with the purpose of entering the life; one came with her lover; 10 "to see New York"; 26 for work and 11 claim that they ran away from home to escape unpleasant conditions and came to New York simply because it was the handiest thing to do. Only 4 were unwilling to answer the question. In none of these cases had we any information which would contradict the statements made by the girls.

We have previously stated that 279 of the total number studied were in the institution when this special study began. We were interested to know how many of them were practising prostitution continuously and living entirely by it. One hundred and sixty-six claim to have been practising it continuously from the time they began; 55 either did not care to answer or gave unsatisfactory answers in the sense that they were obviously misleading; 58 claim to have been practising prostitution intermittently simply to eke out their wages or to get extra money. Thirty-two of the girls who were practising it at intervals and 43 who were practising it continuously, were engaged in trade. Of these, domestic servants were the largest single group, with factory operatives second. The girls who were working at trades excluding domestic service, were for the most part earning small wages; but the number of cases for which we have this data are few, too few on which to base any conclusions. The weekly earnings from prostitution as given by 146 girls who gave a maximum and of 95 girls who gave a minimum, is also to be taken with allowances. See Table XIX. It is our general experience that the majority of prostitutes have little conception of the value of money. They earn it easily and spend it as easily. Even among those who claim to make far more than the wages of even well paid working girls, it is not infrequent to find young women without changes of underclothing. These, of course, are the women who are not patronized by a well-to-do class of men.

As indicative of the character of the girl, their statements as to the reasons for their first sexual offense and of what they believe to be the causes leading up to prostitution as a career are illuminating. One hundred and eight out of 279 claim that their first wrong-doing was because they yielded to a man whom they loved;

A Study of Prostitutes at Bedford

57 admit that it was for pay; 62 claim to have been forced into the first act; 23 yielded where there was no love and where neither money nor force was used, but succumbed through weakness of will; two only state they did it because they liked it; 27 " could not remember why." See Table XXI.

As will be seen when we discuss the mentality of the girls, they are not as a class given to introspection or self-analysis. They are as a rule, incapable of this even if they try. It appeared to us worth while, however, to ask them what they thought were the reasons that led them into an immoral life. It is a very rare thing for a girl to admit that she would be willing to have a younger sister enter the life and this often can be used as a key to secure their willingness to discuss the situation. Two hundred and seventy-nine girls gave 671 reasons. We have grouped them as well as we can. The surprising thing is that very few directly economic reasons are given. It might be supposed that in friendly conversation, a girl would wish to make the greatest possible excuse for herself, and that the one most ready to hand would be the inability to earn a living. But in only 19 cases was this given as an excuse; and by referring to a similar table for street cases, it will be noticed that only 139 out of 1,106 gave a directly economic reason. It will be noted that only 7 out of 671 gave previous use of drink and drugs. As a result of experience, I should say that drink is a consequence rather than a cause of a life of prostitution, although a good many girls have admitted to me that their first wrongdoing occurred after taking an unaccustomed drink. In

Commercialized Prostitution in New York

this connection our medical records at Bedford with regard to the use of alcoholic drinks, drugs and cigarettes, show that at entrance 112 individuals, or 17 percent of the 647 women studied were suffering from one or the other alone, or from combinations, as shown in the following table:

EXCESSIVE USE OF ALCOHOLIC DRINKS, DRUGS AND CIGARETTES

Alcohol	45
Drugs	23
Cigarettes	7
Alcohol and cigarettes	18
Alcohol and drugs	8
Drugs and cigarettes	5
Alcohol, drugs and cigarettes	6

Total	112	17.3%
Not suffering at entrance from effects of above	535	82.6
	647	

Five hundred and thirty-five showed no injurious effects so far as was evident from a physical examination. We cannot give figures as to the exact number who used alcohol or cigarettes in moderation. We believe the number to be high.

Sixteen of the 647 were tubercular and were transferred to institutions for tuberculosis. No examination of the sputum was made except in cases of suspects. Seven others were epileptic and there was one case of chorea (St. Vitus Dance).

Mentality: — Of peculiar value, in view of the public interest in the question of mental defect as a cause of delinquency, is a study of the mentality of our 647 women. Twenty have been pronounced insane by com-

A Study of Prostitutes at Bedford

missions in lunacy and have been transferred to asylums for the insane. Three others will probably have to be transferred; 107 were unhesitatingly pronounced distinctly feeble-minded. Not all of our 647 cases have been examined by our psychologist. One hundred and sixteen, however, have had laboratory tests of various sorts. Among these tests, all have been given the Binet test. The result has been as follows:

MENTALITY BY BINET TEST

Showing mentality of 5 year old child	2
" " " 6 " " "	1
" " " 7 " " "	6
" " " 8 " " "	6
" " " 9 " " "	29
" " " 10 " " "	44
" " " 11 " " "	26
" " " 12 " " "	2
	116

The 44 who have the mentality of a ten year old child and under were unhesitatingly pronounced mentally defective. The 72 showing mentality from ten to twelve years may possibly not be so-called. The 67 others included among the 107 are those so mentally defective that there can be no question as a matter of observation. Fifty-two others are distinctly border line cases. This is the group which gives the most trouble in all reformatory institutions. It is safe to say that 90 percent of all disciplinary difficulties come from cases of this sort. They can be easily divided into at least two groups. Thus divided, 26 are girls who can be taught very little in school, whose general intelligence is low, but who may perhaps be able to learn a certain amount of manual labor; these cannot "stay good" any length of time. The other 26 are those who do well in school, are capable of mastering even such subjects as algebra and bookkeeping, but who have no moral sense or continuity of purpose. Eleven others are also properly in this class but differ from the two preceding groups in the character of their instability. If they were boys they would be tramps. They are all girls who have run away from home, sometimes a number of times, as well as from any place where they are put to service.

The foregoing figures mean that 193 individuals, or 29.8 percent, of the number studied are decidedly mentally defective. This is an extremely conservative estimate.

With the facilities which we are to have in the Laboratory of Social Hygiene under the auspices of the Bureau of Social Hygiene, we expect to get much more definite results not only as to the mentality but also as to the physical condition and the social relations of the young women under our care.

Venereal Disease: — The records of the Bedford Reformatory for girls show that 20.56 percent of the 647 inmates have clinical manifestations of venereal disease. The facts are summarized in the following table:

```
Total number of inmates ..................................... 647
Number free from clinical manifestations of disease ......... 514
Number showing clinical manifestations of disease ........... 133
Of the last named:
Number with syphhilis ............................. 61
            gonorrhœa ........................... 54
            syphilis and gonorrhœa .............. 9
   "     "  disease unnamed ..................... 8
   "     "  chancre ............................. 1
                                                 ———
Total ........................................... 133 (20.56%)
```

A Study of Prostitutes at Bedford

A series of complement fixation tests on blood specimens from 466 of the inmates show, however, that a very much larger number are infected with either syphilis or gonorrhœa or both of these diseases.[3] With the Wassermann test 176, or 37.7 percent gave positive reactions; 273, or 58.6 percent gave negative reactions, and 17, or 3.6 percent gave doubtful reactions. With a modification of the Wassermann technique where the tests were allowed to stand for four hours at ice box temperature to fix complement, instead of the usual one hour at 37°C. in the incubator, 224, or 48 percent gave positive reactions, 212, or 45.4 percent gave negative reactions and 30, or 6.4 percent gave doubtful reactions, showing an increase of 10.3 percent of positive reactions for syphilis over the method of fixing complement at 37°C. The same sera were tested by the complement fixation test for gonorrheal infection with the result that 134 or 29 percent gave positive reactions; 234, or 50 percent gave negative reactions and 98, or 21 percent gave doubtful reactions, fixing complement at 37°C. for one hour. When the ice box method of fixation was used, 306 or 65.6 percent gave positive reactions; 101, or 21.7 percent gave negative reactions and 59, or 12.6 percent gave doubtful reactions, showing an increase of 36.9 percent of positive results over the method of fixing complement at 37°C. in the incubator.

Vaginal smears from the same persons were examined but it was possible to demonstrate the presence of the gonococcus in but five of them, although many of

[3] These tests were made by Dr. Archibald McNeil, of the Research Laboratory, Department of Health, New York City.

them show the presence of numerous pus corpuscles.[4]

The full significance of the results above stated does not appear until the statistics are summarized. Of the 466 girls tested, only 50, that is, 10.7 percent, are found to be free from venereal infection. Practically 90 percent showed infection; 170, or 36.4 percent gave positive reactions for both syphilis and gonorrhœa; 27, or 5.79 percent were positive for syphilis only, and 117, or 25.1 percent were positive for gonorrhœa only.[5]

Offenses: — Not all of the 647 cases studied were committed to Bedford for prostitution; but all were leading the lives of prostitutes in New York City at the time of their commitment and the specific offense which they

---

[4] All smears were prepared and examined in duplicate and were stained by Grams method, pure cultures of staphylococci and colon bacilli being used as controls. In one case the smear was positive and the complement fixation test for gonorrhœa was negative, but as a rule antibodies against the gonococcus do not appear in the blood during the acute stage of the disease, so it may frequently happen that we may have positive smears and negative complement fixation tests in recent cases. At a later period, however, the complement fixation test is almost invariably positive.

The complement fixation tests were all performed in duplicate as a check on any possible errors in technique. The anti-sheep hæmolytic system with inactive sera was used with the alcoholic extract guinea pig heart for an antigen in the syphilis tests and an antigen prepared from ten varieties of gonococci was used in the tests for gonorrhœa.

All of the tests were made in sets of twelve, each set being fully controlled.

The blood specimens were unaccompanied by histories and the laboratory results were not in any way influenced by clinical findings.

[5] These percentages were taken from the combined results of the tests made at both incubator and ice box temperature.

A Study of Prostitutes at Bedford

committed was an incident in the life of prostitution.[6] Table XXIV shows that 105 women or 16.22 percent were convicted of felonies, while 450, or 69.55 percent were convicted of offenses directly connected with prostitution. The 25 cases committed as disorderly children were girls under eighteen years of age whose parents or relatives caused their arrest and brought them into court as the only means of taking them from the life. The 38 commitments for vagrancy were under Subdivision 3 and 4 of Section 887 of the Code of Criminal Procedure, which defines a vagrant as "a person who has contracted an infectious or other disease, in the practise of drunkenness or debauchery, requiring charitable aid to restore him to health" or "a common prostitute who has no lawful employment whereby to maintain herself."

The stories of the following girls will illustrate the relation between prostitution and crime in the cases of women sent to us for felonies or misdemeanors:

A. B. was a girl of eighteen, convicted of manslaughter in the second degree. She was not only leading a life of prostitution but was supporting her lover by it. As is so often the case, she was very fond of the man and intensely jealous when another girl won him away. She bought a sharp knife and carried it for a month before she met the girl, who had tried to avoid her. When at last they met, our girl stabbed her rival so seriously that she died from the effects.

C. D. was also only eighteen years of age. She was

[6] That is to say, the only girls who figure in the present study were girls who were before commitment engaged in prostitution in New York City.

convicted of shooting her lover. The time had come when they were no longer happy together. A quarrel arose on the street over a trivial matter. She wished to go to one place and he to another. Neither would yield. He started across the street to go his own way. She drew a pistol and shot him dead. Asked how she happened to have a loaded pistol in her possession, she said that she has always carried one ever since she came to New York. She thought it necessary for self-protection.

The story of E. F., convicted of grand larceny in the first degree, was as follows: She came north from a southern city thirteen years ago with her mother, who died soon after. She had had a lover before her mother's death. By him she had an illegitimate child. After the child was born he married her but they were not happy together. Another man coaxed her away from her husband. She claims he put her on the street, that she was violently in love with him and supported him by prostitution. Finally she was with a man whose watch she admired and coveted for her lover. She stole it and gave it to her lover in whose possession it was found. Both were convicted.

G. H. was a woman of twenty-four convicted of robbery. She had a husband and two children. The husband was entirely able and willing to support her. She became addicted to the use of opium. She claims it was first prescribed by a physician during an illness. As the habit grew, she stole money from the till in her husband's shop to supply herself with the drug. The resulting friction between herself and her husband finally

A Study of Prostitutes at Bedford

caused her to leave home and enter a life of prostitution. She had been living the life for two years at the time of her arrest for robbing a man of a diamond pin.

Three women, sentenced for corrupting the morals of a minor, had young girls with them whom they had brought to the city for immoral purposes.

The cases of assault were for the most part girls who had engaged in fist fights, usually on account of rivalry.

The attempted suicide was a girl who had tired of the life which she had led since she was fourteen years old and saw no other way out of it. She had made three unsuccessful attempts before she was sentenced to Bedford.

Previous Records:—The law prohibits the sentencing of women to the reformatory who have previously served a term in a state prison. With this limitation the judge has the power of sending those who have served numberless previous sentences for minor offenses if in his judgment there is hope of reform in the particular case. Contrary to the impression of many people, it is a very rare thing for a girl or woman to be sentenced to an institution for what is really a first offense. Never in our experience has a previously innocent girl been so sentenced.

Throwing light on the history of the prostitutes committed to Bedford, Table XXV gives us some information as to the various institutions in which they spent time previous to the Bedford commitment. The first section of the table shows that 305, or 47.1 percent have had previous institution experiences. In cases where these girls have been in more than one institution, this first portion of the table gives the institution in which she

Commercialized Prostitution in New York

has spent the most time. Out of 647 cases, 255, or 39.4 percent only, are not known to have been at least previously arrested. These figures give the data that we know. The probabilities are that the tables understate the facts. The latter half of the table shows the variegated experience of a number of the women. We have no comparable data for the cases from other institutions.

Conclusion: — As this is a statistical study, we have not touched upon various phases of the lives of prostitutes which are of general public interest. This is because we had not sufficiently accurate data to warrant giving figures or percentages. For example, the relation of the women to the men whom they support is a matter where verifiable data are very hard to get. An increasingly large percentage of the women under our care state that they were turning over the whole or a part of their wages to their lovers. In other cases we were pretty well assured that this was the case although it was denied by the girl.

As a result of our twelve years' experience we believe that there is an increasing number of young women who live in furnished rooms and take their patrons to hotels. A larger proportion of prostitutes in our early days lived in houses of ill fame. Now in many instances, even if their work is in these houses, they live outside and go to the houses only for business purposes. A case in point is that of a girl only sixteen years of age who worked in one of the houses conducted by the so-called "syndicate." She was living with a young Italian who had lured her from her home. He conducted her to this house every afternoon at four o'clock, calling

A Study of Prostitutes at Bedford

for her at five or six next morning and receiving her earnings from the woman who ran the house.

A number of the young women included in this study have figured in white slave cases. These commercialized phases of the social evil are dealt with elsewhere in this report.

STATISTICAL TABLES

ACCOMPANYING CHAPTER VIII

These tables comprise (1) *Analysis of histories of cases at Bedford;* the histories in question were carefully compiled from the records and from personal conferences and in so far as possible they were revised and verified in the light of experience, outside inquiry, etc. (2) *Similar analysis of cases from seven institutions in New York State and city other than Bedford;* this material was gathered in different ways. In some institutions two trained investigators interrogated the girls, checking up their replies by the records of the institution wherever possible; in two institutions, information was obtained from the records alone; in one, from the girls alone. (3) *Analysis of histories of street, hotel, and other cases;* these data were obtained by an experienced woman investigator who interviewed the girls under conditions as favorable as possible to her object.

In the matter of earnings, etc., where corroboration was in the nature of things impossible, no responsibility for the accuracy of the statements made by the girls is assumed.

Commercialized Prostitution in New York

TABLE I
BEDFORD CASES
BIRTHPLACE—ANALYSIS OF 647 CASES

Foreign Born		Native Born White		Native Born Colored	
Austria	15	New York City	263	New York City	27
Canada	1	Other parts N. Y. State	39	Other parts N. Y. State	3
Cuba	2	Colorado	1	Alabama	1
England	14	Connecticut	5	Connecticut	1
France	8	District of Columbia	1	District of Columbia	2
Finland	2	Florida	1	Florida	1
Germany	26	Illinois	5	Georgia	2
Holland	2	Iowa	2	Kentucky	1
Hungary	12	Kansas	1	Louisiana	2
India	1	Maine	2	Maryland	2
Ireland	17	Maryland	4	Massachusetts	3
Italy	7	Massachusetts	16	Minnesota	1
Mexico	1	New Jersey	23	New Jersey	2
Norway	1	Michigan	2	North Carolina	10
Nova Scotia	1	Minnesota	1	Pennsylvania	5
Poland	5	Missouri	1	South Carolina	1
Roumania	3	North Carolina	2	Tennessee	1
Russia	32	Ohio	4	Virginia	18
Scotland	2	Oregon	1	Washington	1
Sweden	1	Pennsylvania	22	Unknown	1
Switzerland	2	Texas	1		
Wales	1	Vermont	1		
		Virginia	5		
		West Virginia	2		
		Unknown	1		
TOTAL 156=24.11%		TOTAL 406=62.75%		TOTAL 85=13.14%	

A Study of Prostitutes at Bedford

GRAPH ILLUSTRATING TABLE I

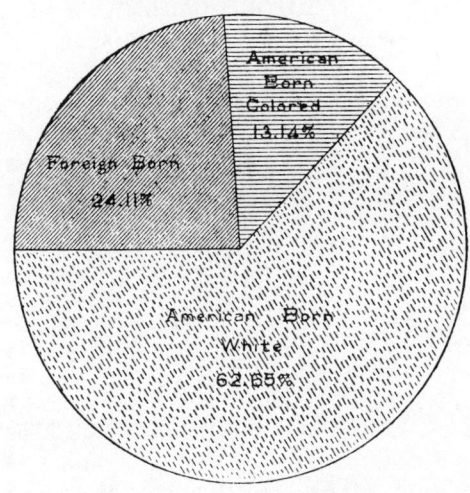

GRAPH ILLUSTRATING TABLE II

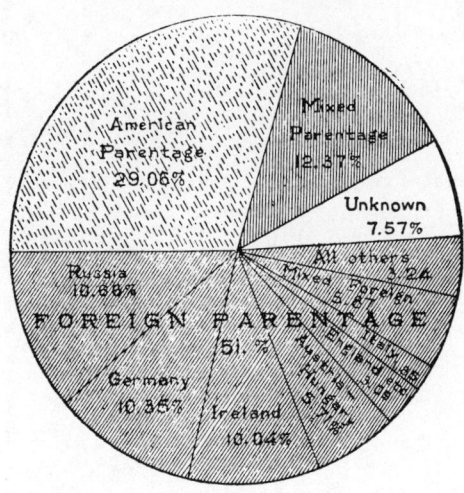

Commercialized Prostitution in New York

TABLE II

BEDFORD CASES

NATIONALITY OF PARENTS IN DETAIL

A. White

I. Both parents foreign, born in the same country

Austria (18 Jews)	22
Bohemia	3
Canada	2
Denmark	2
England	11
Finland	3
France	9
Germany (11 Jews)	67
Holland	3
Hungary	12
India	1
Ireland	65
Italy	12
Norway	1
Nova Scotia	2
Poland	6
Roumania (1 Jew)	2
Russia (57 Jews)	60
Scotland	3
Sweden	2
Switzerland	1
Wales	1

290

II. Both parents foreign, born in different countries

Birthplace of father	Birthplace of mother	
Australia	England	1
Austria	Germany	1
Canada	England	1
Cuba	Spain	1
Denmark	England	1
England	Denmark	1
England	Germany	1
England	Ireland	4
England	Wales	1
France	England	1
France	Germany	1

A Study of Prostitutes at Bedford

TABLE II—*Continued*

II. Both parents foreign, born in different countries—*Continued*

Birthplace of father—Con.	Birthplace of mother—Con.		
France	Irish	1	
Germany	Bohemia	1	
"	Denmark	1	
"	France	1	
" (Jew)	Hungary (Jew)	3	
"	Russia	1	
"	Switzerland	1	
Hungary	German	1	
Ireland	England	3	
"	Scotland	1	
"	Wales	1	
Italy	Roumania	1	
Norway	Ireland	1	
Roumania	Russia	1	
Russia	Austria	1	
Scotland	England	1	
"	Ireland	1	
Spain	Portugal	1	
Wales	Mexico	1	37 327

III. Father of foreign birth, mother, United States

Belgium	United States	1	
Canada	" "	4	
England	" "	6	
Finland	" "	1	
Germany	" "	10	
Ireland	" "	10	
Scotland	" "	2	34

IV. Father born in U. S., mother, foreign

United States	Bohemia	1	
" "	Canada	2	
" "	England	3	
" "	Germany	4	
" "	Ireland	15	
" "	Italy	1	
" "	Norway	1	
" "	Roumania	1	28

TABLE II—*Continued*

V. Father of foreign birth, mother unknown
- Austria 1
- Germany 3
- Ireland................... 2
- Scotland.................. 1   7

VI. Father unknown, mother of foreign birth
- England 2
- France 2
- Germany 2
- Ireland 1   7

TOTAL NUMBER WITH ONE FOREIGN PARENT KNOWN   76

VII. Both parents born in the U. S.   120
VIII. Father born in the U. S., mother unknown ...   5
IX. Father unknown, mother born in U. S.   5
X. Both parents unknown   25

TOTAL WHITE   558

B. *Colored*

I. Both parents of foreign birth

Father's birthplace	Mother's birthplace	
Jamaica	Jamaica	1
Cuba	Cuba	1
West Indies	South America	1

II. One parent of foreign birth

Ireland	United States	1
West Indies	" "	1
United States	England	1
" "	Ireland	1

III. Both parents born in U. S.   68
IV. Father unknown, mother born in U. S..   4
V. Birthplaces of both parents unknown   10

TOTAL COLORED   89
TOTAL NUMBER OF CASES   647

A Study of Prostitutes at Bedford

TABLE III

BEDFORD CASES

NATIONALITY OF PARENTS

Summary

Both parents foreign	Born in the same country	White 290			
		Colored 2	292		
	Born in different countries	White 37		330	51. %
		Colored 1	38		
One parent foreign	Mother U.S.	White 34			
		Colored 2	36		
	Father U.S.	White 28			
		Colored 2	30		
	Mother unknown	White	7		
	Father unknown	White	7	80	12.37%
Both parents born in the U.S.		White 120	18.54%		
		Colored 68	10.52	188	29.06%
One parent born in the U. S., the other unknown	Mother U.S.	White 5			
		Colored 4	9		
	Father U.S.	White	5	2.30% 14	
Both parents unknown		White 25		5.27%	7.57%
		Colored 10		35	
		TOTAL		647	

TABLE IV

COMPARISON AS TO PARENTAGE OF NATIVE POPULATION IN NEW YORK CITY AND AMONG PROSTITUTES AT BEDFORD

Population of New York City* in 1912	No. of Individuals	Percentage of Total Pop.	Bedford Cases 647	No. of Individuals	Percentage of Total Cases
Native white of native parents	921,130	19.3 %	Native white of known native parentage	120	18.5
Native white of foreign parents	1,820,374	38.2	Native white of known foreign parentage (both parents)	327	50.5
Negro—parentage unspecified	91,702	1.92	Negro—total number	89	13.64

*New York Tribune Almanac, 1912.

A Study of Prostitutes at Bedford

TABLE V

BEDFORD CASES

OCCUPATIONS OF THE FATHERS

Professions
Architect	2
Civil engineer	1
Colored preacher	1
Lawyer	1
Minister	1
Music teacher	1
Musician	2
Physician	2
Surveyor	2
Trained nurse	1
Veterinary surgeon	1
TOTAL	15

Own their own Business
Brewer	1
Contractor	5
Fruit dealer	2
Horse dealer	4
Hotel keeper	2
Livery stable keeper	1
Peddler	8
Saloonkeeper	11
Shopkeeper	29
TOTAL	63

Business Positions
Insurance agent	2
Milkman	1
Real estate agent	4
Salesman	21
TOTAL	28

Mechanical Trades
Blacksmith	6
Bricklayer	3
Brickmaker	1
Builder	5
Cabinet-maker	2
Carpenter	13
Carriage-maker	1
Cooper	1
Electrician	2
Engineer (railroad)	4
Engineer (stationary)	15
Gas fitter	1
Glazier	1
Hardwood polisher	1
Iron worker	8
Machinist	7
Mechanic	3
Painter	14
Plasterer	1
Plumber	3
Printer	6
Slate roofer	1
Stone cutter	2
Stone mason	9
Terra cotta worker	1
Tinsmith	2
Walking delegate	1
TOTAL	114

Clothing Trades
Cap maker	4
Cloak maker	2
Designer	2
Finisher on corsets	1
Presser	6
Tailor	22
TOTAL	37

Other Trades
Baker	2
Barber	8
Bartender	2
Basket maker	1
Butcher	10
Carpet layer	1
Cigar maker	10
Draughtsman	1
Mat maker	1
Photographer	1
Reed and rattan worker	1

Commercialized Prostitution in New York

TABLE V—*Continued*

Other Trades—Continued
Shoemaker 10
Watchmaker 1
Weaver 2

TOTAL 51

Clerical Positions
Bookkeeper 3
Clerk of Court 1
Excise officer 1

TOTAL 5

Laborers
Derrick rigger 1
Electric light trimmer . . . 1
Employed on boats 11
Employed on railroad . . . 12
Farmers and farm hands . . 34
Hod carrier 3
Laborer 40
Miner 3
Stableman 3
Street sweeper 2
Teamster 18
Watchman 4

TOTAL 132

Mill and Factory Positions
Factory 13
Mill hand 7

TOTAL 20

Domestic Positions
Coachman 7
Cook 9
Elevator man 1
Gardener 3

Janitor 5
Porter 3
Waiter 7

TOTAL 35

Foreman 7
Asst. Supt. Life Insurance Co. 1
Conductor 2
Sea captain 5

TOTAL 15

In Public Service
Fireman 5
Lighthouse keeper 1
Mail carrier 1
Policeman 5
Soldier 5

TOTAL 17

Miscellaneous
Collector 1
Gambler 1
Sandwich man 1
Telegraph operator . . . 1
Ticket speculator 1
Undertaker 3

TOTAL 8

"Does not work on account of kidney trouble and fainting fits" 1
Unknown 7
No statistics 99

TOTAL 107

TOTAL NUMBER . . . 647

A Study of Prostitutes at Bedford

TABLE VI
BEDFORD CASES
NUMBER OF CHILDREN IN THE FAMILIES FROM WHICH THE GIRLS COME

No. of Children	Cases
1	78
2	95
3	126
4	110
5	95
6	50
7	44
8	22
9	11
10	5
11	5
12	0
13	1
Unknown	5
TOTAL NUMBER OF CASES	647
Average size of family	3.99

GRAPH ILLUSTRATING ABOVE TABLE VI

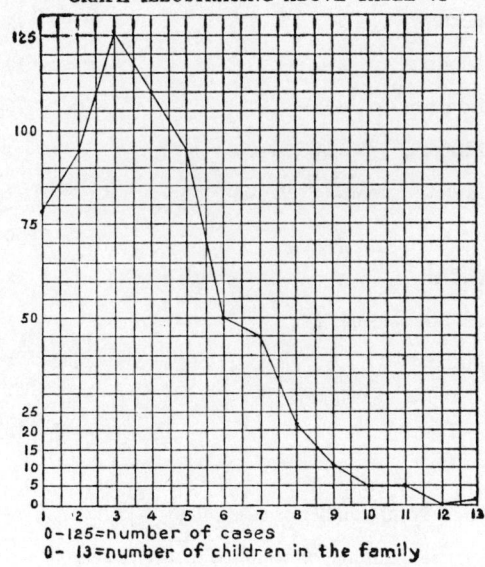

0-125=number of cases
0-13=number of children in the family

Commercialized Prostitution in New York

TABLE VII

BEDFORD CASES

OCCUPATION OF MOTHER

Actress	1
Canvasser	2
Charge of Hotel Linen Room	1
Cook (6 colored)	10
Day's work	46
Domestic—General housework (6 colored)	9
Dressmaker	4
Factory Operatives	11
Housekeeper	4
Janitress	13
Laundress	17
Midwife	6
Milliner	1
Market Woman	1
Nurse	9
Peddler	2
Small Shopkeepers	7
Tailoress	1
TOTAL	145

Total number of cases, 647

Percentage of occupied mothers, 22.4

A Study of Prostitutes at Bedford

TABLE VIII
BEDFORD CASES
EDUCATION

Cannot read or write any language—15 American born	50	7.72%
Reads and writes a foreign language—5 read a little Eng.	32	4.83%
Read and write a little, no further education	192	29.67%
Did not finish primary grades	70	10.82%
Reached but did not finish grammar grades	257	39.72%
Graduated from grammar grades	25	3.86%
Entered, but did not finish high school	13	2.00%
Graduated from high school	4	.77%
One year in normal school	3	.46%
Eight months at college	1	.15%
TOTAL NUMBER OF CASES	647	100.00%

GRAPH ILLUSTRATING TABLE VIII

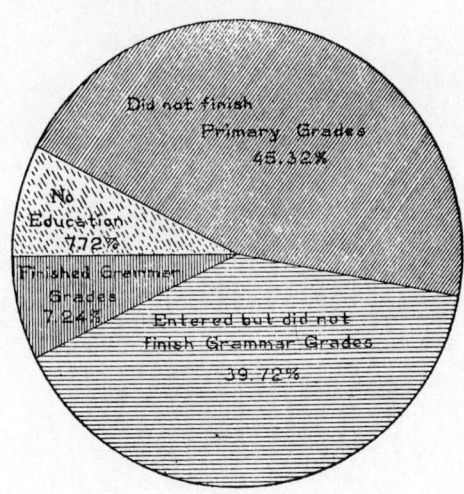

Commercialized Prostitution in New York

TABLE IX   BEDFORD CASES

I Wages before entering prostitution — EARNINGS

	$.50	.75	1.00	1.25	1.50	2.00	2.50	3.00	3.50	4.00	4.50	5.00	5.50	6.00	7.00	8.00	9.00	10
Wages of trades excluding Domestic Service — High 110 cases	.	.	.	.	.	.	.	.	2	11	5	14	7	13	12	15	5	6
Low 110 cases	.	.	1	.	.	3	3	13	9	24	4	23	1	11	3	6	1	4
Wages of Domestic Service — High 52 cases	.	.	.	.	.	.	4	4	5	5	13	9	5	6	7.50 / 1	.	.	.
Low 52 cases	.	.	.	1	1	6	8	13	9	10	3	1	.	.	.	.	.	.

I Wages before entering prostitution. (Continued)

	$11	12	13	14	15	18	20	22	25	30	Highest Wage	Lowest Wage	Average	Mode
Wages of trades excluding Domestic Service — High 110 cases	2	6	.	1	5	1	1	1	2	1	$30.00	$3.50	$8.11	$8.00
Low 110 cases	.	.	.	.	3	.	.	.	1	.	25.00	1.00	5.21	4.00
Wages of Domestic Service — High 52 cases	.	.	.	.	.	.	.	.	.	.	7.50	2.50	4.30	4.50
Low 52 cases	.	.	.	.	.	.	.	.	.	.	5.00	1.25	3.14	3.00

A Study of Prostitutes at Bedford

GRAPHS ILLUSTRATING TABLE IX

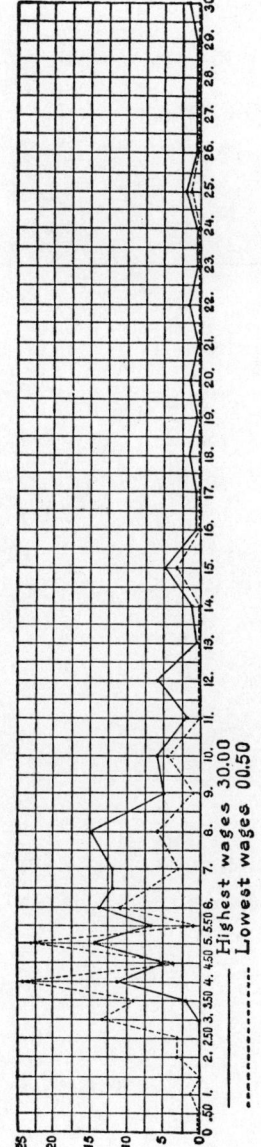

Wages in Trades excluding Domestic Service—110 Cases

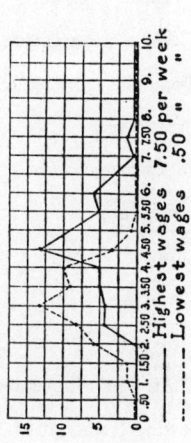

Wages in Domestic Service—52 Cases

Commercialized Prostitution in New York

TABLE X

BEDFORD CASES

OCCUPATIONS

Before entering prostitution	No. of Cases	Percentages
Book-binding	7	1.08
Clerk in small shop	8	1.23
Clerk in department store	40	6.18
Domestic (general housework)	243	37.56
Errand girl	3	.46
Factory operative	127	19.62
Janitress	1	.15
Laundry employee	14	2.16
Manicure	2	.30
Millinery	13	2.00
Office work (not stenographers)	13	2.00
Sewing (handwork)	25	3.86
Steel engraver	1	.15
Telephone operator	9	1.39
Theatrical work (chorus or vaudeville)	18	2.78
Nurse (not graduate)	3	.46
Waitress (in restaurants)	28	4.32
No work	92	14.27
TOTAL	647	

A Study of Prostitutes at Bedford

TABLE XI

BEDFORD CASES

RESIDENCE OF GIRL BEFORE ENTERING PROSTITUTION

Living at home	Giving all they made									53
	Giving part									16
	Supported by parents or husband									32
	No statistics as to money paid									23
										124
Living with relatives	Giving all									15
	Giving part									9
										24
Boarding		$1.50	2.00	3.00	4.00	5.00	5.40	6.00	13.50	No amount given
		1	1	1	3	2	1	1	1	9
										20
Domestics living where they worked										26
								Total		194

TABLE XII

BEDFORD CASES

SOCIAL RELATIONS

Married			193	29.8
Single			454	70.1
		TOTAL	647	

STATEMENT OF 219 WOMEN WITH REGARD TO NUMBER OF CHILDREN

Married women	Pregnant on entering			1
	Miscarriage previous to entering Bedford			18
	Legitimate children	One	66	
		Two	19	
		Three	7	
		Eight	1	
				93
Single women	Pregnant on entering			16
	Miscarriage previous to entering Bedford			18
	Illegitimate children	One	63	
		Two	10	73
	TOTAL NUMBER OF CASES			219
No children, or no record of them				428
		TOTAL		647

A Study of Prostitutes at Bedford

TABLE XIII

BEDFORD CASES

RELIGION

Catholic	266	41.1%
Jewish	123	19.0%
Protestant	252	38.9%
No record	6	.9%

TOTAL NUMBER OF CASES 647

GRAPH ILLUSTRATING TABLE XIII

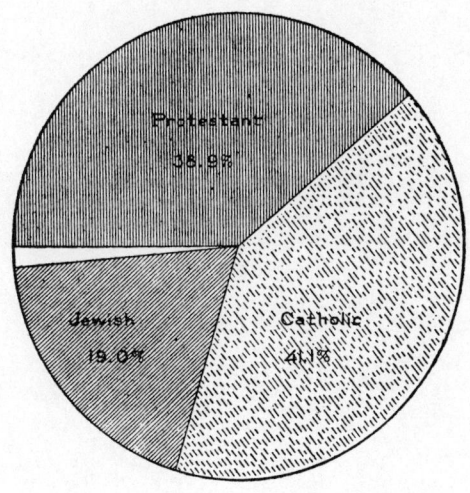

Commercialized Prostitution in New York

Table XIV
BEDFORD CASES
AGE

	I		II		III	
Years of age	Number entering Bedford		First sexual offense		Number entering prostitution	
7	..	......	1	.33⅓%	..	......
9	..	......	1	.33⅓%	..	......
10	..	......	1	.33⅓%	..	......
11	..	......	1	.33⅓%	..	......
12	..	......	4	1.33⅓%	..	......
13	..	......	12	4. %	1	.37%
14	..	......	29	9.66⅔%	3	1.12%
15	12	1.86%	43	14.33⅓%	11	4.08%
16	41	6.34%	61	20.33%	19	7.06%
17	65	10.05%	40	13.33⅓%	40	14.87%
18	47	7.26%	31	10.33⅓%	35	13.01%
19	65	10.05%	28	9.33⅓%	32	11.90%
20	50	7.71%	19	6.33⅓%	28	10.41%
21	61	9.43%	15	5.00%	31	11.52%
22	73	11.28%	3	1. %	22	8.18%
23	48	7.42%	6	2. %	17	6.32%
24	53	8.19%	3	1. %	9	3.35%
25	40	6.18	..	....	10	3.72%
26	22	3.40%	..	....	3	1.12%
27	20	3.09%	1	.33⅓%	6	2.23%
28	22	3.40%	1	.33⅓%	2	.74%
29	24	3.71%	..	....	..	......
30	2	.31%	..	....	..	......
31	1	.15%	..	....	..	......
32	1	.15%	..	....	..	......
Total No. cases	647	99.98%	300	100%	269	100%
Average Age	20 yr. 11.06 mos.		17 yrs. 16 days		18 yrs. 9.18 mos.	

Highest 32	Highest 28	Highest . . . 28
Lowest 15	Lowest 7	Lowest . . . 13
Average 20.09	Average 17	Average . . . 18.7
Mode 22	Mode 16	Mode 17
Mean 23.5	Mean 17.5	Mean 18.5
No. of cases . . .647	No. of cases . . 300	No. of cases .269

A Study of Prostitutes at Bedford

GRAPH ILLUSTRATING TABLE XIV

(*Made from Table of Percentages*)

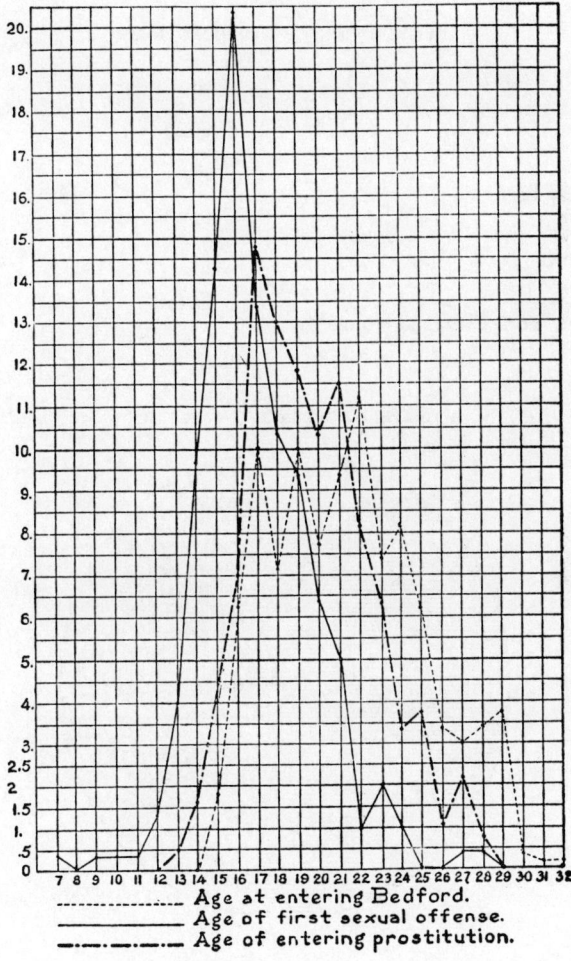

·············· Age at entering Bedford.
─────── Age of first sexual offense.
─·─·─·─ Age of entering prostitution.

Commercialized Prostitution in New York

TABLE XV

BEDFORD CASES

DISTRIBUTION OF AMERICAN BORN

*City born	{ White	341	404	82.48%
	Colored	63		
Country born	{ White	63	85	17.47%
	Colored	22		
Unknown			2	0.05%
	TOTAL		491	

*New York City, 290=59.20%.

GRAPH ILLUSTRATING TABLE XV

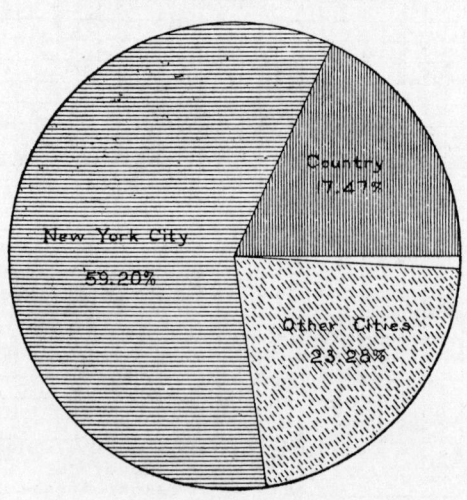

A Study of Prostitutes at Bedford

TABLE XVI

BEDFORD CASES

REASONS FOR COMING TO NEW YORK, OF THOSE BORN OUTSIDE NEW YORK CITY

Ran away to escape home conditions	11
To live with family	78
To obtain work or easier work	26
To practice prostitution	9
To see New York	10
With lover	1
Unknown	4
TOTAL	139

TABLE XVII

BEDFORD CASES

PROSTITUTION: PRACTICED CONTINUOUSLY OR INTERRUPTEDLY

Continuously			166	59.50%
Not continuously	Married	19		
	Living with parents	4		
	Stealing	3		
	Working	32	58	20.79%
No statistics			55	19.71%

TOTAL NUMBER OF CASES CONSIDERED 279

TABLE XVIII

BEDFORD CASES

TRADES COMBINED WITH PROSTITUTION

Trade	No. of Cases	Per cent.
Demonstrator	1	
Clerk in department store	4	
Domestic	22	
Factory operative	17	
Laundry employees	4	
Manicure	1	
Office work	2	
Sewing	2	
Theatrical work	6	
Waitress	8	
Stealing	6	
Received money from husband	2	
Prostitution only	204	73.11
TOTAL	279	

A Study of Prostitutes at Bedford

Table XIX

BEDFORD CASES

WEEKLY EARNINGS FROM PROSTITUTION

	Support Partial	Support	$3	$5	$6	$10	$12	$14	$15	$18	$19	$20	$25	$30	$35	$38	$40	$45	$50
High	2	9	.	2	.	4	.	1	7	.	1	8	3	10	3	1	4	2	24
Low	1	.	1	4	1	7	4	.	8	2	.	5	13	6	3	.	3	.	14

	$55	$59	$60	$63	$70	$75	$90	$100	$110	$120	$125	$150	$200	$240	$250	$300	$400	Total No. cases	Average
High	.	1	12	.	7	7	.	15	1	1	2	5	7	1	2	3	1	146	$71.09
Low	1	.	4	1	2	2	1	6	.	.	1	4	.	.	.	1	.	95	46.02

Commercialized Prostitution in New York

TABLE XX

BEDFORD CASES

EARNED AT THE SAME TIME WITH PROSTITUTION

Weekly Wages	For Board	$.50	$1.00	$2.00	$2.50	$3.00	$3.50	$3.75	$4.00	$4.50	$4.60	$5.00	$5.50	$6.00	$7.00	$8.00	$9.00	$10.00	$11.00	$12.00	$13.00	$14.00	$15.00	$16.00	$17.00	$18.00	Maximum	Minimum	Average	Mode
Wages of occupations excluding Domestic Service — High 34 cases	.	.	.	.	.	1	1	.	2	.	.	6	2	6	3	4	2	2	1	1	1	.	.	.	.	2	$18.00	$3.00	$6.42	$5.00 to $6
Low 34 cases	.	.	.	3	.	5	2	.	6	2	.	10	.	3	.	.	.	.	.	2	.	.	.	.	.	.	12.00	2.00	4.68	5.00
Domestic Service — High 23 cases	.	.	1	1	1	.	1	1	7	2	.	6	2	.	.	.	.	.	.	.	.	.	1	.	.	.	15.00	1.00	4.60	4.00
Low 23 cases	1	.	5	3	7	2	.	.	1	1	.	.	1	.	.	.	.	.	.	.	.	.	.	.	.	.	6.00	.	2.86	3.00

A Study of Prostitutes at Bedford

GRAPHS ILLUSTRATING TABLE XX

Wages in Trades excluding Domestic Service—34 cases

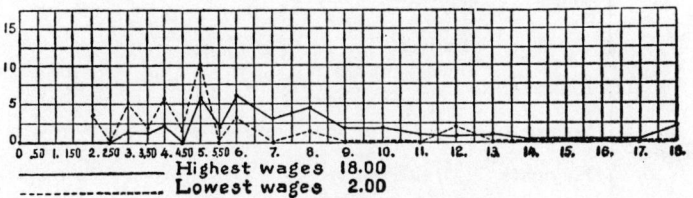

Highest wages 18.00
Lowest wages 2.00

Wages in Domestic Service—23 Cases

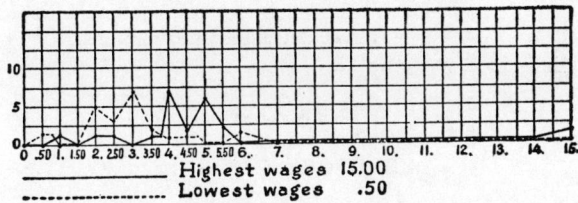

Highest wages 15.00
Lowest wages .50

Table XXI

BEDFORD CASES
CAUSE OF FIRST SEXUAL OFFENSE

Love					108	38.71%
Pay	Married	Living with husband	1	11		
		Separated from "	10			
	Single	Lover	17		57	20.43%
		Playmate	4			
		Stranger	25	46		
Force	Relative			7		
	Lover			27		
	Playmate			3		
	Stranger			25	62	22.22%
Weakness					23	8.24%
Physical predisposition					2	.71%
Unknown					27	9.64%

TOTAL NUMBER OF CASES 279

Table XXII

BEDFORD CASES
MENTAL CONDITION

Insane—Transferred to asylums	20		
Insane tendencies	3		
Feeble-minded (distinctly so)	107		
Border-line—neurotic	26		
Weak-willed—"No moral sense"	26		
"Wild"—truants—run-a-ways	11	193	29.8%

A Study of Prostitutes at Bedford

TABLE XXIII

BEDFORD CASES

CAUSES. REASONS GIVEN BY THE GIRL

A. *In connection with her family*
1. Immorality of the parents 15
2. Incompatibility 39
3. Neglect and abuse 26
4. No mother or father or neither 166
5. Over indulgence 10
6. Over strictness 35
7. Poverty 9
8. Turned out 6
              306

B. *In connection with married life*
1. Death of husband 5
2. Desertion by husband 8
3. Immorality (includes cruelty or criminality) . . . 14
4. Incompatibility 26
5. Husband put girl on street 2
              55

C. *Personal reasons*
1. Bad company 75
2. No sex instruction 10
3. Idle or lonely 5
4. Sick, needed the money 4
5. Ruined anyway 10
6. Lover put girl on the street 10
7. Previous use of drink or drugs 7
8. White slave 2
9. Tired of drudgery 4
10. "Easy money" 17
11. Dances 13
12. Lazy, hated work 20
13. Stage environment 9
14. Love of the life 15
15. Desertion by lover 3
16. Desire for pleasure (theatre, food, clothes) . . . 48
17. Desire for money 38
18. Ashamed to go home after first escapade 1   291

D. *Economic reasons*
1. Can't support herself 5
2. Can't support herself and children 1
3. Couldn't find work 13   19

         TOTAL 671

TABLE XXIV
BEDFORD CASES
OFFENSES

No. Cases, 647

Misdemeanor		Felonies		Other Offenses	
Assault 3rd degree	9	Assault 2nd degree	4	Associating with dissolute persons and in danger of becoming morally deprav'd	50
Attempted suicide	1	Attempted grand larceny	13	Common prostitute	272
Concealing birth of child	1	Burglary 3rd degree	3	Disorderly child	25
Corrupting morals of a minor	3	Felonously selling cocaine	1	Disorderly conduct	44
Indecent exposure	1	Grand larceny, 1st degree	12	Frequenting disorderly houses	6
Keeping a disorderly house	3	Grand larceny, 2nd degree	63	Intercourse with boys	1
Maintaining a place for smoking opium	1	Manslaughter, 2nd degree	3	Public intoxication or habitual drunkard	14
Petit larceny	71	Receiving stolen goods	4	Vagrancy	38
Unlawfully injuring propt'y	1	Robbery	2		
Using vulgar and indecent language in public	1				
TOTAL, 92 or 14.21%		TOTAL, 105 or 16.22%		TOTAL, 450 or 69.55%	

A Study of Prostitutes at Bedford

TABLE XXV

BEDFORD CASES

PREVIOUS RECORDS, SO FAR AS CAN BE ASCERTAINED

Bedford State Reformatory for women	13
Catholic Protectory	4
County jails	6
Florence Crittenton Home	7
Gerry Society	4
House of Good Shepherd, Brooklyn	20
House of Good Shepherd, New York	34
House of Mercy, Inwood	23
House of Refuge, Randall's Island	15
Insane Asylums	2
Magdalen Asylum	16
Massachusetts State Industrial School, Lancaster	3
New York Juvenile Asylum	5
New York State Industrial School, Rochester	3
New York State Training School for Girls, Hudson	6
Orphan Asylum	20
Penitentiaries	7
Sherbourne Prison	1
Washington Square Home	3
Waverly House	4
Wayside Home	13
Workhouse	65
Various other homes for Wayward Girls	31

305   47.1

Say never in institution and never arrested previously 255
Admit one or more previous arrests, but got off with fine, suspended sentence or discharge, and claim never to have been committed 66
Admit having been on probation 21

TOTAL NUMBER OF CASES 647

OF THE ABOVE

Arrested twice, once fined, once on probation	1
In one institution, twice arrested and once on probation	3
In one institution, three arrests and on probation	1
In one institution, several other arrests	3
In one institution, workhouse eight times, six months each	1
In two institutions	30
In two institutions, several other arrests	6
In three institutions	5
In three institutions, several other arrests	2
In four institutions	1
In four institutions, several times Raymond St. Jail	1

Commercialized Prostitution in New York

TABLE XXV—Continued

Six months in workhouse, four times arrested, twice fined	1
Workhouse once, six times arrested and fined	1
Workhouse once, seven times arrested	1
In two institutions, workhouse once, fined three times, and on probation	1
In Madgalen, twice; Good Shepherd, once; 10 days in workhouse; three times arrested; on probation once	1
In workhouse twice; arrested six times; on probation once	1
In one home; workhouse twice; twice fined, and once discharged	1
Workhouse, three terms	1
Workhouse, three terms, six months each; four times fined	1
In three institutions; workhouse, three times; seven other arrests	1
Arrested about 30 times; City prison, 10 weeks; workhouse, 6 terms fined over 20 times	1
Three times on the Island; arrested over 30 times	1
Twice at Good Shepherd, workhouse two terms and arrested nine times	
Two and one-half years House of Refuge, arrested five times; on Island four times	1
Two terms at Hudson; three arrests; workhouse, three months; Bedford for third time	1
House of Refuge, four years; Juvenile Asylum, one year; more than 40 times at the workhouse, once on probation	1

GRAPH ILLUSTRATING TABLE XXVI

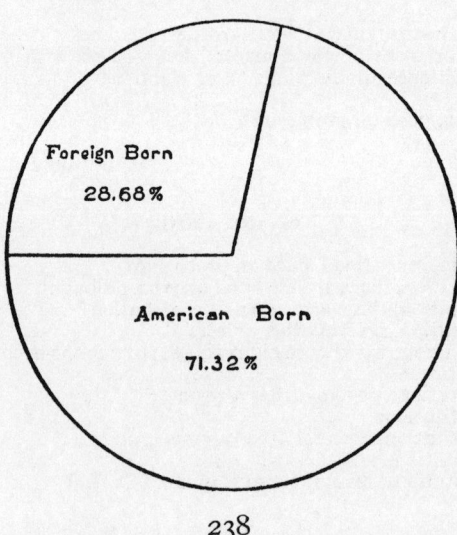

Institutions Other Than Bedford

TABLE XXVI

CASES IN INSTITUTIONS, OTHER THAN BEDFORD

BIRTHPLACE

American Born		*Foreign Born*		
New York City	210	Austro-Hungary	34	
Other parts of N. Y. State	53	Canada	11	
Alabama	2	England-Scotland	9	
Arizona	1	Finland	0	
Arkansas	1	France	4	
California	6	Galacia	2	
Colorado	1	Germany	24	
Connecticut	4	Holland	0	
Delaware	2	India	0	
District Columbia	3	Ireland	12	
Florida	3	Italy	6	
Georgia	3	Mexico	1	
Illinois	4	Poland	9	
Indiana	2	Roumania	2	
Iowa	0	Russia	46	
Kansas	1	Sweden	5	
Kentucky	2	Switzerland	2	
Louisiana	0	Venezuela	1	
Maine	0	West Indies	7	
Maryland	5	Total No. foreign born	175	28.68%
Massachusetts	24	" " American "	435	71.31%
Michigan	1			
Minnesota	1	TOTAL	610	
Mississippi	1			
Missouri	0			
New Hampshire	1			
New Jersey	17			
North Carolina	6			
Ohio	3			
Oregon	0			
Pennsylvania	23			
Rhode Island	2			
South Carolina	7			
Tennessee	0			
Texas	3			
Virginia	8			
Vermont	0			
West Virginia	0			
Wisconsin	2			
Unknown	33			
TOTAL	435			

Commercialized Prostitution in New York

TABLE XXVII

CASES IN INSTITUTIONS, OTHER THAN BEDFORD

DISTRIBUTION BETWEEN CITY AND COUNTRY OF 147 CASES, BORN IN THE UNITED STATES

City born	85	57.82%
Country born	62	42.18%
TOTAL	147	
Born in cities of New York	52	
Born in cities of other states	33	
TOTAL		85
Born in country, New York State	1	
Born in country, other states	61	
TOTAL		62
		147

TABLE XXVIII

CASES IN INSTITUTIONS, OTHER THAN BEDFORD

REASONS FOR COMING TO NEW YORK OF 400 CASES BORN OUTSIDE THE CITY, AMERICAN AND FOREIGN

Ran away to escape home conditions	4
To live with family or husband	63
To obtain work, or easier work	57
To practice prostitution	42
To see New York	10
With lover	11
Unknown or not given	213
TOTAL NUMBER CASES	400

Institutions Other Than Bedford

Table XXIX
CASES IN INSTITUTIONS, OTHER THAN BEDFORD
EDUCATION

Does not read or write in any language	68	11.15%
Reads and writes a foreign language	20	3.28%
Reads and writes English, no further education	335	54.92%
Finished fifth grade	34	5.57%
Finished Grammar grades	74	12.13%
Entered High School or Business courses	36	5.90%
Unknown	43	7.05%
TOTAL NUMBER OF CASES	610	100%

Table XXX
CASES IN INSTITUTIONS, OTHER THAN BEDFORD
OCCUPATIONS

Before entering prostitution 662 cases used			After entering prostitution 497 cases used	
Artist				1
Book-binding	1			
Canvasser	2			
Chambermaid	34			5
Clerk in small store	9			
Companion	1			
Department store	70	10.57%		10
Errand girl	1			1
Factory	215	32.46%		24
Domestic service	117	17.67%		20
Laundry	16			1
Librarian	1			
Manicure	4			2
Massage	1			
Millinery	12			2
Nurse girl	34			1
Office work	20			0
Palmist	1			
Salvation Army worker	1			
Sewing	16			4
Steel Engraver	1			
Stenographer	8			
Teacher	1			
Telephone operator	13			
Theatrical work	20			3
Waitress	53			6
No work	10			
			Supported by prostitution only	353
			Supported by husband or parents	23
	TOTAL	662	Stealing	11
			Unknown	30
			TOTAL	497

Commercialized Prostitution in New York

TABLE XXXI

CASES IN INSTITUTIONS, OTHER THAN BEDFORD

AGE

Years of age	Number entering Institution	First sexual offense	Number entering prostitution
6	..	1	..
7	..	1	..
8	..	..	..
9	..	1	..
10	..	2	..
11	2	5	3
12	2	9	1
13	..	7	..
14	7	33	7
15	7	67	32
16	20	59	45
17	28	83	67
18	43	77	73
19	54	56	59
20	51	35	66
21	31	31	37
22	54	32	35
23	41	12	25
24	54	10	24
25	31	7	13
26	31	11	9
27	20	3	8
28	28	6	6
29	15	1	1
30	23	5	4
31	14	2	2
32	14	1	2
33	6	..	..
34	7	..	..
35	1	..	1
36	5	3	1
37	2	..	..
38	1	..	..
39	2	..	..
40	4	1	1
TOTAL	598	561	522
Highest Age	40	40	40
Lowest Age	11	6	11
Average	22.66 years	17.95	19.60

Institutions Other Than Bedford

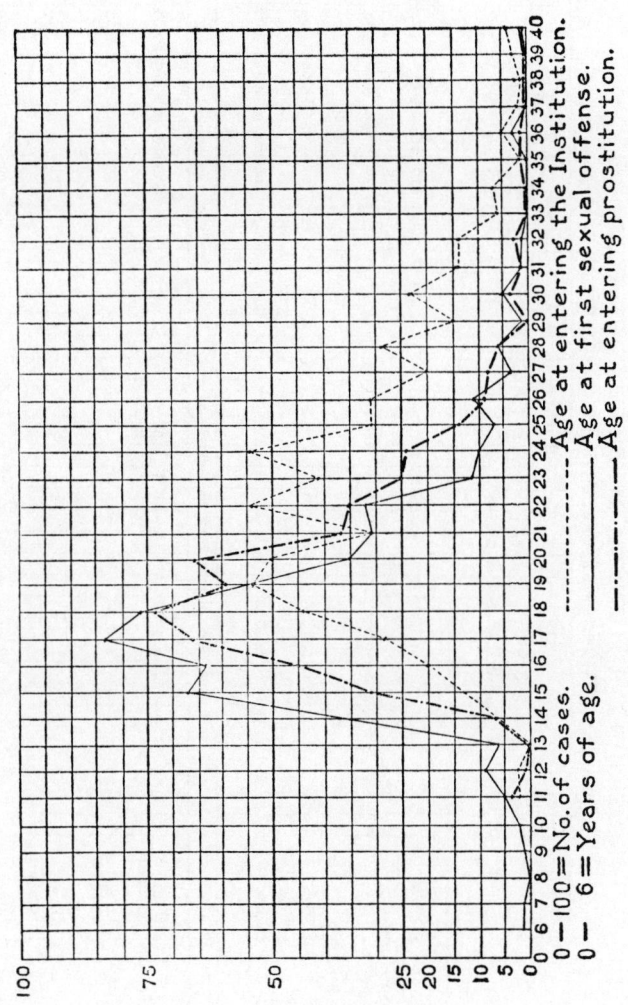

GRAPH ILLUSTRATING TABLE XXXI

Commercialized Prostitution in New York

TABLE XXXII
CASES IN INSTITUTIONS, OTHER THAN BEDFORD
WEEKLY EARNINGS—BEFORE ENTERING PROSTITUTION

		Living	$.50	$1.00	$1.50	$2.00	$2.50	$3.00	$3.50	$4.00	$4.50	$5.00	$5.50	$6.00	$7.00	$8.00	$9.00	$10.00	$11.00	$12.00	$13.00	$14.00	$15.00	$18.00	$20.00	$22.00	$25.00	$30.00	$50.00	$70.00	Highest wage	Lowest wage	Mode, wage of greatest frequency	Average wage	Mode
Wages of Trades excluding Domestic Service	High 377 cases	..	..	1	..	..	..	6	..	5	..	14	..	9	..	4	2	28	4	27	2	4	14	..	7	1	5	1	..	1	$70	$1.00	$6.00	$8.10	$6.00
	Low 377 cases	..	1	2	4	14	14	14	..	20	..	57	..	60	48	22	22	8	..	10	..	1	4	..	..	..	..	1	..	..	30	.50	5.00	5.53	5.00
Wage of Domestic Service	High 156 cases	2	..	..	..	..	..	20	..	17	..	73	..	48	15	22	2	8	..	..	..	1	4	..	4	..	1	1	..	..	20	.50	5.00	3.99	5.00
	Low 156 cases	4	2	7	..	11	22	15	17	19	26	22	7	6	2	..	1	1	..	..	..	1	..	..	..	..	..	..	..	..	14	Liv'g	4.50	3.63	4.50

COMBINED WITH PROSTITUTION

		Living	$.50	$1.00	$1.50	$2.00	$2.50	$3.00	$3.50	$4.00	$4.50	$5.00	$5.50	$6.00	$7.00	$8.00	$9.00	$10.00	$11.00	$12.00	$13.00	$14.00	$15.00	$18.00	$20.00	$22.00	$25.00	$30.00	$50.00	$70.00	Highest wage	Lowest wage	Mode, wage of greatest frequency	Average wage	Mode
Wages of Trades excluding Domestic Service	High 63 cases	..	..	..	..	..	..	2	..	..	..	2	..	..	..	..	..	3	..	6	..	..	6	..	2	..	1	1	..	1	$70	$3.00	$6.00	$9.98	$6.00
	Low 63 cases	..	..	..	..	..	2	2	2	5	..	8	..	12	3	8	2	3	..	..	..	..	3	..	..	..	1	..	..	..	25	3.00	5.00	6.83	5.00
Wage of Domestic Service	High 15 cases	..	..	1	2	..	..	3	..	1	..	3	..	2	2	2	..	..	..	..	..	..	1	..	..	..	..	..	..	..	15	2.00	..	5.10	..
	Low 15 cases	1	..	..	5	..	2	2	..	2	..	4	..	..	2	..	..	1	..	..	..	..	..	..	..	..	..	..	..	..	10	.50	2.50	3.70	2.50

Institutions Other Than Bedford

GRAPH ILLUSTRATING TABLE XXXII
Earnings in Trades excluding Domestic Service

——— Highest wages 377 cases
·········· Lowest wages 377 cases

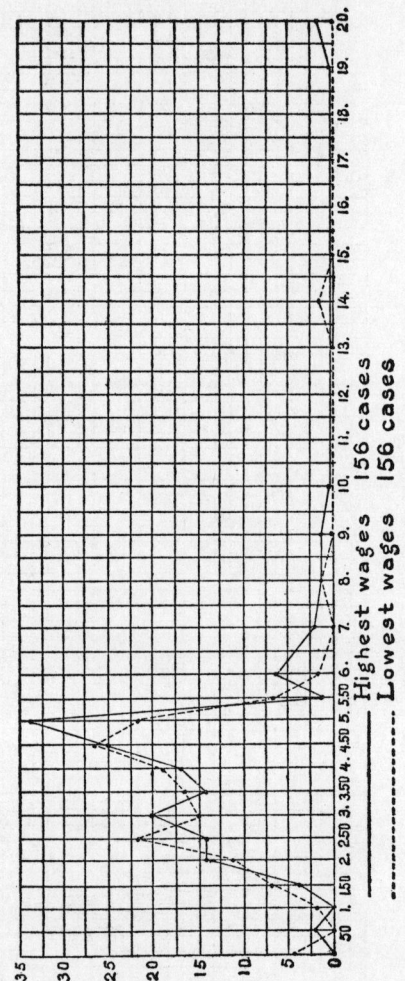

GRAPH ILLUSTRATING TABLE XXXII
Wages in Domestic Service

Institutions Other Than Bedford

TABLE XXXIII

CASES IN INSTITUTIONS, OTHER THAN BEDFORD

SOCIAL RELATIONS

No children		214
Miscarriages and abortions		36
Legitimate children	One .... 28 Two .... 7 Three .... 5 Four .... 1 Five .... 2 Eight 1	44
Illegitimate children	One .... 66 Two .... Three 2	68
Unknown		135
TOTAL NUMBER OF CASES WHERE STATISTICS ARE GIVEN		497

TABLE XXXIV

CASES IN INSTITUTIONS, OTHER THAN BEDFORD

RESIDENCE OF GIRL BEFORE ENTERING PROSTITUTION

Living at home	Giving all they made ...... 66 Giving part 62	128
Living with relatives	Giving all they made ...... 0 Giving part 22	22

BOARDING AMOUNT PAID PER WEEK

$1.00	$1.50	$2.00	$2.50	$3.00	$3.50	$4.00	$4.50	$6.00	
2	4	4	6	31	12	12	9	17	
$5.00	$7.00	$8.00	$10.00						
1	3	..	3						104

Total number cases, where statistics are given 254

Commercialized Prostitution in New York

Table XXXV
CASES IN INSTITUTIONS, OTHER THAN BEDFORD
CAUSE OF FIRST SEXUAL OFFENSE

Love				231	37.86%
Pay	Married	Living with husband	6		
		Separated from husband	10		
		Widow	51		
		Put on street by husband	10	77	12.78%
	Single		48	125	20.49%
Force	Relative		11		
	Lover		5		
	Playmate		3		
	Stranger		43	62	10.16%
Weakness				26	4.26%
Physical predisposition				41	6.72%
Unknown				125	20.49%

TOTAL NUMBER OF CASES 610

Table XXXVI
INSTITUTION CASES, OTHER THAN BEDFORD
PROSTITUTION, PRACTICED CONTINUOUSLY OR OCCASIONALLY

			No. cases	Percent
Continuously			445	72.95
Occasionally	Working girls	48		
	Married women	27	75	12.29
Unknown			14	2.30
Cases omitted, first offenders, etc.			76	12.46

TOTAL NUMBER OF CASES 610

Institutions Other Than Bedford

TABLE XXXVII

CASES IN INSTITUTIONS, OTHER THAN BEDFORD

WEEKLY EARNINGS FROM PROSTITUTION

	Partial Support	Support	0–2	$5	$10	$15	$20	$25	$30	$35	$40	$45	$50	$55	$60
High..	.	.	.	2	1	10	6	20	11	5	5	1	36	.	5
Low..	4	77	3	8	18	21	20	35	11	3	9	.	28	.	4

	$65	$70	$75	$80	$90	$100	$120	$125	$150	$200	$250	$400	$500	Total No. Cases	Average
High..	.	4	18	5	2	41	4	3	20	6	3	2	1	211	$81.91
Low..	.	2	17	10	4	43	.	4	10	1	2	.	.	334	53.06

249

Commercialized Prostitution in New York

Table XXXVIII

CASES IN INSTITUTIONS, OTHER THAN BEDFORD

DISPOSITION OF EARNINGS FROM PROSTITUTION

To lover or any one acting as pimp, except husband { All given	138	
	Part given	9	147
To husband		31
To parents or children		45
To self		216
Unknown		171
	TOTAL	610

Table XXXIX

CASES IN INSTITUTIONS, OTHER THAN BEDFORD

DISEASES INCIDENTAL TO PROSTITUTION
(Clinically Determined)

	Cases	Percent.
No disease	75	47.4
Syphilis	25	
Gonorrhea	49	
Syphilis and gonorrhea	9	52.5
TOTAL NUMBER OF CASES	158	

Only institution cases are counted in which a physical examination has been given. All are taken from the records of Waverly House and the Church Mission of Help. But all of their cases were not examined. That is, out of 158 cases where they deemed an examination desirable 52.5 per cent. were found to be diseased.

Institutions Other Than Bedford

TABLE XL

CASES IN INSTITUTIONS, OTHER THAN BEDFORD

CAUSES. REASONS GIVEN BY THE GIRL

A. *In connection with her family*
1. Neglect or abuse 41
2. Immorality of parents 25
3. Over strictness 21
4. Over indulgence 3
5. Poverty 27
6. Incompatibility (quarrels, nagging, etc.) 27
7. Father, mother or near relative put girl in life . . . 6
8. Turned out of the house . . . . 18 — 168

B. *In connection with married life*
1. Incompatibility 8
2. Non-support 24
3. Immorality (including cruelty or criminality) . . . 29
4. Desertion 12
5. Death 16
6. Husband put girl in the life . . . . 26 —115

C. *Personal reasons*
1. "Ruined anyway" 15
2. Lover put girl in the life 80
3. Desertion by lover 33
4. White slave (put into life by force) 21
5. Bad company 108
6. Dances and shows 23
7. Love of excitement or a good time 58
8. Lazy, won't work 12
9. Love of money (a business enterprise) 3
10. Idle or lonely 0
11. No sex instruction 6
12. Ashamed to go home after first escapade 23
13. Not satisfied with one man 7
14. "Born bad"—enjoys the life 2
15. Previous use of drugs or drink 11
16. Stage environment 9
17. Tired of drudgery (usually housework) 16
18. "Easy money" 58
19. Love of clothes . . . . 7 —492

TABLE XL—*Continued*

D. *Economic reasons*
1. Can't support herself 67
2. Can't support herself and children or parents . . . 37
3. Can't live according to her standards 17
4. Out of work, can't get work (often because of). . . 60
5. Ill health or defect 53
6. Not trained for skilled work and above the unskilled   2   236

TOTAL   1011

GRAPH ILLUSTRATING TABLE XLI

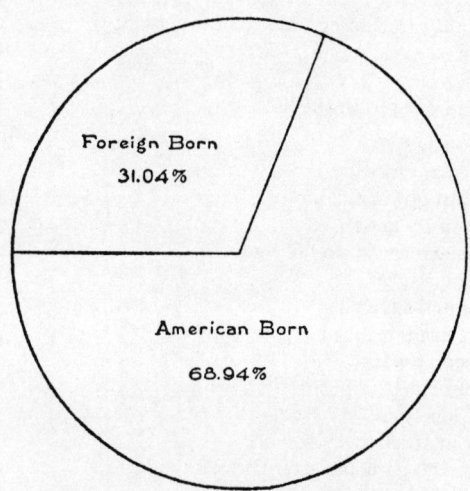

252

Street Cases

TABLE XLI
STREET CASES
BIRTHPLACE

American Born		Foreign Born	
New York City	234	Austria-Hungary	35
Brooklyn	20	Belgium	1
Staten Island	1	Bohemia	1
Other cities in New York	36	Canada	13
New York State (country)	53	Denmark	1
California	8	England-Scotland	32
Colorado	5	France	13
Connecticut	26	Galacia	12
Delaware	2	Germany	72
District of Columbia	1	Ireland	29
Florida	2	Italy	8
Georgia	2	Holland	1
Illinois	14	Poland	4
Indiana	1	Russia	107
Iowa	1	Roumania	7
Kansas	2	Sweden	5
Kentucky	10	Switzerland	3
Louisiana	5		
Maryland	8	TOTAL	
Maine	3	Foreign born	344 31.04%
Massachusetts	25	American born	762 68.94%
Michigan	13		
Mississippi	1	GRAND TOTAL, 1106	
Missouri	10		
Nebraska	1		
New Hampshire	2		
New Jersey	63		
Ohio	35		
Pennsylvania	95		
Rhode Island	6		
South Carolina	3		
Tennessee	2		
Texas	4		
Vermont	7		
Virginia	20		
Washington	1		
West Virginia	6		
Wisconsin	3		
Unknown	31		

TOTAL AMERICAN BORN, 762

Commercialized Prostitution in New York

TABLE XLII

STREET CASES

EDUCATION	No. Girls
Does not read or write in any language	127
Reads and writes a foreign language	10
Reads and writes English, no further education	687
Reads and writes, how much more not given	222
Graduated from grammar grades, at least	46
Some special education { 4 stenographers, 2 translators, 1 linguist }	7
TOTAL NUMBER CASES	*1099

*Note: 7 cards, no information.

TABLE XLIII

STREET CASES

PROSTITUTION. PRACTICED CONTINUOUSLY OR OCCASIONALLY

	No. Cases	Percent.
Continuously	1049	94.84+
Occasionally { Working girls 26, Married women 7 }	33	2.98+
Unknown	24	2.17+
TOTAL NUMBER CASES	1106	

Street Cases

Table XLIV
STREET CASES
AGE

Years of age	Number at present age	First sexual offense	Number entering prostitution
6	...	2	1
8	...	2	..o
10	...	2	..o
12	...	11	...
13	...	3	...
14	...	71	6
15	...	85	26
16	...	167	114
17	1	189	176
18	12	147	223
19	40	94	123
20	66	61	110
21	88	38	72
22	131	29	44
23	137	15	22
24	205	15	30
25	57	15	21
26	98	15	23
27	46	8	11
28	74	5	10
29	44	...	...
30	36	3	2
31	3	...	...
32	15	1	3
33	7	1	1
34	13	...	...
35	8	1	1
36	3	...	...
37	...	1	1
38	2	1	1
40	11	...	...
42	1	...	...
44	3	...	...
49	2	...	...
50	3	...	...
Not given	...	124	81
TOTAL	1106	1106	1106
Highest Age	50	38	38
Lowest Age	17	6	14
Average	25 62+ yrs.	17.87+ yrs.	19.44 yrs.
Mode	24	11	18
Mean	33.5	22	25

Commercialized Prostitution in New York

TABLE XLV
STREET CASES
WEEKLY EARNINGS FROM PROSTITUTION

Weekly Earnings	Highest	Lowest
$75.00	76	17
$70.00	39	6
$65.00	21	7
$60.00	80	23
$55.00	38	12
$50.00	90	81
$45.00	34	24
$40.00	73	53
$35.00	12	64
$30.00	25	80
$25.00	23	75
$20.00	22	103
$15.00	5	58
$10.00	2	85
$5–$7	..	59
0–$3	..	23
Support	3	19
Partial Support	..	..

Weekly Earnings	Highest	Lowest
$1,000	1	..
$500.00	6	..
$400.00	3	..
$300.00	15	..
$250.00	20	2
$200.00	86	1
$175.00	9	..
$150.00	84	10
$125.00	22	4
$120.00	..	..
$110.00	22	..
$100.00	103	43
$95.00	2	..
$90.00	22	4
$85.00	23	..
$80.00	19	10
No. Cases Used	1022	863
Average	97.725	35.80

Street Cases

TABLE XLVI
STREET CASES
OCCUPATIONS

	Before Entering Prostitution	After Entering Prostitution
Artist	4	4
Artists' model	2	3
Canvasser	5	4
Chambermaid	9	1
Clerk in small store	28	16
Companion	1	1
Department store	117	68
Errand girl	1	....
Factory	72	21
Domestic service	27	20
Laundry	2	....
Librarian	1	....
Manicure	6	4
Massage	2	2
Millinery	13	2
Nurse girl	8	1
Office work	25	18
Palmist	2	2
Sewing	17	5
Stenographer	31	27
Storekeeper	1	2
Teacher	9	6
Telephone operator	9	5
Theatrical work	72	88
Trained nurse	4	3
Translator	1	1
Waitress	18	8
No work	518	....
Unknown	101	33
Supported by prostitution only	....	677
Supported by husband or family	....	83
Stealing	....	1
TOTAL NUMBER CASES	1106	1106

Commercialized Prostitution in New York

TABLE XLVII

STREET CASES

CAUSES OF FIRST SEXUAL OFFENSE

Love			441	39.87%
Pay	Married	Living with husband	51	
		Separated from husband	41	
		Widow	33	
		Put on street by husband	28	153	13.84%
	Single		116	269	10.49%
Force by	Relative		26	2.35%
	Lover		1	.09%
	Playmate		2	.18%
	Stranger		32	2.89%
Weakness (yielded to importunities)			34	3.07%
Physical predisposition			84	7.60%
Unknown			217	19.62%
		TOTAL NUMBER CASES	1106	

Street Cases

Table XLVIII
STREET CASES
CAUSES. REASONS GIVEN BY THE GIRL

A. *In connection with her family*
  1. Neglect or abuse 20
  2. Immorality of parents 36
  3. Over strictness 52
  4. Over indulgence 11
  5. Poverty 36
  6. Incompatibility (quarrels, nagging, etc.) 20
  7. No mother or no father, or neither 12
  8. Father, mother or near relative put girl in the life . . 10
  9. Turned out of the house 21   218

B. *In connection with married life*
  1. Incompatibility 31
  2. Non-support 34
  3. Immorality (including cruelty or criminality) . . . 39
  4. Desertion 34
  5. Death 14
  6. Put girl in the life 61   213

C. *Personal reasons*
  1. Ruined anyway 32
  2. Lover put girl in the life 144
  3. Desertion by lover 40
  4. White slave (put in life by force) 6
  5. Bad company 61
  6. Dances and shows 1
  7. Love of excitement or a good time 103
  8. Lazy, won't work 49
  9. Love of money (a business enterprise) 50
  10. Idle or lonely 19
  11. Ashamed to go home after first escapade 13
  12. "Born bad"—enjoys the life 116
  13. Previous use of drugs or drink 1
  14. Stage environment 36
  15. Tired of drudgery (usually housework) 42
  16. "Easy money" 58
  17. Love of clothes 85   866

D. *Economic reasons*
  1. Can't support herself 33
  2. Can't support herself and children or parents . . . 55
  3. Out of work 42
  4. Ill health or defect 9   139

                                             Total   1436

In many cases, more than one reason was given, which explains the large *total*.

TABLE XLIX

RANK NUMERICALLY OF DIFFERENT COUNTRIES CONTRIBUTING TO POPULATION OF NEW YORK CITY COMPARED WITH THEIR CONTRIBUTIONS TOWARD 2363 PROSTITUTES

I	II	III	IV	V
Foreign born population of New York City	Bedford 647 cases 156 foreign born	Other Institutions 610 cases 175 foreign born	Street Prostitutes 1106 cases 344 foreign born	Combined 2363 cases 664 foreign born
1. Russia	Russia	Russia	Russia	Russia
2. Italy	Austria-Hungary	Austria-Hungary	Germany	Germany
3. Germany	Germany	Germany	Austria-Hungary	Austria-Hungary
4. Austria-Hungary	Ireland	Ireland	England-Scotland	Ireland
5. Ireland	England-Scotland	England-Scotland	Ireland	England-Scotland
6. England-Scotland	France	Canada	France-Canada (equal)	France-Canada (equal)
7. France	Italy	Italy	Italy	Italy
8.		France		

Combined Cases

TABLE L

COMPOSITION OF THE POPULATION OF NEW YORK CITY AS TO BIRTHPLACE COMPARED WITH BIRTHPLACE OF 2363 PROSTITUTES

	I	II	III	IV
Population of New York City	*1910** 4,766,883	Percentage of population	Prostitutes 2363 cases	Percentage of prostitutes
Native White	2,741,504	57.3%	1586	67.1
Foreign White	1,927,720	40.43	664	28.0
Negro	91,702	1.92	113	4.78
All other	5,957	.12	..	..
Of the foreign born		*Percent. entire pop.*		
Russia	485,600	10.18	197	8.33
Italy	340,400	7.14	21	.88
Germany	279,200	5.85	122	5.12
Austria-Hungary	265,500	5.57	110	4.65
Ireland	252,500	5.29	58	2.45
England-Scotland	104,100	2.18	57	2.41
France	18,200	.38	25	1.05
Canada	....	,.	25	1.05

*Preliminary Bulletin issued by U. S. Census Bureau (Census of 1910) Dec. 29, 1911.

TABLE LI

COMPARISON OF EARNINGS AT PREVIOUS OCCUPATIONS OF BEDFORD CASES WITH THOSE OF OTHER INSTITUTIONS AND WITH THE STREET CASES

		Average		
Bedford	Domestic service	High $4.50 / Low 3.00	with board	52 cases / 52 "
	Other occupations	High 8.00 / Low 4.00		110 " / 100 "
Other Institutions	Domestic service	High 5.00 / Low 4.50	with board	156 " / 156 "
	Other occupations	High 6.00 / Low 5.00		377 " / 377 "
Street Cases	Domestic service	High 5.43 / Low 4.29	with board	30 " / 27 "
	Other occupations	High 13.92 / Low 9.88		420 " / 332 "

TOTAL CASES CONSIDERED:
Domestic service 238
Other occupations . . . . 907—1145

CHAPTER X

PREVENTIVE, REFORMATIVE, AND CORRECTIONAL AGENCIES IN NEW YORK CITY

THE agencies working to meet the need of wayward and professional delinquent women and girls in New York City are both private and public, direct and indirect. Work in this field can rarely be strictly characterized as either preventive, reformative or correctional. Almost all the agencies in question do both a preventive and a reformative work, though, in the main, the tendency toward preventive work is stronger than that toward rescue work. The following account is not exhaustive, but aims to deal with the representative institutions in each field.

(a) THE WORK OF PREVENTION

Preventive agencies cover a very wide range, beginning of course with the home and family, the school and the church; but important as these and similar institutions are, they are too general to come within the scope of this chapter. There are, however, certain societies and institutions which exert a potent though indirect influence,— among them the New York Society for the Suppression of Vice, the Society for the Prevention of Crime and the New York Society for the Prevention of Cruelty to Children. A few institutions render more direct serv-

Commercialized Prostitution in New York

ice,— the Association for Befriending Children and Young Girls and the Children's Aid Society, for example. These, with the Home for the Friendless, the Sheltering Arms, the girls' departments of the Catholic Protectorate, the Juvenile Asylum, and other organizations maintain homes for the young. There are, moreover, numerous settlements with a hold on the young through kindergartens, clubs, and friendly services, doing a quiet but constantly effective preventive work; independent girls' clubs, thirty special ones in New York, providing opportunities for friendship, recreation and training; some societies, such as the Girls' Friendly, offering attractions to girls who have few advantages in their homes. The work of the Committee on Amusements and Vacation Resources of Working Girls has been active in the difficult dance hall problem, previously shown to be an important factor in the exploitation of prostitution. The Travelers' Aid Society, which assists incoming women of all classes at railway stations and docks, is a valuable safeguard. This society definitely helped 18,562 persons in the year 1912. Of these, 5,161 were from seventeen to twenty-five years of age, and nearly all women. The Council of Jewish Women, active along similar lines, in 1912 aided 10,120 women and children entering the port of New York. Of these, 6,101 were unmarried girls; 1,533 were illiterate. Personal care is bestowed on every case; the girls are located suitably and afterwards visited. Similar work for traveling colored girls is done by a department of the National League on Urban Conditions among Negroes. The Big Sisters assist girls who have already come to the point of grave danger. Work-

Preventive Agencies

ing along the lines already marked out by the big Brothers' Movement, women of devoted abilities are taking little girls who have already yielded to temptation and endeavoring to win them to useful lives.

Homes for working girls and women, though touching this need indirectly, touch it strongly. There are many of these homes, maintained by philanthropic and religious boards of women; seventeen hundred women are accommodated in them. Their economic value has long been realized; their moral and social importance is beginning to be appreciated. Their usefulness as preventive agencies probably varies with the degree of experience, resourcefulness, and sympathy possessed by those who are directly in charge.

Among the more definitely preventive agencies may be mentioned, first, societies of a national scope which aim to create healthy sentiment by emphasizing the grave dangers of the social evil. Such are the American Federation of Sex Hygiene and the Society of Sanitary and Moral Prophylaxis, operating through meetings, lectures and printed matter; the American Vigilance Association, which, originally organized to secure legislation and law enforcement as respects the white slave traffic, has now extended its operations so that it is actively engaged in a propaganda that touches the entire field of commercialized vice; it publishes a monthly periodical, *Vigilance*.

Prominent among local organizations is the Committee of Fourteen, originally organized for the suppression of the Raines Law Hotels, now occupied in combating all manifestations of commercialized sexual vice in New York. It endeavors to secure more vigorous and effective action by all departments of state and city government having power to suppress vice; and it also strives to improve conditions in saloons and hotels through the influence and control over such places exercised by brewers and surety companies.

Two societies doing important work in other lines are strongly interested in educational preventive work — the New York Probation Association and the Church Mission of Help. Both make special appeal to churches, to societies, and to clubs of women. The Probation Association organizes among working girls protective leagues, fourteen of which leagues have been started. Their main purpose is to secure the help of girls in protecting other girls. They endeavor to raise the tone of conversation in places where girls assemble and work. Lectures on sex hygiene are given, wholesome recreation is encouraged, and higher ideals of life cultivated. The Church Mission of Help organizes bands of women, principally in Episcopal churches, to study the needs of wayward girls and to give help as they are able. Both of these societies encourage parents, guardians, and girls in need to come to them for advice and help, thus making their work more personal.

The foregoing direct agencies mainly exert their preventive influence on the public *en masse*. The more definite and concrete examples of preventive work appear in the work of homes which concern themselves with individuals in distress. They take girls, some of them very young girls, who are subject to bad influences, who are incorrigible, or who for various reasons find difficulty in their home life. Of such homes there are several.

Preventive Agencies

Those reaching the larger numbers are represented by the Children's Department of the House of Mercy and the House of the Good Shepherd. For colored girls the work on the larger scale is done by the Howard Orphan Asylum, which maintains a house at Kings Park, Long Island. The smaller homes, of which there are at least six in New York, deal more personally with the individual girl. Their capacity ranges from 25 to 75. Of this type is the Free Home for Young Girls, managed by an incorporated association of church women. The inmates, mostly sent by guardians and friends, are from eleven to seventeen years of age. A real home life is maintained. Most of the girls attend the public schools. All are taught sewing, simple cooking, laundry work, and housework. They remain two or three years and are sent out to friends or to situations with approved surroundings. In Brooklyn the Training School and Home for Young Girls cares for and trains girls by a method similar to that of the Free Home. Two of these homes are partly preventive and partly reformative — the House of the Holy Family and the Washington Square Home. The first named is conducted by the Association for Befriending Young Girls, under the immediate charge of the Sisters of the Divine Compassion, and cares for 75 young girls, mostly Roman Catholics. Instruction in ordinary school branches is given. Physical exercises, manual training, and domestic science are taught. Special attention is given to the matter of amusements; religious as well as friendly care is provided. Provision is made for all girls leaving the home. Correspondence with Sisters and visits to the home are encouraged. This home cared for 177 girls in 1912.

The Washington Square Home is a non-sectarian institution. It provides a home for indefinite periods for girls who have erred or who are in danger of so doing. They come voluntarily to the home. Twenty-seven can be accommodated and the home is usually full. Of the 64 received in 1912, fifty were Protestants, 12 Roman Catholics, and 2 Hebrews. The average age of the girls is 18. Instruction in housework, laundry, and plain sewing is given. Girls are kept as long as necessary to train for self-support.

All these homes maintain good discipline and friendly relations. The girls usually go out equipped to live and with a strong appreciation of what has been done for them. Unfortunately their facilities are very limited in consequence of the meager resources. Usually from three to eight girls occupy a room when, as a matter of principle, each girl should be given her own cubicle. Moreover, the capacity is far below what is required.[1] Even as it is, valuable preventive results have been accomplished in case of those girls who have been reached.

(b) REFORMATIVE WORK

The border line between preventive and reformative work is in theory definite and clear; in practice, as illustrated by institutions, it is rather hazy. These institutions and homes endeavor to help women who have actually yielded to temptation or to force of circumstances.

[1] See page 281.

Preventive Agencies

They are susceptible of division along several lines. Some are small, under religious or private control, and for the most part reach the less demoralized class. There are also larger establishments, which receive both girls committed by the court and girls who enter voluntarily. Among the former may be mentioned the Margaret Strachan Home, the Midnight Mission and St. Michael's Home, and the New Shelter for Young Women, quite recently opened.

The Margaret Strachan Home cares for 24 girls temporarily. They come voluntarily, through doctors and mission friends, remain from one to six months, receive certain training under religious influences, and are sent out to maternity hospitals or to friends. There were 80 girls in the home in 1911, most of them under twenty years of age. For twenty-nine years this home has been conducted under the management of an association of religious women. The Wayside Home in Brooklyn provides a home for friendless girls and serves as a reformatory for Protestant young girls in Kings County. It emphasizes home care and practical training.

The St. Michael's Home is at Mamaroneck. It is operated under the Protestant Episcopal Church by the Sisters of St. John the Baptist. It cares for 60 girls at a time, most of them for the space of two years. Instruction in school branches and in housework and home making is given. Girls come through parents and guardians, a few by commitment. Many of them are discovered by the missionary visitor. They go out to proper places equipped for usefulness.

Of the larger institutions there are four,— the House

of the Good Shepherd, the House of Mercy, the New York Magdalen Benevolent Society and the Ozanam Home for Friendless Women. All of these receive wayward women of all kinds, and the House of the Good Shepherd and the House of Mercy receive little girls from dangerous surroundings. While they do not seek for committed cases, such are accepted. The Magdalen Society is the oldest home of this kind, having been founded in 1833.

The Ozanam Home in Brooklyn under the leadership of Roman Catholic women offers shelter and help to those who wish to reform. The work is of a temporary nature in that inmates do not as a rule remain in the home over three weeks. In the year 1912, six hundred and sixty-seven were cared for at public charges and 198 at private charges.

The House of the Good Shepherd can care for 500 women and girls, making it the largest institution of the kind. No account is taken of race, color, or creed, although probably the majority of its wards are Catholic. The girls are divided into classes according to their condition and purpose of entering the institution. Some look forward to giving their lives to religious service; others are to be trained for useful work and to be discharged when it is best. Volunteers leave at any time. The training covers usual school work, laundry, cooking, embroidery and lace making. Physical and recreational needs are cared for.

The House of Mercy does a similar work under the guidance of the Protestant Episcopal Church. The capacity of this house is 110. At the close of 1910 there

Preventive Agencies

were 107 inmates. These come, some of free will, others by commitment. The department for women is entirely separate from that for young girls, which, conducted as the work of St. Agnes Guild, is referred to above. The women are given practical training in domestic service and do the work of the large laundry which is a source of income. Attention is given to recreation, religious training and to the life after leaving the institution.

The Magdalen Benevolent Society Home cares for about 100 women, the larger part of whom are committed by magistrates. Erring women under 30 years of age also come voluntarily into the home for six months or more. Suitable school and practical training is given, physical and recreational wants are met, moral influences are exerted, and women go out to situations approved by the management. Unmarried mothers with babies are received and trained. This home is non-sectarian in its management and in its work.

All institutions dealing with erring women have to receive in larger or smaller numbers unmarried girls expecting to become mothers. There are, however, certain homes specially devoted to this class of women. The Heartsease Work for Friendless Women in this city, the St. Faith's Home at Tarrytown, and Lakeview House at Arrochar, Staten Island, are perhaps the best examples. To these the girls come voluntarily or are directed by relatives, friends and charitable workers. St. Faith's Home, though smallest in capacity and in total numbers cared for during the year, is representative in respect to the policy pursued. From 15 to 17 can be accommodated, and 39 girls were cared for in 1912, twenty-four of whom were received during that year. Mothers with their children are kept for two years in most cases. They are taught all kinds of home work and especially nursery work. Instruction in the fundamental branches of school work is given as well as lessons in hygiene, in dress, and in the expenditure of and accounting for money. Safe places are provided for all leaving the home. The home is managed by a board of women and an advisory board of men. It is largely supported by Episcopalians and the work is done by members of that church.

Lakeview Home, operated under the direction of the Council of Jewish Women, does a similar work for Hebrew girls. It emphasizes industrial training and personal work. It cares for 25 women and girls and 24 infants at a time. The total number cared for in 1912 was 60 girls and 45 infants.

The Heartsease Work is undenominational, though definitely religious. In addition to the care of women with babies, it provides a temporary home for erring women and endeavors to fit women for work. It cared for 204 cases in the year 1911-12. Forty were mothers with infants, 61 were girls becoming mothers, 14 girls were convalescing, and 20 girls were seeking employment. There were 9 infants without mothers. The home provides classes for instruction, social entertainments, and religious services.

Definite work to reform this class of women done by three religious organizations may be mentioned here,— that of the Chinatown Settlement, the Rescue Mission in Doyers Street, and of the Salvation Army. These organizations are in a position to touch those more deeply

Preventive Agencies

involved in vice; but the majority of the girls they reach are not prostitutes.

The Chinatown Settlement offers a home and friendly relations to girls drawn into Chinatown. It affords entertainments, religious teaching, and practical training. It brings to the home an average of 75 different girls per month. Two thousand calls on girls were made in 1912. It has a small country place for summer use.

The Rescue Society reaches girls through mission services, clubs, and classes. Two thousand, seven hundred and forty-eight women were touched by the services in 1911.

The Salvation Army maintains rescue and industrial homes in Manhattan and Brooklyn, as it does in all the chief cities of the land. The home in Manhattan cares for 50 women and is always full. Some midnight rescue work is done; but the girls actually taken from the streets are few. This work, which formerly depended largely upon religious results in meetings, now accomplishes more by personal influence of workers. The girls are of all nationalities, their average age, 25. So far as possible, the different classes are separated in the home. Of 115 inmates in one year 60 were betrayal cases, 19 were cases of prostitution, and 27 girls were under serious temptation. Capable girls are trained and sent out to service. The leaders state that perhaps 80 percent are reformed. The Army also maintains a home at Tappan on the Hudson for young girls about to become mothers. This work was formerly the Door of Hope and is still in charge of Mrs. Whittemore. The Army also does a preventive work for young girls on its farm in Spring Valley.

Commercialized Prostitution in New York

The two homes that probably touch the problem of the prostitute and commercialized traffic in women more closely than any others are Waverly House and the Florence Crittenton Home. The leaders in these homes are in close relation to the magistrates' courts and both take care of witnesses in white slave cases pending in the Federal Court.

Waverly House is under the management of the New York Probation Association. It accommodates 18 girls, who come through the courts, as above mentioned, and through philanthropic and religious organizations. Two hundred and nine were cared for in the house in 1912. They remained from one day to three months, for Waverly House is a temporary home and not a reformatory. Most of the girls are young, the largest group between sixteen and eighteen. With the exception of the court witnesses, girls are placed in such permanent institutions or positions as will meet their needs. Personal attention and careful study are most prominent in this house. Classes in the useful arts, English, and music are provided. One night each week is "play night," and entertainments of all kinds are provided. The higher spiritual truths are brought to the girls through a Sunshine Circle. Through the Employment Bureau the girls of the house, as well as many who have been arrested, those in moral danger, and many difficult and incorrigible girls, find situations.

The Florence Crittenton Mission in this city is one of many homes of the same name situated in the larger cities of this country. It formerly engaged in a rescue mission work for both men and women. Its work is now limited

Preventive Agencies

to the care of erring women. The home contains 16 rooms, each occupied by two or more persons. The girls are probationers, girls released on suspended sentences, witnesses in white slave cases, and women discharged by the courts; a few come from cafés and from the streets. During an entire year, 501 girls passed through the home, some staying but a few hours, others remaining for the year. They range in age from fourteen to twenty-five years. A night school is maintained, as well as classes in physical culture and the useful arts. A Helping Hand Class makes scrap books and small articles for sick children. The pleasure side of life is met by entertainments, and religious services are regularly held. The disposition of the 501 girls above mentioned was as follows:

Situations	183
Sent home	185
Deported	17
In care of organizations	58
Committed to institutions	19
Left against wishes	17
In Home	22
	501

The work is financed and managed by the National Florence Crittenton Mission.

Though not placed strictly under the reformative heading, certain fundamental phases of the work of the Probation Association and the Church Mission of Help may here be presented. As stated above, the sphere of these societies is largely that of clearing houses. They study carefully the girls who come to them and make of them the disposition best suited to their needs. The time of study allows opportunities for personal helpfulness and it is well improved.

Commercialized Prostitution in New York

The Church Mission of Help began its work by a prolonged study of 229 cases of wayward girls who were more or less connected with the Episcopal Church. Parental and good home conditions were sadly lacking in most cases. On the basis of this study the society began its work of information to the church and of helpfulness to the girls. During the year 1912 it was in touch with 352 girls, of whom 148 were under its direct care, 58 were cared for on leaving institutions, and 103 were in institutions. Two hundred and six of these girls were connected with the Episcopal Church. Twelve other religious bodies were represented, while a small number of the girls had no religious affiliations. All cases are referred, where possible, to the churches with which they are or were connected. The work of this society is largely personal. Besides locating girls in homes and institutions, employment is found for those fitted for it. Some court work is done. In addition to paid workers, an increasing number of trained volunteers are being used. Besides the care of the church girl and the work of education and prevention done by this society, its service of visitation in institutions is most valuable. The visits of sympathetic women to girls in institutions pave the way for a useful service in their social reinstatement later.

The wider work of the New York Probation Association, which deserves mention here, is in the form of a careful study of all the cases with which it has to do. A thorough physical examination is given each girl by a physician. A mental examination follows and cases are placed under the direct supervision of a skilled neurologist and psychologist. Careful records of all facts

Preventive Agencies

are kept. The discovery of physical and mental weakness, often after prolonged study, leads to a definite course of action. Such scientific results are not only valuable in the practical treatment of the individual girl, but furnish a basis on which the courts act, and are of wide usefulness to the student of the conditions which lead to moral delinquency.

(c) CORRECTIONAL WORK

There are three main correctional agencies in New York City: the New York State Training School for Girls at Hudson, the State Reformatory for Women at Bedford and the Workhouse. A real work of correction is also accomplished in the case of those committed to the House of the Good Shepherd, the House of Mercy, and the Magdalen Benevolent Society Home. The State Farm for Women, to be situated at Valatie, is not yet established, and the House of Detention, in connection with the Night Court for women, which would serve as an intermediary to correctional agencies, is not yet available.

The New York State Reformatory for Women at Bedford Hills, New York, was opened for commitment in May, 1901. It is supported entirely by state appropriations. It receives women between the ages of sixteen and thirty years from the First, Second, Third and Ninth Judicial District, *i. e.*, Greater New York, Long Island and the tier of counties on each side of the Hudson River as far north as Albany. Over 80 percent of its inmates come from Greater New York. A woman of suitable age may be committed by any judge or magistrate for any offense over which he has jurisdiction, except murder in the first and second degrees, provided, however, that the woman has not previously been convicted of a felony.

The institution is situated in the heart of Westchester County — 39 miles north of New York City. Here the State owns 192 acres of land and leases an additional 57 acres. It has at the present time a capacity for 340 inmates, with a population of 505; the expenditure for maintenance last year was $4.06 per week per capita. It is built on the cottage plan. This permits of classification, whereby the younger girls are separated from the older women and the less innocent from the more hardened offenders.

The idea of the institution is that of a good industrial school. There are book schools in which the inmates receive instruction in reading, writing, arithmetic, nature study, etc. Physiology and sex hygiene are taught by the resident physician. All the work of the farm, including the care of the cattle, pigs and other live-stock, is performed by the inmates, with the exception of the plowing. Much out-door work of a constructive character is carried on, both for its physical effects and for mental and moral results. In this constructive work is included a milk house, silo, stairways and sidewalks made of concrete. Industrial training in laundry work, various branches of needle work, cooking and other branches of domestic science is given. The inmates have musical and dramatic clubs. Their religious needs are met by services conducted by clergymen of their respective denominations.

The Board of Managers constitute a Board of Parole

Preventive Agencies

and while the inmates are all committed for a maximum of three years, they may be paroled at any time, if in the judgment of the Board of Managers, such action is considered to be for their best interest. Parole officers find suitable homes and suitable work for the paroled women and follow them up carefully until the expiration of the parole period.

The New York State Training School receives girls under sixteen years of age from the entire state. Those from New York City come through the Children's Court. The equipment of the school is very good, the chief need being for more room. The cottage system used accommodates 385 girls, in separate sleeping rooms. It is, however, necessary to use other buildings and parts of buildings for housing purposes. The households are practically independent of each other, thereby offering, as far as possible, the conditions and spirit of a real home.

The methods of work and the life in the school are most commendable. A personal and individual interest in each girl is manifest from the time of commitment through the school life and for years after the school is left. By careful study each one is placed in the cottage and environment where she will receive the most help and the best training. Changes to insure development are made, as necessary. A girl's grading depends on her conduct and proficiency. Discipline is varied, with the principle always in mind that the individual and not the offense is to be treated. Humiliation and loss of self-respect are avoided, if possible. The living conditions and training seem excellent. The girls do the cottage work, changes being so arranged as to give all a thorough experience in housework. School sessions of fifteen hours weekly in the morning and eight weekly in the afternoon prevail. The morning session is the book school, the afternoon the industrial school. Cooking, plain sewing, dressmaking, physical culture, gardening, and vocal music are carefully taught. Religious instruction is given by representatives of various churches under direction of the state. Amusements are afforded at proper times, are well arranged and heartily indulged in. That there is a spirit of pride and enthusiasm in work and a feeling of happiness in the life is quite believable when one realizes that so many old girls wish to visit the school that they cannot be accommodated. The records show that the delinquent girl of normal mind can be and is cured. Girls of sub-normal mind are still to some extent cared for in this school; but they should be in a special institution.

The Workhouse receives about 75 percent of all women prisoners convicted of offenses related to prostitution in the magistrates' courts in this city. In the year 1912, three thousand, five hundred and thirteen women charged with soliciting and loitering were committed to the Workhouse for periods up to six months. About 50 percent of these, as shown by the fingerprint process, are repeaters, each of whom had been arrested from two to eight times. The life in the Workhouse is generally conceded to be not only useless but actually harmful. The Chief Magistrate of the city has stated in print the following: " The present Workhouse, through no fault of the Commissioner or its officers, is a poor

Preventive Agencies

place for these women. The building does not meet the requirements for these cases. A new institution should be provided; not a lounging, unsanitary place, but a real workhouse, looking to reformation as well as punishment."

The reformatories in 1912 received through the courts 286 women. To Bedford were committed, 108; to the House of Mercy, 4; to the House of the Good Shepherd, 100; to the Magdalen Home, 74. Most, though not all these cases, were strictly related to prostitution. Through the Children's Court of the city, of the 120 cases charged with tendency to moral depravity and convicted in the year 1912, sixty-two were committed to institutions and 58 were placed on probation. Girls under sixteen committed to the House of the Good Shepherd numbered 64, to the House of Mercy, 57, and to the Training School at Hudson, 32; but not all of these cases involved immorality.

The following table summarizes the institutions for friendless and wayward girls, in so far as they are described in the text; though numerous, their capacity and resources are obviously quite inadequate to the need:

Preventive Agencies

Name	Object	Capacity	Total Cared For 1 Year	Sources of Support	Expenses
Heartsease Work	Prevention and reformation	25	204	Contributions	$ 3,300
House of the Holy Family	Prevention and reformation	75	177	City grant, contributions, sewing-room, etc.	13,850
Washington Square Home for Friendless Girls	Prevention and reformation	27	85	Investments, city grant, contributions	6,160
Margaret Strachan Home	Reformation of first cases. Training	24	80	Investments, contributions	3,238
House of the Good Shepherd	Protection and reformation	500	880	County grants, industrial dept.	100,690
House of Mercy	Protection and reformation	110	183	Investments, city grant, laundry, etc., contributions	22,247
New York Magdalen Benevolent Society	Reformation	106	237	City grants, laundry, etc., contributions	27,690
St. Michael's Home	Reformation and training	60	88	Investments, contributions	8,000
Waverley House	Temporary care	26	209	Contributions, investments, fees	22,371
Salvation Army Rescue Home	Reformation and training	50	115	Sewing, room, etc., contributions	7,652
Door of Hope	Shelter and reformation	25	56	Contributions, sewing	3,451
Chinatown and Bowery Settlement	Care and reformation	6	84	Contributions	3,059
Florence Crittenton Mission	Reformation	36	907	Contributions	9,319
New Shelter	Reformation	20	140	Private patron	
St. Faith's Home	Shelter and reformation	17	31	Contributions	7,404
Lakeview Home	Care for first offenders	25	60 (plus 45 infants)	Subscriptions, contributions	8,476
St. Katherine's Homes	Shelter and reformation	13	13 (plus 13 infants)	Subscriptions and contributions	3,531
Ozanam Home for Friendless Women	Care and reformation	100	865	City grants, industrial dept., contributions	8,957
Wayside Home	Reformation and training	21	67	City grants, contributions	
Free Home for Young Girls	Care and prevention	30	53	Invests. funds, contrib't's	5,402
Brooklyn School and Home for Young Girls	Care and prevention	30	94	City grants, contributions	8,000
New York State Training School for Girls	Correction and reformation	335	440	State grants	99,278
State Reformatory for Women	Correction and reformation	340 Daily average, 422.	763	State grants	89,721

Appendices

Appendices

Appendix

APPENDIX I

SUMMARY OF PLACES IN MANHATTAN WHERE PROSTITUTION WAS FOUND TO EXIST DURING PERIOD OF INVESTIGATION (JANUARY 24TH TO NOVEMBER 15TH, 1912)

Places	Number of Buildings	Different Vice Resorts in Them	Number of Investigations Made
Parlor Houses	142	142	441
Massage Parlors	70	75	78
Tenements	578	1172	1245
Furnished Rooms	112	112	148
Hotels	105	105	560
TOTALS	1007	1606	2472

APPENDIX II

SUMMARY OF PLACES IN MANHATTAN CATERING TO PROSTITUTION—INVESTIGATED JANUARY 24TH TO NOVEMBER 15TH, 1912

Places	Number of Different		Number of Prostitutes Counted
	Addresses of Buildings	Investigations Made	
Saloons, cafes and concert halls	308	1304	2689
Miscellaneous places allied with prostitution	71	145	385
Semi-public places used by prostitutes	20	35	150
TOTALS	399	1484	3224

Appendix

APPENDIX III

SUMMARY OF INMATES COUNTED AND ESTIMATED AT PLACES IN MANHATTAN WHERE PROSTITUTION WAS REPORTED DURING PERIOD OF INVESTIGATION FROM JANUARY 24TH TO NOVEMBER 15TH, 1912

Places	Number of Inmates Counted	Inmates Estimated but not seen	Total Including those Counted and Estimated
Parlor Houses	1686	2609	2609
Massage Parlors	153	..	153
Tenements	2294	2976	2976
Furnished Rooms	227	..	227
Hotels	583	..	583
	4943	5585	6548

Commercialized Prostitution in New York

APPENDIX IV
MONTHLY EXPENSES OF THIRTY ONE-DOLLAR PARLOR HOUSES

Address	Mmes. or House-keepers	Maids	Cooks	Butcher & Grocer	Light-house	Gas & Electricity	Telephone	Rent	Entertainment Tickets	Total
No. — W. 18th	$140	$104	$40	$160	$120	$35	$15	$150	$50	$814
No. — W. 24th	132	80	40	160	100	20	8	175	20	735
No. — W. 25th	48	78	34	140	60	18	8	200	20	606
No. — W. 25th	148	148	40	200	40	25	10	208	20	839
No. — W. 25th	65	88	47	148	82	32		208	35	705
No. — W. 25th	160	76	32	120		25	8	125	25	571
No. — W. 28th	136	116	32	140	100	30	15	110	50	729
No. — W. 28th	248	88	40	140	120	25		110	50	821
No. — W. 31st		80	40	120		35	8	208	25	516
No. — W. 35th	192	78	34	200	84	30	10	150	20	798
No. — W. 40th		52	32	48		12	6	125		275
No. — W. 40th		56	40	60		12		125		293
No. — W. 40th	128	80	36	120	72	35	12	125	20	628
No. — W. 56th	172	112	48	180	60	35	15	175		797
No. — 6th Ave.	72	60	44	140	100	25		200	50	691
No. — 6th Ave.	108	100	48	120	60	15	10	208	20	680
No. — 6th Ave.	128	80	40	120	120	30		175	40	733
No. — 6th Ave.	60	64	48	200		20	10	166	25	593
No. — 6th Ave.	120	60	32	140		25	8	150	20	555
No. — 6th Ave.	64	48	32	48	80	15		150		437
No. — 6th Ave.	128	54	40	140	60	25	10	150	35	667
No. — 6th Ave.	128	120	44	180	100	35	15	175	50	847
No. — 6th Ave.	60	44		180	72	20	6	225	20	627
No. — W. 24th	72	96	36	80	160	20	10	175	25	674
No. — W. 26th	168	120	36	180	60	40	15	150	50	819

Appendix IV Continued on Next Page

Appendix

APPENDIX IV.—Continued
MONTHLY EXPENSES OF THIRTY ONE-DOLLAR PARLOR HOUSE—Continued

No. — W. 27th	60	52	40	100	80	25	8	175	30	570
No. — W. 28th	60	76	40	160	120	25	10	200	50	741
Na. — W. 28th	60	56	48	140		12		125		441
No. — W. 36th	160	88	40	140	80	30	10	150	50	748
No. — W. 36th	180	80	36	120	80	25	10	150	25	706
Monthly Totals	$3197	2434	1139	4124	2010	746	237	4943	825	19665
Year's Total	$41561	31642	14807	53612	26130	8952	2844	59316	9900	248764

APPENDIX V
MONTHLY EXPENSES OF TEN DISORDERLY APARTMENTS IN TENEMENT BUILDINGS

Address	Maids	Light-house, bell boys, etc.	Butcher & Grocer	Gas & Electricity	Telephone	Rent	Total
No. — W. 43rd St.	$36	$.	$ 60	$10	$ 8	$ 75	$189
No. — W. 45th St.	32	.	60	10	8	125	235
No. — W. 49th St.	64	.	75	12	8	100	259
No. — W. 50th St.	64	10	80	10	.	100	264
No. — W. 55th St.	64	.	60	12	15	110	261
No. — W. 58th St.	44	.	55	8	.	36	143
No. — W. 58th St.	52	.	60	8	5	50	175
No. — W. 58th St.	44	230	100	10	6	50	440
Na. — W. 60th St.	60	.	60	8	5	75	208
No. — W. 65th St.	32	.	40	7	5	60	144
Monthly Totals	$492	240	650	95	60	781	2318
Year's Totals	$6396	3120	8450	1140	720	9372	29198

APPENDIX VI

MONTHLY EXPENSES OF EIGHT FIVE-DOLLAR PARLOR HOUSES

Address	House-keepers	Maids	Cooks	Butcher & Grocer	Piano Player	Cab Boy	Gas & Electricity	Telephone	Rent	Total
No. — W. 38th	$152	$112	$40	$200	$88	$56	$45	$12	$166	$871
No. — W. 41st	152	104	48	250	100	.	45	15	210	924
No. — W. 46th	140	96	44	240	80	48	45	15	230	938
No. — W. 46th	136	144	44	200	80	48	60	15	225	952
No. — W. 46th	80	128	40	200	80	.	45	12	175	760
No. — W. 47th	144	88	44	240	.	40	45	20	250	871
No. — W. 49th	200	88	40	240	.	.	40	20	200	828
No. — W. 52nd	140	112	48	240	80	60	40	15	150	885
Monthly Totals	$1144	872	348	1810	508	252	365	124	1606	7029
Year's Total	$14872	11336	4524	23530	6604	3276	4380	1488	19272	89282

Appendix

APPENDIX VII

CONDITIONS ON THE STREETS OF MANHATTAN IN MONTHLY PERIODS FROM JANUARY 24TH TO NOVEMBER 15TH, 1912, SHOWING STREET WALKERS COUNTED, AND NUMBER WHO SOLICITED MEN INVESTIGATORS

Period	All Streets in Manhattan			Broadway		
	Street Walkers Counted	Street Walkers who Solicited Investigators	Number of Reports	Street Walkers Counted	Street Walkers who Solicited Investigators	Number of Reports
Jan. 24th to Feb. 24th	482	104	157	38	8	9
Feb. 24th to Mar. 24th	492	133	149	105	25	22
Mar. 24th to Apr. 24th	490	104	129	195	25	28
Apr. 24th to May 24th	883	117	214	435	46	74
May 24th to June 24th	1203	118	259	562	40	69
June 24th to July 24th	696	72	245	479	25	114
July 24th to Sept. 1st	1048	52	201	593	20	87
Sept. 1st to Oct. 1st	451	45	69	209	18	22
Oct. 1st to Nov. 1st	738	34	134	352	16	55
Nov. 1st to Nov. 15th	276	14	39	207	12	12
TOTALS	6759	793	1596	3175	235	492

Of the total number of street walkers counted, over 47% were on Broadway.
Of the total number of street walkers who solicited investigators, nearly 30% were on Broadway.
Of the total number of reports on streets, about 31% related to Broadway.

APPENDIX VIII

NUMBER OF REPORTS ON STREET WALKING IN MANHATTAN, DURING PERIOD OF INVESTIGATION FROM JANUARY 24th TO NOVEMBER 15th, 1912, ACCORDING TO POLICE PRECINCTS

Precincts	Jan. 24 to Feb. 24	Feb. 24 to Mar. 24	Mar. 24 to Apr. 24	Apr. 24 to May 24	May 24 to June 24	June 24 to July 24	July 24 to Sept. 1	Sept. 1 to Oct. 1	Oct. 1 to Nov. 1	Nov. 1 to Nov. 15	Total Six Months	Percentage
1	.	.	.	.	.	7	3	.	2	.	12	.75
2	.	.	.	.	.	7	2	.	3	.	12	.75
5	.	.	.	.	.	.	.	.	1	.	1	.07
6	.	.	.	1	3	1	1	.	.	.	7	.45
7	.	.	.	.	.	.	.	.	.	.	.	.
8	.	.	.	.	.	.	.	.	.	.	.	.
10	.	.	.	.	.	2	.	.	.	.	2	.13
12	.	.	1	4	.	3	.	.	.	.	8	.50
13	1	7	2	4	.	1	4	1	6	1	8	.50
14	22	.	.	.	.	1	8	.	1	1	6	.38
15	3	.	18	14	26	14	4	1	.	.	117	7.33
16	.	.	1	.	.	1	15	4	.	.	11	.70
17	.	10	2	16	4	16	12	2	.	.	3	.20
18	18	13	8	21	32	11	15	14	13	.8	112	7.02
21	24	22	8	13	28	13	51	28	7	2	132	8.25
22	17	21	8	73	64	69	3	.	10	.	140	8.75
23	35	2	28	.	21	2	37	.	40	13	422	26.40
25	1	.	.	14	38	59	11	7	18	7	31	1.95
26	.	13	13	29	12	11	4	.	6	.	225	14.08
28	4	13	13	14	5	4	.	.	2	3	81	5.08
29	1	3	1	.	.	.	.	.	.	.	23	1.45
31	1	.	.	.	.	.	.	.	.	.	.	.
32	3	10	7	15	10	11	20	5	11	2	94	5.90
33	1	.	2	3	1	1	.	.	.	.	8	.50
35	.	.	.	.	.	.	1	.	.	.	1	.07
36	.	18	4	5	9	5	9	5	9	2	.	.
39	9	5	5	.	3	.	.	.	.	.	75	4.70
40	3	.	.	2	1	3	.	.	.	.	16	1.02
43	14	12	7	.	2	2	.	2	3	.	45	2.82
	157	149	129	214	259	244	201	69	134	39	1596	100.00

APPENDIX VIII

POLICE RULES REGARDING DISORDERLY PLACES

Captains of Police Precincts. It is the duty of a police captain to report to the police commissioners on the fifth of each month:

1. Steps taken to enforce provisions of the Penal Law with reference to disorderly houses within his precinct.

2. Steps taken to enforce the Penal Law and Greater New York Charter regarding concert saloons, dives and other places where disorderly, degraded or lawless people congregate.

3. Steps taken to enforce the Liquor Tax Laws and ordinances relating to various crimes above mentioned.

No. 55 Under Rule 42.—When any room or building in any part or portion within the precinct is known to the captain to be kept, used, or occupied for purposes of prostitution, assignation, or other immoral purpose, he must give notice in writing to the owner, lessee or occupant, that such room or building is so used, and that it is a misdemeanor.[1]

No. 56 Under Rule 42.—If the occupation and use of such premises shall continue the captain will obtain warrants for and cause the arrest of such owner, lessee or

[1] See Rules and Regulations of the Police Department, 1908, page 115.

occupant for a misdemeanor and cause them to be prosecuted as required by law.[2]

No. 100 Under Rule 42.—Captains will make charges of neglect of duty against any patrolman under their command who fails to discover a serious breach of the peace occurring on his post, during his tour of duty; or who shall fail to arrest any party guilty of such offense.[3]

No. 13 Under Rule 45.—If a policeman is on duty on a post where houses of ill-fame are suspected to exist, he should be careful to restrain acts of disorder, prevent soliciting from windows, doors or on streets, and arrest all persons found so doing, also carefully observe all other places of a suspicious nature, obtain evidence as to the character and ownership of such houses, by whom frequented and report results of his observation to his commanding officer.[4]

[2] Ibid., page 115.   [3] Ibid., page 120.   [4] Ibid., page 130.

APPENDIX IX

PARLOR HOUSES: ADDITIONAL DATA

X 25. Sixth Avenue — a one-dollar house.

March 5, 12.40 A. M. The investigator visited this place at the solicitation of X 26, a lighthouse stationed at the corner of Sixth Avenue and 29th Street. He counted 14 inmates and bought a pint bottle of beer for 25 cents from the madame. The names of some of the inmates are Mignon, Helen, Violet and Georgette.

March 6, 1912, 11 P. M. This house is reported as running about a year. Names of some of inmates: Alice, Louise and Mabel.

May 25, 1912. Rosie, X 27, was an inmate here on this date.

July 21, 1912. Flora, X 28, and Violet, X 29, were inmates here on this date.

August 25, 1912. The proprietors are X 30, and X 31. The madame is X 32.

X 7. James Slip.

At 2 P. M. on April 10, 1912, there were seven inmates in the receiving parlor. One of these girls said there were three more, making ten in all. All were dressed in the regular parlor house costume and all claimed to possess medical certificates. Tony, X 8, is said to be connected with this house, and reaps the profits from the business. The girls receive one-half of what they make, *i. e.*, twenty-five cents from every visitor. The sanitary conditions are very bad.

X 33. Sixth Avenue — a one-dollar house.

February 5, 1912. X 34, the proprietor of this place, is a power in the Tenderloin. One of his women, whose name is Rosie, is madame at this address.

February 6, 1912. The investigator counted 8 inmates. Some of the inmates' names are Daisy, Rose and Bertha. The house is open night and day.

February 19, 1912. 1.30 A. M. The investigator counted 14 inmates. The madame was stationed in the hall with her ticket puncher.

February 24, 1912. An inmate in this house told the investigator that Dr. X 35 is the physician employed by the house.

April 4, 1912. X 36 was an inmate on this date.

July 9, 1912. X 37 was an inmate on this date.

July 15, 1912. X 38 and X 39 were inmates on this date.

X 41. West 24th Street — a one-dollar house.

February 2, 1912. 9.30 P. M. to 10.45 P. M. The investigator counted nine men entering.

February 19, 1912. 9.30 P. M. The investigator counted 14 inmates. The Madame is X 42. The names

Appendices

of some of the inmates on this date are Pearl, Marie, Clara and Sadie.

March 24, 1912. The physician for this place is X 43.

May 24, 1912. The proprietor of the resort is X 44.

May 25, 1912. X 45, an inmate here on this date claims that this is a good "money house."

(X 46.) *West 25th Street — a one-dollar house.*

February 1, 1912. 9 to 9.30 P. M. The investigator counted 9 inmates.

February 24, 1912. 2 A. M. The investigator counted 12 inmates and estimated 16. The proprietors are X 47 and X 48.

March 1, 1912. 9.30 P. M. The investigator counted 14 inmates. X 49 is said to be a proprietor.

March 19, 1912. 8.45 P. M. The investigator counted 14 inmates.

March 29, 1912. The investigator was present when a young thief, X 50, sold the madame, X 51, a dress he claimed to have stolen from a department store. X 35 is the house doctor here. The house is conducted by X 52.

X 51, the madame of this place, is the wife of X 47, the proprietor. X 43 is the physician. The investigator estimated the number of inmates as 19. Gussie often acts as madame.

April 16, 1912. X 53, the girl of X 54 is the assistant madame and housekeeper here.

X 59. *West 25th Street — a one-dollar house.*

February 1, 1912. 10.30-11.30 P. M. The investigator counted 11 inmates. The house is kept by X 17 in partnership with X 34. The names of some of the inmates on this date are Ruth, Elsie, and Margarita.

February 6, 1912. X 17, keeper of this place, has two other houses.

February 25, 1912. 9.15 P. M. The investigators counted 20 inmates. Eight pimps were present. The names of two of the girls on this date were Edith and May.

March 19, 1912. The investigator counted 14 inmates.

March 23, 1912. 1 A. M. The investigator counted 21 inmates and estimated 24. X 17 is the madame, also proprietor together with X 34. The house physician on this date is X 43. X 60 is a man said to be connected with this place. The names of some of the inmates on this date are Cora, Ruth, Violet, Lottie, Sophie, Blanche, and Mamie.

April 24, 1912. The names of some of the inmates on this date are X 61, X 62, and X 63.

May 24, 1912. X 2, who is an inmate of this house and has a country-wide reputation, does an exceedingly large business.

June 18, 1912. X 17, the madame, is in partnership with X 34.

July 12, 1912. The names of two inmates on this date are X 64 and X 65.

July 16, 1912. The investigator counted 12 inmates and estimated 16.

X 67. West 25th Street — a one-dollar house.

February 1, 1912. 9.30-10.30 P. M. The investigator

Appendices

counted 6 inmates and estimated 8. Annie acts as madame.

February 8, 1912. The proprietors of this place are X 68 and X 69.

February 19, 1912. 12.05 A. M. The investigator counted 12 inmates. Liquor is sold in this house on the quiet. The names of some of the inmates on this date are Marie, Laura, Mary, and Nellie.

February 23, 1912. 12.20 A. M. The investigator counted 10 inmates. X 49 is said to own a part interest in this place. Liquor not sold on this date.

March 2, 1912. 12.15 A. M. The investigator counted 10 inmates and estimated 17. Cigarettes sold but no liquors. The names of some of the inmates on this date are X 70, Rosie, Grace and Mabel.

March 19, 1912. 8.15 P. M. The investigator counted 19 inmates. Bessie acted as madame. X 69 and X 72 are reported as the proprietors of this place.

June 10, 1912. 11.20 P. M. The investigator counted 12 inmates and estimated 15. The proprietors are X 72 and X 73. Names of inmates on this date are Anna, Grace and Rose.

June 13, 1912. The investigators counted 13 inmates and estimated 15. The names of some of the inmates on this date are Marcelle, Grace, Dollie and Fannie. The place was formerly owned by X 72, X 69 and another. X 72 forced X 69 out and is now the chief owner. The share of X 69 was sold to X 73.

June 19, 1912. Inmate Nellie says she turns her earnings over to her pimp, X 74.

July 11, 1912. The names of three inmates on this date are X 75, X 76 and X 77.

X 78. *West 27th Street — a one-dollar house.*

February 8, 1912. The proprietors of this place are X 68, X 69 and X 72.

February 25, 1912. 8.30 P. M. The investigator counted 12 inmates.

March 4, 1912. 12.15 A. M. The investigator counted 16 inmates. The investigator was solicited to go here by a lighthouse, X 79. The proprietors are X 68 and X 69. The names of some of the inmates on this date are Ray, Matilda, Jennie, Belle and Georgie.

March 6, 1912. The investigator witnessed X 69 in conversation with a patrolman. X 68 is the chief owner.

March 24, 1912. The investigator counted 16 in-inmates. The physician of this place is X 80. The inmates pay him $1 per visit.

June 19, 1912. 11.30. The investigator was given a card to this place. X 69 forced X 72 out and bought his interest.

June 28, 1912. The investigator was handed a card to this place by a woman on Seventh Avenue near 28th Street. He saw another card on the sidewalk near West 27th Street on Seventh Avenue.

July 12, 1912. The names of three inmates of this house on this date are X 81, X 82 and X 83. The name of the owner of the property as given in the tax book for 1912 is X 84.

Appendices

X 16. West 31st Street — a one-dollar house.

February 8, 1912. 4.15 P.M. The investigator was approached on the street by a woman "runner" and given cards to above address. She said she had 5 or 6 girls there and she invited him to follow her. The investigator said he might call in the evening, and she told him to ring the bell on the stoop.

February 14, 1912. 12 P.M. The investigator counted 8 inmates, and was told there were 12 working here. The investigator had been solicited to come here by a cab driver, X 85.

February 16, 1912. The madame's name is Rose.

February 20, 1912. 9.20 P.M. The investigator was solicited on Sixth Avenue by a woman "runner" to enter this house. She had been stopping other men. The investigator counted 6 inmates. Mamie acted as madame. The names of some of the inmates on this date are Goldie, Ella, and Richmond.

March 7, 1912. 1.30 A.M. The investigator saw a prostitute who solicits on Sixth Avenue take four different men to this address within an hour, the first floor of which is a house of prostitution run by Madame Rose.

April 24, 1912. The name of the madame is X 86. The proprietors are X 34 and X 17.

May 14, 1912. X 86, the real madame, conducts this house on a 20 percent basis for X 34.

May 24, 1912. X 88 drunkard, lighthouse and procurer, works for X 34 at this address. He usually stands in front of X 89.

June 12, 1912. 3.00 A.M. The investigator talked

Commercialized Prostitution in New York

with two men who had just come from this house. An inmate had shown one of the men her card punched with holes indicating that she had entertained 60 men that night.

July 10, 1912. The place is reported as closed, probably on the instructions of X 34. X 90 and X 17 are interested here.

July 15, 1912. The name of an inmate at this house on this date is X 91. The name of the owner of this property as given in the tax book for 1912 is X 92.

X 93. *West 40th Street — a one-dollar house.*

March 8, 1912. 10.40 P. M. The investigator counted 5 inmates. The name of the madame is Rosie; proprietor, X 94. The names of some of the inmates on this date are Ethel, Della, Josie and Maria.

March 14, 1912. 12.30 A. M. The investigator was taken to this place by X 95. This place is running very quietly.

May 14, 1912. X 96 and his brother, X 94, are partners in the house.

June 12, 1912. The name of an inmate on this date is X 97. The name of the owner of this property as given in the tax book for 1912 is X 98.

X 99. *West 40th Street — a one-dollar house.*

February 1, 1912. 11.30 P. M. The investigator saw men go in and out of this place. He was unable to gain admittance.

February 13, 1912. 10.00 P. M. The investigator saw five men enter in half an hour.

Appendices

February 16, 1912. 10.00 P. M. The investigator counted 2 inmates and estimated 8. The madame's name is Rosie. The proprietor of the place is X 100. The name of the owner of the property as given in the tax book for 1912 is X 101.

X 102. *West 40th Street.*

February 1, 1912. X 103, partner of X 44, has practised prostitution and run houses for ten years.

February 6, 1912. The investigator counted 12 inmates. The proprietors are X 44 and X 103, who also acts as housekeeper. X 44 hangs out at X 104.

April 27, 1912. 9.00 P. M. The investigator counted 5 inmates and estimated 6. The price of the house is $2 and $5. Drinks are sold — $2 for an ordinary round, and $5 for a quart of champagne. The name of the madame is X 105. The names of some of the inmates on this date are Mignon, Lucy, Emma and Fifi. The name of a man connected with the house is X 106. The owner of the property is X 108.

APPENDIX X

TENEMENTS: ADDITIONAL DATA

(a) SOLICITING

February 24, 1912, investigator visited a cider stube in a tenement building at X 128, St. Mark's Place. A waitress solicited him to enter a rear room for immoral purposes. The woman who conducts this stube is X 127, this being the name of the woman mentioned in the letter quoted in Chapter II. The investigator says in his report that X 127 was formerly with X 126 at X 125, East 5th Street.

There are 13 families living at X 128, St. Mark's Place. In these families are 7 boys under 16 and 14 girls under 16. Five single young men and 3 single young women over 16 also live in this tenement house.

On February 21, 1812, between 7 and 8 P. M., investigator was solicited by a waitress in a cider stube in a tenement at X 129, East 6th Street. The stube is in the basement and the proprietress said she would send out for a young girl, but as she had previously been in trouble because of a 15 year old girl, she did not want to take another chance.

There are 38 families living at this address, with 20 boys and 20 girls all under 16 years of age. Seven single men and 9 single women over 16 also live in this tenement.

Appendices

X 130 lives at X 131, West 102nd Street, with a friend who has a furnished apartment. The janitress is named X 132, and X 130 says she does not pay any attention to what goes on in the tenement so long as the girls do not become too bold. Some of the prostitutes have been in his tenement as long as 10 years.

X 130 is a chorus girl during the regular season. She has been with several well known companies.

X 133 is the janitor at X 134, West 28th Street. Four street walkers bring men to their rooms in this building for immoral purposes. One of these women said that they each paid $5 per week to the janitor for the privilege of using their rooms in this way. The janitor has a family consisting of his wife and three children. One boy is 10 and the eldest girl 17 years of age.

On February 13, 1912, between 3.30 and 4.30 P. M., two colored girls who appeared to be 17 and 18 years of age respectively were soliciting men on the street to enter a tenement house at X 136, West 40th Street. The children from Public School No. X 137, a short distance away, were playing along the street on their way home. The colored girls were particularly insistent and talked in loud tones intermingled with vile remarks and oaths. Some of the children who did not appear to be more than 10 or 11 years old noticed the two colored girls and laughed at them, pointing their fingers.

Seven colored families live in this tenement. The prostitutes who solicited offered to reduce the price to 50 cents if the hallway were used. On March 4, 1912, a colored girl entered the hallway with a white man.

Commercialized Prostitution in New York

The conditions in this building are extremely unsanitary. The hallways are dark and full of odors, the stairs in a state of dilapidation.

X 138 and a younger girl rented two rooms in a tenement at X 139, East 122nd Street. On January 30, 1912, about 9.15 P. M., X 138 solicited the investigator on the street to accompany her to this tenement for immoral purposes. The girls paid $4 per week for the rooms and the landlord had told X 138 that they could bring men into the house if they desired. A man by the name of Louis has tried several times to induce X 138 to enter a house of prostitution. "This man," said the girl, "is a swell dresser and wears diamonds." He even went so far one night as to impersonate a detective and threatened to arrest her for soliciting on the street, thinking in this way to frighten her into complying with his request. X 138 said that he receives $50 for every girl he secures for houses.

The investigator called at this address again on February 1 for the purpose of talking further with X 138 and tried to obtain a description of the procurer of whom she spoke. The hour was 5 P. M. As he entered the hallway a boy about 11 or 12 years of age asked him whom he wanted to see. "Mrs. X 140 has been out and so has Mrs. X 141," said the boy, "and now there are only two w—— on the top floor." Four families live at this address, in which there are 2 boys and 1 girl under 16.

Mrs. X 118 lives on the third floor of a tenement at X 117, West 58th Street. Mrs. X 118 has two daughters; one, a girl of 18, is divorced from her husband

Appendices

whom she met when her mother conducted a similar business on West 49th Street, and lives here with her mother. The other daughter, X 142, is 15 years of age. On February 24, 1912, about 1 A. M., investigator saw a young man talking to X 142 in the rear of the flat. X 118 said X 142 is attending a business school, but different young men who are customers declare that she works in a candy factory. One day a business man who had been a customer received a letter from X 118 urging him to call. He showed the letter to the investigator, and declared that X 142 had written it at the dictation of her mother who he knew could not write English. In fact, the writing was in an immature hand, and the letter poorly composed.

One of the inmates here, X 143, lives at X 144, East 94th Street and uses X 118 flat in which to meet two steady customers at stated intervals. She has been a clandestine prostitute for several months.

X 118 has a list of addresses of girls in a book which she keeps in her bureau. There are 10 families in this tenement. One of the tenants, a Mrs. X 145, told an investigator that on several occasions the police have been called into the house to stop the noise. She further said that the landlord, X 146, knows the character of some of the tenants and charges them high rentals.

(b) DIFFERENT INVESTIGATIONS OF SAME ADDRESS

As was the case with parlor houses, many tenements were investigated at different times in order to show that the business was systematically conducted:

Commercialized Prostitution in New York

X 147. *Broadway.*

July 27, 1912. X 155, prostitute, told the investigator she "answers calls for this place. $5. Wine sold."

July 30, 1912. X 154, prostitute, told the investigator she "receives men here, $5, $10, $20."

August 1, 1912. X 150, prostitute, told the investigator that "this place is owned by a colored woman; X 149-a, white woman has charge." Prices charged are $3, $5 and $10.

August 1, 1912. There are two apartments in X 147 Broadway owned by colored women. One, X 148, and her sister, X 149-a. These women have white girls conducting the resorts while they, the owners, keep in the background. One apartment, 3rd floor, inside, is operated under the name of X 149. The other is one or two flights above on the same side. Both send for girls supposed to be $3, $5, and $10.

August 8, 1912. 10 P. M. Business and residential district. Six story red brick building. Madame X 148. The investigator counted 2 inmates. Price $5. Girls get half. Drinks $5. Inmates wear gowns and claim to have health certificates. Names of inmates, Stella and Ellen. Girls claim to pay weekly board of $15. Rent paid is $105.

August 15, 1912. X 152, prostitute, told the investigator she "takes friends here."

August 29, 1912. X 156, prostitute, told the investigator she "meets many a good man through this house. Two other apartments here where I see men."

August 29, 1912. X 156., prostitute, told the in-

Appendices

vestigator she "makes many a dollar right in the house. Four good places here."

X 157. West 27th Street.

February 6, 1912. 8.30-9 P. M. Investigator reports this former house of prostitution now occupied by families.

March 18, 1912. 2:30 P. M. Investigator solicited by inmate Blanche on 27th Street and Seventh Avenue and went to her apartment one flight up, east. Counted two inmates. Price of place $1. Names of inmates, Blanche (madame) and Bella. Name of owner of property as given in the tax book for 1912 is X 158.

X 159. West 28th Street.

March 5, 1912. 9.50 P. M. Investigator counted 6 street walkers accosting men in the vicinity and using the premises for purposes of prostitution. Investigator was solicited by one, Jennie, to enter premises. Price of woman and room $1. Owner of this property as given by the tax book for 1912 is X 161. The previous owner was X 162.

Reports from other sources:

Tenement house, double family tenement, janitor giving women privileges after 10 P. M. for a weekly consideration. A procurer by the name of X 163 living on the premises has shipped his girl Rosie to Pittsburg, Pa., into a disorderly house there.

February 1, 1912. Flat house for street walkers.

Commercialized Prostitution in New York

Tenement House Department report, June 18, 1909. Disorderly house, prostitution alleged, no basis. July 2, 1909: Disorderly house, prostitution alleged, no basis.

X 164. *West 28th Street.*

February 8, 1912. Investigator reports prostitution discontinued here.

March 17, 1912. Tenement house inhabited by about 10 families. 12.15 A. M. Investigator solicited by two French women on street near the stoop of premises to enter this house. Price of women $1. Soliciting from street and windows. Owner of property as given in the tax book for 1912 is X 165.

Reports from other sources:

February 1, 1912. Ground floor, French flats. Almost on every floor " business " is carried on.

Tenement House Department report, January 8, 1910. Disorderly house, second floor. Cause of complaint removed.

Police report June 18, 1909. Disorderly house, prostitution alleged. No basis.

August 19, 1912. Prostitution is practised in this house. Rosie, prostitute, resides in a flat one flight up, and a woman named X 166, also a prostitute, lives on the floor above Rosie. The investigator was solicited from the window of this house.

X 167. *West 29th Street.*

March 24, 1912. 8.30 P. M. Investigator was solic-

Appendices

ited by several colored women in front of this address to come to their rooms. Counted five women soliciting. Price of women 50 cents. Owner of the property as given in the tax book for 1912 is X 168.

Reports from other sources:

Tenement. Some apartments occupied by prostitutes.

X 169. West 29th Street.

March 9, 1912. Investigator reported about eight families and eight children in this building, mostly colored. House appeared all right at this visit.

Reports from other sources:

February 1, 1912. Some apartments occupied by prostitutes.

Tenement House Department report, March 9, 1910: Disorderly house. Fourth floor, front, west, X 170. No action necessary. Police report.

X 171. West 29th Street.

February 2, 1912. A colored woman named X 172 lives in this house and keeps girls. She lately moved from X 173 when X 174 (well known to investigator) was her pimp.

March 4, 1912. Investigator visited this building. Estimated seven families, mostly colored, living here. Saw two suspicious women on first floor. Owner of this property as given in the tax book for 1912 is X 175.

Reports from other sources:

Tenement House Department. February 8, 1910.

Disorderly house, basement. Cause of complaint removed.

Police report. February 24, 1910. Disorderly house, basement, east side, front. X 176, cause of complaint removed.

Police report. November 9, 1911. Disorderly house. Prostitution alleged. Cause of complaint removed.

X 177. West 29th Street.

April 19, 1912. A prostitute, X 178, lives at this address and uses her apartments for immoral purposes.

June 19, 1912. 1:10 A. M. Investigator solicited on street by colored women to go to apartment in this building. Price of women 50 cents.

Reports from other sources:

Tenement House Department. November 9, 1911. Disorderly house, prostitution alleged. Cause of complaint removed.

Police report. January 27, 1909. Disorderly house, second floor, front, west. X 179. Cause of complaint removed.

Police report. April 13, 1909. Disorderly house, rear, second floor, east. X 180 and X 181. Cause of complaint removed.

X 182. West 29th Street.

February 6, 1912. Investigator reports this a tenement occupied by colored families and prostitutes. On third floor, east, X 172, who is a maid in the house of prostitution at X 183, is a prostitute and has had a

Appendices

white man living with her for several months. Investigator visited her apartment with this man and was solicited by X 172 to stay with her. Two other women were in the rear room at the time.

March 4, 1912. Investigator reports about six families (Italian and colored) in this tenement. Suspicious women on third floor, among them X 184, a widow.

March 9, 1912. Investigator reports building mostly occupied by colored people. Two suspicious women on fifth floor.

Reports from other sources:

Tenement House Department. July 25, 1910. Disorderly house, third floor, X 200. Cause of complaint removed.

Police report and police officer. November 9, 1911. Disorderly house, prostitution alleged. No action necessary.

December 26, 1911. Disorderly house, prostitution alleged, second floor, west, cause of complaint removed.

X 185. *West 30th Street.*

February 2, 1912. 6.30 P. M. Investigator saw men entering this place.

March 4, 1912. Investigator reported three families living here. House appeared quiet.

August 21, 1912. Investigator reports some of the rooms evidently used by street walkers. Outside door locked.

Reports from other sources:

February 1, 1912. Bed house.

Commercialized Prostitution in New York

X 186. *West 37th Street.*

March 18, 1912. 4.40 P. M. Investigator counted 6 inmates, all colored. He was solicited on 37th Street between Seventh and Eighth Avenues to enter premises. Price 50 cents. Names of inmates, Hannah and Eliza.

May 1, 1912. 5 A. M. Investigator was solicited to go to second floor of this building by two colored prostitutes standing on the steps of this building. Price 50 cents.

August 24, 1912. Colored prostitutes solicit here day and night from windows of this house and on street in front. Thieves and pimps hang out on corner. Name of owner of this property as given in the tax book for 1912 is X 187.

Reports from other sources:

Tenement House. Colored women carry on business at all hours of the day and night with the purpose of robbery chiefly in view.

August 17, 1912. Place occupied by colored prostitutes. Saw them soliciting from windows on all floors of this building.

APPENDIX XI

HOTELS: ADDITIONAL DATA

X 214. *Sixth Avenue.*

February 8, 1912. 10.30 P. M. Investigator solicited to go here by prostitute; price $1.

Investigator solicited by prostitute in front of this hotel to enter premises, March 11, 1912. 9.20 P. M. Investigator counted 6 street walkers in vicinity of this hotel. He was solicited by prostitutes in front of place; price of woman $2, price of room $1 to $2.

March 18, 1912. 12 M. Investigator counted 4 street walkers loitering in the vicinity of this hotel. He was solicited by one of them to enter this place. Price $2, price of room $1.50.

March 23, 1912. 7.30 P. M. Investigator counted 8 street walkers loitering on Sixth Avenue, in the vicinity of this hotel. He was solicited by one on the corner of Sixth Avenue and —— Street to enter this hotel. A police officer stood across the street at the time. Price $2, price of room $1.50 to $2.

May 4, 1912. 3 P. M. Investigator counted 6 street walkers loitering in vicinity of this hotel, on Sixth Avenue. All approached men. He was solicited on the corner of Sixth Avenue and —— Street by a prostitute to enter this hotel. Price $2, price of room $2. A

Commercialized Prostitution in New York

police officer stood across the street at the time investigator was solicited.

The investigator stood near the entrance of this hotel for 30 minutes and saw 6 women whom he believed to be prostitutes enter the hotel with men. It is said on good authority that the receipts in this hotel on Saturday nights were as high as $400.

May 6, 1912. 5 P. M. Investigator counted 5 street walkers loitering in vicinity of this hotel on Sixth Avenue. All approached men. He was solicited by one of these in front of the hotel to enter the premises. Price $2, room $2.

May 9, 1912. 7 P. M. Investigator counted 4 street walkers on Sixth Avenue in the vicinity of this hotel. All approached men. He was solicited by one to enter the premises. Price $2, price of room $2.

May 13, 1912. 6.30 P. M. Investigator counted 4 street walkers on Sixth Avenue in the vicinity of this hotel. All of these women approached men. He was solicited by one in front of the hotel to enter premises. Price $2, price of room $2.

May 22, 1912. 7.15 P. M. Investigator counted 6 street walkers on Sixth Avenue, in the vicinity of this hotel. All approached men. One of the women solicited him on the corner of Sixth Avenue and —— Street to enter the premises.

May 28, 1912. 12 P. M. Investigator counted 7 street walkers on Sixth Avenue in the vicinity of this hotel. All approached men. He was solicited to enter the premises. Police officer was in sight at the time of solicitation.

Appendices

May 30, 1912. 6.30 P. M. Investigator counted 5 street walkers on Sixth Avenue in the vicinity of this hotel. All approached men. He was solicited by one at the corner of Sixth Avenue and —— Street to enter the premises.

June 3, 1912. 2 P. M. Investigator counted 4 street walkers on Sixth Avenue in the vicinity of this hotel. All of these women approached men. He was solicited by one within 100 feet of an officer at the corner of Sixth Avenue and —— Street to enter the premises. Price $2, room $2.

June 7, 1912. 2 P. M. Investigator counted 5 street walkers on Sixth Avenue in the vicinity of this hotel. All approached men. He was solicited by one at the corner of Sixth Avenue and —— Street to enter premises.

June 10, 1912. 2 P. M. Investigator counted 7 street walkers on Sixth Avenue in the vicinity of this hotel. All approached men. He was solicited by one of these women at the corner of Sixth Avenue and —— Street to enter the premises. Price of woman $2, price of room $2. Officer was in sight at the time of solicitation.

The following prostitutes are among those who use this hotel for immoral purposes:

May 22, 1912, Lena X 219.
May 28, 1912, Christie X 218.
May 31, 1912, Rosie X 217.
June 26, 1912, Becky X 220.
July 15, 1912, Annie X 222.
August 2, 1912, Rosie X 221.
August 15, 1912, Anna X 212.

August 15, 1912, Betty X 216.
August 16, 1912, Gussie X 223.
Reports from other sources:
Reported owners are X 224, X 225 and X 226. C X 227, manager.
Proprietors are X 28, X 225 and X 229. Dive of worst kind.
The premises also appear under the address —— W. —— Street. Bed house.
February 1, 1912. Bed house.
August 19, 1912. This place is a noted assignation hotel.

X 230. *West 35th Street.*

February 13, 1912. 11.15 P. M. Investigator counted 3 street walkers in vicinity of this hotel. He was solicited to enter premises by a prostitute at the corner of Broadway and —— Street. Price of room $1. He also saw four couples enter here in half an hour, the women being street walkers. Saw prostitute pick up a man on Seventh Avenue and take him to premises.

February 15, 1912. 9.00 P. M. Investigator was solicited by a street walker on Broadway between 35th and 40th Streets to enter premises.

February 20, 1912. 2.00 P. M. Clerk of this hotel sentenced to two months' imprisonment. It is said the proprietor is a fugitive from justice.

April 10, 1912. Investigator met men who appeared to be cadets near premises. Hotel said to be run by X 231. The proprietor is said to be X 225.

Appendices

April 26, 1912. 1.00 A. M. Investigator counted 5 street walkers on Seventh Avenue between —— and —— Streets. All approached men. He was solicited by one at the corner of Seventh Avenue and —— Street to enter premises. Price of woman $3. Price of room $2. This woman lives at X 238, West 34th Street. X 232 is the rebate clerk at this hotel, and this duty takes up his whole time.

May 3, 1912. Investigator counted three street walkers on south side of —— Street towards Broadway. Two stopped men. Investigator was solicited by one to enter premises. Price of woman $2, room $2.

May 6, 1912. 11.00-12.00 P. M. Investigator counted 10 street walkers in the entrance to this hotel and in the doorways near-by. Four approached men. Investigator was solicited by one on the street near the hotel to enter premises. Price of woman $2, room $2. Investigator saw 5 suspicious couples enter this hotel in half an hour and 3 girls unescorted. Men lookouts in doorways across the street.

May 9, 1912. 7.45 P. M. Investigator counted 5 street walkers on Seventh Avenue between —— and —— Streets. All accosted men. He was solicited by one, in sight of an officer across the street, to enter the premises. price of woman $2, room $2.

May 11, 1912. 2.00 A. M. Investigator counted fifteen street walkers on Broadway between —— and —— Streets. All approached men. He was solicited by three of these prostitutes to enter premises. Price of women $2, $3; price of room $1, $1.50.

May 15, 1912. 6.50 P. M. Investigator counted 5

Commercialized Prostitution in New York

street walkers on Seventh Avenue between —— and ——
Streets. All approached men. He was solicited by one
at the corner of Seventh Avenue and —— Street to enter
premises. Price of woman $2, price of room $2.

May 18, 1912. 1.30 A. M. Investigator counted 6
street walkers on —— Street near Broadway. Three accosted men. Investigator was solicited by one on the
southwest corner of —— Street and Broadway to enter
premises. Price of woman $2, price of room $2. The
name of the woman who solicited the investigator is
Blanche X 233; she lives with her pimp at X 239, West
38th Street, third floor.

May 20, 1912. 7.10 P. M. Investigator counted 6
street walkers on Seventh Avenue between —— and ——
Streets. All approached men. He was solicited at the
corner of Seventh Avenue and —— Street to enter premises. An officer passed by them during this solicitation.
Price of woman $2, price of room $2.

May 23, 1912. 7.15 P. M. Investigator counted 4
street walkers on Seventh Avenue between —— and ——
Streets. All approached men. He was solicited by one
at the corner of Seventh Avenue and —— Street to enter
premises. Price of woman $2, price of room $2.

May 29, 1912. 7.45 P. M. Investigator counted 6
street walkers on Seventh Avenue between —— and ——
Streets. All approached men. He was solicited by one
at the corner of Seventh Avenue and —— Street within
100 feet of an officer to enter premises.

May 31, 1912. 8.00 P. M. Investigator counted 8
street walkers on Seventh Avenue between —— and ——
Streets. All approached men. He was solicited by one

Appendices

at the corner of Seventh Avenue and —— Street within sight of an officer to enter premises.

June 1, 1912. 8.00 P. M. Investigator counted 5 street walkers on Seventh Avenue between —— and —— Streets. All approached men. He was solicited by one at the corner of Seventh Avenue and —— Street to enter premises. Price of woman $3, price of room $2. Investigator talked with X 231, part owner in this hotel. He complained about business, saying it was "too hot."

June 4, 1912. 7.35 P. M. Investigator counted 6 street walkers on Seventh Avenue between —— and —— Streets. All approached men. He was solicited by one at the corner of Seventh Avenue and —— Street to enter premises. Price of woman $2, price of room $2.

June 7, 1912. 7.30 P M. Investigator counted six street walkers on Seventh Avenue between —— and —— Streets. All approached men. He was solicited at the corner of Seventh Avenue and —— Street, within sight of an officer, to enter premises. Price of woman $2, price of room $2.

June 8, 1912. 8.15 P. M. Investigator counted 13 street walkers on Seventh Avenue between 34th and 40th Streets. All approached men. The investigator was solicited twice, once within sight of an officer, to enter the premises of this hotel. Price of woman $2, price of room $2.

June 11, 1912. 8.15 P. M. Investigator counted 6 street walkers on Seventh Avenue between —— and —— Streets. All approached men. He was solicited at the corner of Seventh Avenue and —— Street, within 200 feet of an officer, to enter premises. Price of woman $3, price of room $2.

June 15, 1912. 8.00 P. M. Investigator counted 6 street walkers on Seventh Avenue between —— and —— Streets. All approached men. He was solicited by one at the corner of Seventh Avenue and —— Street, within sight of an officer, to enter premises. Price of woman $2, price of room $2.

June 17, 1912. 8.30 P. M. Investigator was solicited by a street walker on Sixth Avenue near —— Street to enter premises. Price of woman $2, price of room $2. The following prostitutes are among those who frequent and use this hotel for immoral purposes:

May 25, 1912, Anna X 234.
May 28, 1912, Sarah X 235.
May 31, 1912, Louise X 236.
June 6, 1912, May X 237.

Reports from other sources:

August 19, 1912. Notorious assignation hotel.

X 215. *West 28th Street.*

February 7, 1912. 11.00 P. M. Investigator solicited to enter premises.

February 7, 1912. 9.15-9.30 P. M. Investigator solicited at the corner of Sixth Avenue and —— Street to enter premises. Price of woman $1. Price of room $1.50.

February 7, 1912. 1.15 P. M. Investigator was solicited by street walker on Sixth Avenue near —— Street to enter premises. Price of woman $1. Price of room $1.50.

Appendices

February 7, 1912. 1.15 P. M. Investigator solicited by a prostitute on 28th Street to enter the premises. Price of woman $1, price of room $1.

February 7, 1912. Evening. Investigator asked clerk price of room for himself and was told $2.50, a prohibitive rate.

February 10, 1912. 8.30 P. M. Investigator solicited by prostitute to enter premises.

February 19, 1912. 2.00 A. M. Investigator solicited by street walker on Broadway between 31st and 32nd Streets to enter premises. Price of woman $3 for the rest of the night. Price of room $1.

March 11, 1912. 9.20 P. M. Investigator counted 9 street walkers within 50 feet of this hotel. All approached men. He was solicited by one of the prostitutes at the entrance of the hotel to enter the premises. Price of woman $2. Price of room $1.50.

March 11, 1912. 11.25 P. M. Investigator counted 2 street walkers at the corner of Sixth Avenue and —— Street in the vicinity of this hotel. He was solicited by one to enter premises. Price of woman $3, price of room $1.50.

March 11, 1912. 9.00 P. M. Investigator counted 9 street walkers in the vicinity of this hotel. He was solicited by one on the west side of Sixth Avenue between —— and —— Streets to enter premises. Price of woman $2, price of room $1.50.

May 1, 1912. 3.30 P. M. Investigator counted 11 street walkers on Sixth Avenue in the vicinity of this hotel. Three approached men. Investigator was solicited by one on Sixth Avenue within sight of an officer to enter premises. Price of woman $1. Price of room $1.

May 1, 1912. 2.00 P. M. Investigator counted 6 street walkers on Sixth Avenue between —— and —— Streets in the vicinity of this hotel. All approached men. He was solicited by one at the corner of Sixth Avenue and —— Street to enter the premises. Price of woman $2, price of room $2.

May 8, 1912. 5.00 P. M. Investigator counted 6 street walkers on Sixth Avenue between —— and —— Streets. All approached men. He was solicited by one at the corner of Sixth Avenue and —— Street to enter premises. Price of woman $2, price of room $2.

May 13, 1912. 6.45 P. M. Investigator counted 5 street walkers on Sixth Avenue between —— and —— Streets. All approached men. He was solicited by one at the corner of Sixth Avenue and —— Street to enter premises. Price of woman $2, price of room $2.

May 15, 1912. A man sold obscene photographs in the toilet room of this hotel. He had a bundle of such pictures.

May 15, 1912. 5.30 P. M. Investigator counted 4 street walkers on Sixth Avenue between —— and —— Streets, in the vicinity of this hotel. All approached men. He was solicited by one at the corner of Sixth Avenue and —— to enter premises. Price of woman $2, price of room $2.

May 23, 1912. 11.00 A. M. Investigator counted 5 street walkers on Sixth Avenue between —— and —— Streets in the vicinity of this hotel. All approached men.

Appendices

He was solicited by one at the corner of Sixth Avenue and —— Street to enter premises. Price of room $2, price of woman $2.

May 24, 1912. 11.00 A. M. Investigator counted 6 street walkers on Sixth Avenue between —— and —— Streets in the vicinity of this hotel. All approached men. He was solicited by one within sight of an officer at the corner of Sixth Avenue and —— Street to enter premises. Price of woman $2, price of room $2.

May 31, 1912. 1.30 P. M. Investigator counted 5 street walkers on Sixth Avenue between —— and —— Streets. All approached men. He was solicited by one at the corner of Sixth Avenue and —— Street. Price of woman $2, price of room $2.

June 1, 1912. 1.30 A. M. Investigator counted 7 street walkers on Sixth Avenue between —— and —— Streets. Six of these women approached men. Investigator was solicited by one of them at the corner of Sixth Avenue and —— Street within sight of an officer, to enter premises. Price of woman $2, price of room $2.

June 4, 1912. 10.45 A. M. Investigator counted 5 street walkers on Sixth Avenue between —— and —— Streets in the vicinity of this hotel. All approached men. He was solicited by one within sight of an officer at the corner of Sixth Avenue and —— Street to enter premises. Price of woman $2, price of room $2.

June 6, 1912. 1.30 P. M. Investigator counted 6 street walkers on Sixth Avenue between —— and —— Streets. All approached men. He was solicited by one at the corner of Sixth Avenue and —— Street within sight of an officer, to enter premises. Price of woman $2, price of room $2.

June 8, 1912. 11.30 A. M. Investigator counted 6 street walkers on Sixth Avenue between —— and —— Streets. All approached men. He was solicited by one at the corner of Sixth Avenue and —— Street to enter premises. Price of woman $2, price of room $1.50.

June 13, 1912. 11.30 A. M. Investigator counted 5 street walkers on Sixth Avenue between —— and —— Streets. All approached men. He was solicited at the corner of Sixth Avenue and —— Street, within sight of an officer, to enter premises. Price $3 for woman, price of room $2.

June 15, 1912. 11.30 A. M. Investigator counted 6 street walkers on Sixth Avenue between —— and —— Streets. All approached men. He was solicited by one at the corner of Sixth Avenue and —— Street, within sight of an officer, to enter premises. Price of woman $2, price of room $2.

The following prostitutes are among those who frequent this hotel for immoral purposes:

April 24, 1912, Laura X 240.
July 29, 1912, Mamie X 241.
August 2, 1912, Marion X 244.
August 12, 1912, Kate X 243.
August 15, 1912, Anna X 212.
August 15, 1912, Betty X 216.
August 15, 1912, Mrs. K. X 242.
August 16, 1912, Gussie X 223.

Reports from other sources:

Appendices

Bed House. Hotel and disorderly house. Proprietor X 245. License issued in the name of X 245-a. One of the worst places in the city. X 245 is manager.

February 1, 1912. Bed house, hotel and disorderly house; proprietor X 245, license issued in the name of X 245-a. X 245 is manager.

August 19, 1912. A notorious assignation place.

APPENDIX XII

SALOONS: ADDITIONAL DATA

FEBRUARY 2, 1912. A man entered the rear room of saloon X 275. With him was a porter from a house of prostitution at X 173, West 27th Street. Prostitutes here were especially vulgar and obscene. A waiter in this place, named X 277, knew the prostitutes by name and encouraged the men to sit at the tables with these women and treat them to drinks. The proprietor, named X 278, also attempted to " drum up " trade between the prostitutes and the men.

February 4, 1912. Between the hours of 7.15 and 10 P. M. the same conditions prevailed with variations. One prostitute who was intoxicated exposed herself. The waiter did not offer any objections to this exhibition.

May 1, 1912. At 12 P. M. a stranger entered the rear room of saloon at X 279, West 42nd Street. The waiters appeared to be familiar with certain girls who were unescorted.

May 23, 1912. 2 P. M. A special officer attached to a notorious saloon and dance hall accompanied a man to this place. He told him it was a resort for pimps, pickpockets, cheap crooks and prostitutes. The dancing on this evening was vulgar and obscene. There were several young girls present between 17 and 20 years of age

Appendices

who gave vile exhibitions. At 3 A. M., six pimps invited the man to go to a saloon at X 280, Seventh Avenue. When they reached this place the pimps talked to several prostitutes. One of these girls was called May. While the young man sat at the table with one of these women, she attempted to steal a $2 bill from one of his pockets. When he remonstrated one of the pimps called to his five companions and said, "Come on, fellows, let's go through him." When they found the man did not have any more money they threw him out of the door and jostled him on the sidewalk. The man threatened to call a policeman who was standing on the opposite side of the street and they laughed, saying, "Go ahead, call the cop and see if he will come over." The man yelled "police" three or four times and the pimps said, "Holler louder, he won't bother us, we stand in."

June 6, 1912. 2.30 A. M. Thirteen girls were sitting at the tables in the rear room. Jack X 281, a waiter in this resort, who lives at X 282, Second Avenue, stated that the boss, Joe X 283, has a small room in the rear where a few of his friends play cards and "roll" dice.

February 20, 1912. 2 A. M. Concert hall at X 288, West 39th Street. Manager is X 289. The door at this house is guarded by George X 290. A chain on the door. The dances were vulgar and obscene. Carrie X 291 solicited a man to go to a furnished room at X 292 West 39th Street. A pickpocket stole a watch, a stickpin, and $9 in money from one of the men in the place.

Commercialized Prostitution in New York

February 24, 1912. 3.50 A. M. During the night there were over 100 men and 16 white and colored prostitutes at the tables. A negro named Albert X 293 pointed out the proprietor, whose name is X 294.

April 11, 1912. 4 A. M. Same conditions prevail.

April 19, 1912. 4.30 A. M. Same conditions prevail.

March 29, 1912. Saloon at X 848, Sixth Avenue. It is said that X 849, the manager of this place, bails out the girls who solicit in his saloon. X 850, living at — West 96th Street said that madames send to this rear room for girls. Following are some of the girls who solicit in this saloon: Hope X 852, May X 853, Bessie X 854, Elizabeth X 855, X 856, Nellie X 857, Mattie X 858, Marie X 859, and X 877.

May 16, 1912. Twenty unescorted women counted in the rear room. Several girls solicited investigator to go to the X 860 hotel at — Sixth Avenue, to the X 861 Hotel at — Sixth Avenue, and to different flats.

June 3, 1912. 9.15 P. M. Fifteen unescorted women in this rear room. Two women from this saloon solicited men to go to the X 862 Hotel,— Sixth Avenue.

July 25, 1912. Nine unescorted women, among them being Ellen X 863 and Mildred X 864.

July 27, 1912. Seven unescorted women. One of these is Catherine X 865.

August 14, 1912. May X 866 soliciting in the rear room.

August 15, 1912. 9. P. M. Nine unescorted women. Dancing was vulgar.

August 28, 1912. Eleven unescorted women. One

Appendices

of these was Lottie X 850, who said she had been soliciting in this rear room for years.

August 30, 1912. Seventeen unescorted women. One of these is Beatrice X 867.

September 24, 1912. Lottie X 850 was again in this rear room with others, among whom was Cora X 868.

September 26, 1912. Fifteen unescorted women. One of these was Sue X 869.

October 5, 1912. Four unescorted women. One of these by the name of May X 870 said that she had been coming to this place for 15 years or more.

October 9, 1912. Among the seventeen unescorted women was Lottie X 850, previously mentioned.

October 11, 1912. Nine unescorted women. One of these was Rose X 871.

October 30, 1912. Several unescorted women. Four left the saloon with men. One of the women was Anna X 872.

November 1, 1912. Lottie X 850 was again in this saloon with other unescorted women.

November 4, 1912. Eleven unescorted women. One named Mamie X 873 said, "I have my steady friends come here — they know where to find me." Another girl was Celia X 874.

November 19, 1912. Eleven unescorted women. One of these was Lena X 875, another Clara X 876.

Previous records:

Proprietors of this place have given cash bond.

Concert place and saloon. Women gather here to solicit trade, without interference from the management.

Commercialized Prostitution in New York

January 26, 1912. Between 6.30 and 8.30 P. M. X 878, East 14th Street. Number of unescorted women in the rear room. Waiters assist girls in finding customers. One of the women named X 877 solicited investigator to go to X 893 Hotel at — Third Avenue.

February 2, 1912. 11.05 P. M. Twenty unescorted women in rear room. Many solicited investigator to go to hotel.

April 8, 1912. During the evening eleven unescorted women sat at separate tables. One prostitute said she would go to a hotel for $2.

May 14, 1912. May X 879, living at — East 13th Street, was soliciting in this rear room.

May 20, 1912. Nine unescorted women. One of these was Annie X 880, known as X 880-a, living at — East 15th Street.

May 25, 1912. The following prostitutes were seen in this place: Ida X 881, Annie X 882.

May 29, 1912. Lettie X 888 was soliciting in this rear room.

June 5, 1912. Seven unescorted women. One of these, Emma X 884, said that she meets some good men in this place. Another girl was Minnie X 885.

June 8, 1912. Pauline X 886 was engaged in soliciting in this rear room.

August 7, 1912. Three unescorted women. One of these was Emma X 887.

September 26, 1912. Five unescorted women. One of these was Rose X 888.

October 2, 1912. Five unescorted women. One of these was Mary X 889.

Appendices

October 3, 1912. Mary X 889 was again in this saloon.

Previous records:

February 1, 1912. Café and rear room. Women enter without escorts and solicit men in this place.

January 13, 1912. The proprietor of this place has given cash bond.

February 13, 1912. 9 to 12 P.M. X 890, W. 40th Street. Ten unescorted women at the tables. Six of these women beckoned to investigator to come to their tables. A number of these girls have been seen soliciting on Broadway. During the evening 7 couples left this place and went to the Hotel X 891. At 12 P.M. on this date, X 892, a prostitute, solicited investigator to go to a hotel.

June 8, 1912. Number of unescorted women in this saloon.

Previous records:

This place is on the police list, alleged disorderly. Proprietor has given a cash bond.

APPENDIX XIII

MISCELLANEOUS PLACES: ADDITIONAL DATA

February 6, 1912. 3 A. M. Pool room and barber shop at X 300, West 28th Street. Conducted by two or three men who sell liquor without a license at 5 cents per glass. One of the customers in the place solicited a man to go to a house of prostitution at X 25, Sixth Avenue. The man's name is X 301.

A man by the name of X 302 conducts a pool parlor and cigar store at X 303, Second Avenue. A pimp named X 304, frequents this place. X 305, another pimp, was at this place on February 5, 1912.

About nine years ago a woman named Rosie X 306 opened a hair dressing parlor on Second Avenue. She now has the same kind of a parlor at X 307, Second Avenue. It is a rendezvous for prostitutes, and Rosie's husband is a bail bondsman for these women when they are arrested. Rosie sells these women dresses, hats, kimonos, feathers, and hair goods, either for cash or on the instalment plan. One of the methods used by X 306 to draw trade is to allow messages and mail for prostitutes and their pimps to be delivered at her parlor. One of the prostitutes is the wife of X 308. She is a street walker and also a shoplifter. Becky X 309 and her sister Sarah, who

Appendices

solicit on the Bowery, both go to Rosie's to have their hair dressed.

February 9, 1912. Twenty-five pimps, gamblers and crooks were in the restaurant at X 311, Second Avenue. The chief amusement of these men is gambling, playing such games as stuss, poker, and "klobiosh." These pimps receive at this place telephone messages from their women on the streets or in vice resorts, and make arrangements in connection with arrests and other deals. Among the pimps who were seen here at different times were Louis X 312, Harry X 313, Joe X 314, Sam X 315, Joe X 316, and Sam X 317.

APPENDIX XIV

SHIPPING WOMEN: ADDITIONAL DATA

X 47, alias X 47-a, who is part owner in X 46 West 25th Street, has had his woman in England, Russia, South Africa, Dallas, Texas, and Seattle, Washington. He travels back and forth between South Africa and New York.

X 431 took his woman, X 432, to Africa and China, and now has her in a house of prostitution in Texas, the city being either Dallas or Fort Worth.

X 316, alias X 316-a, alias X 316-b, sends his women out to western cities of this country.

X 433, a pimp, had a German girl for his woman and sent her to Denver, Colorado. She "threw him down" and now he has another girl named Ida, whom he broke into the business of prostitution. When she was in Philadelphia she is said to have made as much as $200 for him every week. He then sent her west. She returned, and he sent her west again.

X 434, the wife of X 435, a pimp, has been sent out west. One week she sent X 435 $150. Formerly she was with him in Portland, Oregon, Salt Lake City, Utah, and Billings, Montana.

X 402, alias X 402-a, has sent his woman to South Africa and to Brazil.

X 47-a took his wife, Ida, to South Africa seven years ago.

Appendices

Ray, the wife of X 407, alias X 407-a, is now in Providence, Rhode Island, in a house of prostitution.

X 406, alias X 406-a, has just returned from Denver. X 436 once took her to Philadelphia; when the houses there were broken up and they were arrested, they " skipped " their bail.

X 410, owner of a house of prostitution, has sent his woman to South Africa, Philadelphia and St Louis. He has a house in Philadelphia, which is now conducted by one of his women, Rosie.

X 437, alias X 437-a, alias X 437-b, has sent his women to the western cities of this country. One of his women at the present time is X 438, alias X 438-a, alias X 438-b.

X 439, who is part owner of the house of prostitution at X 426, Sixth Avenue, has sent his woman Minnie to Alaska three times, and it is said that each time she came back with between $4,000 and $5,000, all of which she gave to him.

X 73, who is a part owner of the house of prostitution at X 67, West 25th Street, sent his girls to all the cities of the west — Seattle, Tacoma, Denver, San Francisco — and also to Philadelphia.

X 440, alias X 440-a, pimp, has traveled with several of his women all over the country. He is now located in Boston.

X 441 conducts a house of prostitution on Percy Street, Philadelphia.

X 442 conducts a house of prostitution in Paterson, New Jersey. X 443 and X 444 have sent girls to him there.

X 445, who is part owner in a house of prosti-

Commercialized Prostitution in New York

tution at X 441, Montrose Avenue, Brooklyn, has sent his women to Omaha, Philadelphia and St. Louis. Lena, one of his girls, is now in Philadelphia; she has been in Omaha and St. Louis.

X 110 has conducted a house of prostitution in South Africa, and at present is interested in X 109, West 40th Street — a house of prostitution.

X 145-a, alias X 415, who is a part owner in X 416, West 36th Street, has been in South Africa, with his woman, from which place he went to Chicago.

X 34, partner in at least 11 houses of prostitution, has sent his woman, X 87, to Seattle, Tacoma, Portland, and other cities of the west. He also sent another woman, X 86, west over practically the same route.

X 69, who is partner with his brother, X 68, in the house of prostitution at X 78, West 27th Street, had a woman named Becky, whom he sent to the western cities of this country.

X 446 recently sent his woman to Stockton, California. She sent him $150 and he followed her to that city. Since then they have been in Seattle, San Francisco, and other western cities. In going from one city to another with his woman, X 446 was apprehended by the authorities and sentenced to one year in prison.

X 429, who hangs out at X 400, Second Avenue, sent his woman to El Paso, Texas. The immigration authorities arrested her and are at this writing still holding her. X 429 also has a girl in Buenos Ayres at the present time.

X 447 has had his girl in San Diego, Denver, Wilkes-

Appendices

barre, Pennsylvania. At the present time she is in California.

X 448, who owns X 499, East 13th Street, has been in houses of prostitution in San Francisco and Seattle.

X 450, who is now in New Orleans, had his girl there. She is now in New York City with a return ticket to New Orleans.

X 451, who now has X 452 as his woman, has sent women to houses of prostitution in New Orleans, Fort Worth, and Houston. X 452 lately returned from Texas.

X 424, alias X 424-a, has left with his woman for South Africa.

X 387, alias X 387-a, part owner of X 425, West 28th Street with his brother, X 424, alias X 424-a, had his wife in a house in South Africa, where he ran houses of prostitution.

X 453, alias X 453-a, has sent his woman Jennie to houses of prostitution in Denver, Spokane, Seattle, Tacoma and other western cities. She was in Denver four months ago. When in Spokane it is said she made $2,700 in two or three months.

X 443, alias X 443-a, has taken his woman Becky to Philadelphia. It is now supposed that she is either in Globe, Arizona or Havana, Cuba.

X 454 has a girl in New Orleans; she left him when he took a married woman to that city. X 454 has another girl named Rosie in a city in the west.

X 455 sent his girl Ida to Brazil, from whence she has returned. He is thinking of sending her back to Brazil.

Commercialized Prostitution in New York

X 328-a has a girl Sophia in New Orleans. She is about 24 or 25 years of age, 5 feet 6 inches tall, weighs about 135 pounds, dark hair, was born in Russia and has been in the United States about 7 or 8 years.

X 428 has had two women. One woman left him. The other woman is in Panama and he expects her back soon. He has had her in houses of prostitution in Chicago, New Orleans, Brazil and Panama.

X 385 had a woman whom he sent to Brazil. She returned, but with another pimp.

X 456 has been unfortunate. He sent three women west and lost all of them.

X 390 has sent his women to western cities to work in houses of prostitution four or five times.

He has also taken his girls to houses of prostitution in Chicago, and has one girl there at the present time.

X 453-a has had his woman Jennie in cities of the west three or four times. X 453-a is part owner in X 459, West 24th Street.

X 427, a pimp, sent his woman Fanny to Butte, Montana, about five weeks ago, from which place she sent him $150, the first week.

X 444 sent his woman to Panama five years ago and she left him.

X 314 has had his women in houses of prostitution in Seattle and Philadelphia.

X 460 has had his women in houses in Boston, Philadelphia and New Orleans.

X 461 has had his women in houses in Philadelphia and Boston.

Appendices

X 439, partner in X 426, Sixth Avenue, a house of prostitution, sent his woman Ida to Tacoma, Washington. For a protracted period she is said to have sent him $100 every week.

INDEX

Amusement Parks, 75.

Business of Prostitution, 112;
  Receipts, 126-133.

Cadet, 87.
Call Houses in Tenements, 29.
Census, Tenements, 26.
Chicago Vice Commission, 111.
Cider Stubes in Tenements, 30.
Conditions in 1907, 10.
Concert Halls in Amusement Parks, 75.
Committee of Fourteen, 34.
Correctional Work, 277.
Customers, 13, 108, 111.

Dance Halls, 67, 76.
Davis, Katharine Bement, 173.
District Attorney, 123.

Excursion Boats, 73.
Exploiters, The, 77, etc.

Fifty-cent Houses, 16, etc.
Five and Ten Dollar Houses, 42, etc.

Hotels, Disorderly, 33 etc.; Appendix XI.

Independent Benevolent Association, 41.
Inmates, Numbers of; Appendix, III.

Investigators' Reports, 140-142.
Investigation, Period of, 4.

Key, Explanation of, 7.

Law, Tenement House, 24.
Leasing Property, 113.
Lighthouse, 7.
Liquor Licenses, Revocation of, 161; Sale of in Vice Resorts, 15.
Lookouts, 12.

Madames, 92, etc.
Massage Parlors, 45, etc.
Medical Certificates, 9.
Miscellaneous Places, 59; Appendix XIII.
Morals Survey Committee, 111.

One Dollar Houses, 17, etc.
Owners of Houses, etc., 77; of Property, 114.

Parks, 73.
Parlor Houses, 4, etc.; Appendix IX.
Pimps, 64, 87.
Places which Cater to Vice, 52; Appendix II.
Police Precincts, Reports of Police on, 138-139.
Police Rules and Regulations, 137; Appendix VIII.

343

Index

Police Commissioner, 123.
Prevention Agencies, 263, etc.
Procurers, 85.
Prostitutes, Professional in Manhattan, 100; personal histories, 101; birthplaces, 101, 102, 198, 209, 253; nationality of parents, 210-213; previous occupations, 102, 103, 112, 241, 257; reasons for entering life, 103, 235, 251, 259; salaries in occupations, 105, 106, 220, 244; age of first sexual offense, 106, 226, 234, 242; age when entering life, 107, 255; length of time in business, 108; earnings from prostitution, 232, 249, 256; committed to Bedford Reformatory, 173.
Prostitution, the Police and the Law, 137.
Public Parks, 76.

Reformation Work, 268.
Renting Property, 113, 114.
Runners, 12.

Saloons, Disorderly, 53; Appendix XII.

Shares, Trading in, 118.
Shipping Women, 85; Appendix XIV.
Social Evil in Chicago. Report on, 111.
Special Sessions, 160, 161.
Stars in Parlor Houses, 7.
State Reformatory at Bedford Hill, 173, etc., 277.
Stolen Goods, Buyers of, 97.
Streets, Soliciting, 65; Appendix VII.
Street Walkers, Receipts of, 121.

Tenements, Vice Resorts in, 24; Appendix V, Appendix X; department records, 144.
Trading in Shares, 118.

Venereal Diseases in New York City Hospitals, 134-136; at Beford Reformatory, 198, etc.; other institutions, 250.
Vice Resorts in Parlor Houses, 3; in Tenements, 24; Massage Parlors, 45.

Watchboys, 12.
White Slaves, 85.

PATTERSON SMITH REPRINT SERIES IN
CRIMINOLOGY, LAW ENFORCEMENT, AND SOCIAL PROBLEMS

1. Lewis: *The Development of American Prisons and Prison Customs, 1776-1845*
2. Carpenter: *Reformatory Prison Discipline*
3. Brace: *The Dangerous Classes of New York*
4. Dix: *Remarks on Prisons and Prison Discipline in the United States*
5. Bruce et al: *The Workings of the Indeterminate-Sentence Law and the Parole System in Illinois*
6. Wickersham Commission: *Complete Reports, Including the Mooney-Billings Report.* 14 Vols.
7. Livingston: *Complete Works on Criminal Jurisprudence.* 2 Vols.
8. Cleveland Foundation: *Criminal Justice in Cleveland*
9. Illinois Association for Criminal Justice: *The Illinois Crime Survey*
10. Missouri Association for Criminal Justice: *The Missouri Crime Survey*
11. Aschaffenburg: *Crime and Its Repression*
12. Garofalo: *Criminology*
13. Gross: *Criminal Psychology*
14. Lombroso: *Crime, Its Causes and Remedies*
15. Saleilles: *The Individualization of Punishment*
16. Tarde: *Penal Philosophy*
17. McKelvey: *American Prisons*
18. Sanders: *Negro Child Welfare in North Carolina*
19. Pike: *A History of Crime in England.* 2 Vols.
20. Herring: *Welfare Work in Mill Villages*
21. Barnes: *The Evolution of Penology in Pennsylvania*
22. Puckett: *Folk Beliefs of the Southern Negro*
23. Fernald et al: *A Study of Women Delinquents in New York State*
24. Wines: *The State of the Prisons and of Child-Saving Institutions*
25. Raper: *The Tragedy of Lynching*
26. Thomas: *The Unadjusted Girl*
27. Jorns: *The Quakers as Pioneers in Social Work*
28. Owings: *Women Police*
29. Woolston: *Prostitution in the United States*
30. Flexner: *Prostitution in Europe*
31. Kelso: *The History of Public Poor Relief in Massachusetts: 1820-1920*
32. Spivak: *Georgia Nigger*
33. Earle: *Curious Punishments of Bygone Days*
34. Bonger: *Race and Crime*
35. Fishman: *Crucibles of Crime*
36. Brearley: *Homicide in the United States*
37. Graper: *American Police Administration*
38. Hichborn: *"The System"*
39. Steiner & Brown: *The North Carolina Chain Gang*
40. Cherrington: *The Evolution of Prohibition in the United States of America*
41. Colquhoun: *A Treatise on the Commerce and Police of the River Thames*
42. Colquhoun: *A Treatise on the Police of the Metropolis*
43. Abrahamsen: *Crime and the Human Mind*
44. Schneider: *The History of Public Welfare in New York State: 1609-1866*
45. Schneider & Deutsch: *The History of Public Welfare in New York State: 1867-1940*
46. Crapsey: *The Nether Side of New York*
47. Young: *Social Treatment in Probation and Delinquency*
48. Quinn: *Gambling and Gambling Devices*
49. McCord & McCord: *Origins of Crime*
50. Worthington & Topping: *Specialized Courts Dealing with Sex Delinquency*

PATTERSON SMITH REPRINT SERIES IN
CRIMINOLOGY, LAW ENFORCEMENT, AND SOCIAL PROBLEMS

51. Asbury: *Sucker's Progress*
52. Kneeland: *Commercialized Prostitution in New York City*
53. Fosdick: *American Police Systems*
54. Fosdick: *European Police Systems*
55. Shay: *Judge Lynch: His First Hundred Years*
56. Barnes: *The Repression of Crime*
57. Cable: *The Silent South*
58. Kammerer: *The Unmarried Mother*
59. Doshay: *The Boy Sex Offender and His Later Career*
60. Spaulding: *An Experimental Study of Psychopathic Delinquent Women*
61. Brockway: *Fifty Years of Prison Service*
62. Lawes: *Man's Judgment of Death*
63. Healy & Healy: *Pathological Lying, Accusation, and Swindling*
64. Smith: *The State Police*
65. Adams: *Interracial Marriage in Hawaii*
66. Halpern: *A Decade of Probation*
67. Tappan: *Delinquent Girls in Court*
68. Alexander & Healy: *Roots of Crime*
69. Healy & Bronner: *Delinquents and Criminals*
70. Cutler: *Lynch-Law*
71. Gillin: *Taming the Criminal*
72. Osborne: *Within Prison Walls*
73. Ashton: *The History of Gambling in England*
74. Whitlock: *On the Enforcement of Law in Cities*
75. Goldberg: *Child Offenders*
76. Cressey: *The Taxi-Dance Hall*
77. Riis: *The Battle with the Slum*
78. Larson *et al*: *Lying and Its Detection*
79. Comstock: *Frauds Exposed*
80. Carpenter: *Our Convicts.* 2 Vols. in 1
81. Horn: *Invisible Empire: The Story of the Ku Klux Klan, 1866-1871*
82. Faris *et al*: *Intelligent Philanthropy*
83. Robinson: *History and Organization of Criminal Statistics in the United States*
84. Reckless: *Vice in Chicago*
85. Healy: *The Individual Delinquent*
86. Bogen: *Jewish Philanthropy*
87. Clinard: *The Black Market: A Study of White Collar Crime*
88. Healy: *Mental Conflicts and Misconduct*
89. Citizens' Police Committee: *Chicago Police Problems*
90. Clay: *The Prison Chaplain*
91. Peirce: *A Half Century with Juvenile Delinquents*
92. Richmond: *Friendly Visiting Among the Poor*
93. Brasol: *Elements of Crime*
94. Strong: *Public Welfare Administration in Canada*
95. Beard: *Juvenile Probation*
96. Steinmetz: *The Gaming Table.* 2 Vols.
97. Crawford: *Report on the Pentitentiaries of the United States*
98. Kuhlman: *A Guide to Material on Crime and Criminal Justice*
99. Culver: *Bibliography of Crime and Criminal Justice: 1927-1931*
100. Culver: *Bibliography of Crime and Criminal Justice: 1932-1937*